ANTHROPOCENE FEMINISM

Center for 21st Century Studies

Richard Grusin, Series Editor

ANTHROPOCENE FEMINISM

Richard Grusin, Editor

CENTER FOR 21ST CENTURY STUDIES

University of Minnesota Press
Minneapolis
London

Published by the University of Minnesota Press
111 Third Avenue South, Suite 290
Minneapolis, MN 55401-2520
http://www.upress.umn.edu

Printed in the United States of America on acid-free paper

The University of Minnesota is an equal-opportunity educator and employer.

24 23 22   10 9 8 7 6 5 4 3

Library of Congress Cataloging-in-Publication Data
Names: Grusin, Richard A., editor.
Title: Anthropocene feminism / Richard Grusin, editor, Center for 21st Century Studies.
Description: Minneapolis : University of Minnesota Press, [2017] |
Series: 21st century studies | Includes bibliographical references and index.
Identifiers: LCCN 2016022218 | ISBN 978-1-5179-0060-1 (hc) |
ISBN 978-1-5179-0061-8 (pb)
Subjects: LCSH: Feminist anthropology. | Feminist theory.
Classification: LCC GN33.8 .A67 | DDC 305.4201—dc23
LC record available at https://lccn.loc.gov/2016022218

Contents

Introduction

Anthropocene Feminism: An Experiment in Collaborative Theorizing

RICHARD GRUSIN

What do we mean by "anthropocene feminism"? Separately, each of the two terms has a clear enough import, but what does it mean to put them together? This was the question set out in fall 2013, when Rebekah Sheldon, Dehlia Hannah, Emily Clark, and I gave name to a concept that we felt was just beginning to emerge amid the various ways in which artists, humanists, and social scientists had taken up the concept of the Anthropocene in the second decade of the twenty-first century. We came up with the concept as the name and initial provocation for the 2014 annual spring conference at the Center for 21st Century Studies (C21) at the University of Wisconsin–Milwaukee, which I then directed and with which we have all in different ways been affiliated over the past several years. The essays that make up this book have their origins in that conference and reflect the experimental spirit with which we approached its organization.

Coined in the 1980s by ecologist Eugene F. Stoermer, and popularized at the inception of the twenty-first century by Nobel Prize–winning atmospheric chemist Paul Crutzen, the Anthropocene is the proposed name for a new geological epoch defined by overwhelming human influence upon the earth. More specifically, the Anthropocene would mark a new epoch for the earth's lithosphere, its crust and upper mantle. Much of the initial evidence for this new lithospheric epoch came from geomorphology, particularly the recognition that large-scale impacts on the earth's surface from such human activities as mining, construction, and deforestation had come to surpass the effects of nonhuman forces. Recently, the Anthropocene has come to refer more broadly to the effects of climate change and the ongoing possibility of a "sixth extinction."[1] Many scientists would place the beginning of the Anthropocene at the Industrial Revolution in the late eighteenth century. Some would put it as far back as the beginning of agriculture, while others trace it to the mid-twentieth century—with the splitting of the atom or, citing Rachel Carson, the invention and widespread use of chemical insecticides and pesticides.

Although a formal decision about whether the Anthropocene should be added to the geological series as a new epoch is not expected from the International Commission on Stratigraphy until after this book has gone to press, the concept of the Anthropocene has already been picked up and expanded by other scientists, chiefly but not exclusively geologists and planetary ecologists. Perhaps even more enthusiastically, the idea of the Anthropocene has caught fire in the imagination of artists, humanists, and social scientists, for whom it has provided a powerful framework through which to account for and depict the impact of climate change in a variety of media forms and practices. Both inspired by and suspicious of the often uncritical (and sometimes uninformed) adaptation of this proposed geological periodization, we wanted to put together a conference that would both challenge and embrace the possibilities of this new geological epoch.

In many ways, we realized, the Anthropocene is a strikingly resonant reiteration of a feminist problematic powerfully articulated in 1985 by Donna Haraway, whose "Manifesto for Cyborgs" sees humans, nonhumans, culture, and nature as inextricably entangled and warns that the consequences of attempts to dominate human and nonhuman nature can be at once devastatingly successful and productively perverse.[2] Indeed, the concept of the Anthropocene has arguably been implicit in feminism and queer theory for decades, a genealogy that is largely ignored, or, worse, erased, by the masculine authority of an institutional scientific discourse that now seeks to name our current historical moment the Anthropocene. By the same token, feminists have long argued that humans are dominating and destroying a feminized earth, turning it into standing reserve, capital, or natural resource to devastating ends. We were concerned, therefore, that this recent articulation of the Anthropocene, even as it affirms those arguments in many ways, could deprive feminism of some of the ethical ground on which such indictments are based, evident in recent efforts by scientists, geoengineers, and futurists, for example, to bring about what has begun to be called a "good Anthropocene."[3] Insofar as early feminism begins with a critique of nature, a critique of the idea that gender differences were biological, that gender was natural, how does feminism address the definition of the human as a geological force, the embrace of the naturalness of "man"?

This tension between feminist and other critiques of science has already been anticipated in ecofeminism and feminist science studies. Ecofeminism in particular has a robust liberatory history, built around its recognition of the parallels between the structural binaries supporting the oppression of women and those supporting the exploitation of nature. Ecofeminists such as Vandana Shiva, Val Plumwood, and Greta Gaard have long been concerned to point out structural homologies between patriarchy, capitalism, racism, and technoscience, each of which depends on enforcing hierarchical dualisms between dominant and oppressed entities, often on behalf of the mutual liberation of women and nature.

A similar tension informs the relationship between feminist new materialists in the twenty-first century and contemporary Anthropocene theory. Feminist new materialism has taken the articulation of a postnatural condition in the form of a new geological age as calling for rigorous and sustained attention to global, ahuman forces of ecological change as well as to local spaces of vulnerability and resistance. In naming humans as the dominant influence on the planet at least since industrialization, proponents of the Anthropocene recognize that humans must now be understood as climatological or geological planetary forces that operate just as nonhumans would, independent of human will, belief, or desires. In addressing the climatological and ecological catastrophes consequent upon this new geological era, however, scientists and engineers continue to rely on many of the same masculinist and human-centered solutions that have created the problems in the first place, whether through offsetting carbon emissions, by developing new and cleaner energy sources, or, most dramatically, through the heroic agency of geoengineering.

In contradistinction to the too often unquestioned masculinist and technonormative approach to the Anthropocene taken by technoscientists, artists, humanists, or social scientists, we created the concept of *anthropocene feminism* to highlight the ways in which feminism and queer theory might offer alternatives to these approaches. Dehlia Hannah's provocative claim that much contemporary art operates according to philosophical logics of scientific experimentation led us to imagine the conference (and, by extension, this book) as something of an experiment, a kind of scholarly and artistic crucible in which we would bring the Anthropocene together with feminist theory to see what might result from the interactions among these competing conceptual formations. Because feminist theory has long been concerned with the anthropogenic impact of humans, particularly men, on nature, we invited participants to explore what current interest in the Anthropocene might mean for feminism, in its evolving histories, theories, and practices, as well as what feminist theory might offer technoscientific understandings of and approaches to the Anthropocene. More to the point, the conference (like this book) was designed to highlight both why we need an anthropocene feminism and why thinking the Anthropocene must come from feminism.

We approached this experiment with two questions: What does feminism have to say to the Anthropocene? How does the concept of the Anthropocene impact feminism? In exploring how feminism has already anticipated this concept, we asked what it might yet have to offer. How can feminism help us to historicize, challenge, or refine the current understanding of the Anthropocene? What do new materialist feminism or ecofeminism (to name just two) add to (or detract from) current humanistic understandings of the Anthropocene? What do feminism and queer theory have to say to the claim that humans now act as a geological force in ways that are independent of or indifferent to social, cultural, or political will or intent? Equally important, in considering how the Anthropocene impacts feminism, we began with a prior question: is there (or should there be) an "anthropocene" feminism? Put differently, does the claim that we have entered a new epoch in which humans are a major geological force on the planet call for a reconceptualization of feminism? Does feminism require a new formulation specific to the age of the Anthropocene, a new historical or period designation? How should feminism and queer theory in an anthropogenic age take up an altered relation to—an increased attention to or concern for—the nonhuman world?

As important as it is for us to ask and answer these questions—and it is vitally important—we also need to stress the continued flourishing of speculation and imagination as forms of queer and feminist knowledge production. For example, the question of where and when the Anthropocene should be said to begin (where the "golden spike" should be placed) is part of what we take anthropocene feminism to be calling into question.[4] Counter to the technoscientific desire for specificity, definition, and fact, we coined the term *anthropocene feminism* as an experiment or provocation, expressing a survivalist ethos in regard to the masculinist and patriarchal urge to proclaim mankind an agent of major change. We conceived of anthropocene feminism as an ethos of disruption and hoped that one of the forms that an anthropocene feminism could play would be the assembling of small-scale systems or the claiming of responsibility for all human and nonhuman actants toward a goal of mutual thriving.[5] Think of this book, then, as one such experiment, a small-scale assemblage of different voices, speaking from different discursive communities, offering a variety of results from the laboratory or field, results that productively raise as many new questions as they answer the ones we initially posed.

Among the scholars who figure prominently in the essays that make up *Anthropocene Feminism* are two not explicitly feminist scholars, Michel Foucault and Dipesh Chakrabarty. Perhaps unexpectedly, Foucault is the most cited author in the collection—in part but by no means solely because he is central to Lynne Huffer's essay "Foucault's Fossils." Long aligned with feminist theory, Foucault's formative concept of biopower proves crucial to several authors in working through anthropocene feminism. Huffer sees Foucault's understanding of biopower as offering the key to a nonvitalist, even nonhuman, understanding of both the Anthropocene and feminist theory, reading his discussion of fossils in *The Order of Things* as a way to critique the concept of life that motivates two competing strains of feminist theory. For Elizabeth Povinelli, Foucault's notion of biopower, and *History of Sexuality* generally, offers an important entryway into the Anthropocene but needs to be expanded to include a theory of geopower or geontology. Rosi Braidotti as well sees Foucault's biopolitics as central to thinking about the sexual politics of the Anthropocene, particularly in her development of the concept of *zoe* power; Braidotti credits his antihumanism (along with Deleuze's) as instrumental in forming her own critical posthumanism.

Dipesh Chakrabarty's work is also frequently engaged by the volume's authors, particularly his groundbreaking essay "The Climate of History: Four Theses." Unlike Foucault, Chakrabarty is often taken as a foil, serving throughout the volume as a touchstone, or more frequently an object of critique, interrogation, disagreement, or revision, for thinking a feminist Anthropocene. Stacy Alaimo addresses Chakrabarty most extensively, challenging his four theses for ultimately separating out the human from the biological, geological, or technical, even as the Anthropocene insists on their inseparability. When, in another essay, Chakrabarty does take up humans as a "brute force," Alaimo notes from an alternate angle that seeing humans solely as force elides meaningful differences among different human groups, histories, and practices and hence cannot do justice to the complex heterogeneous assemblages of humans and nonhumans that she sees as the true mark of anthropogenic climate change. Myra Hird and Alexander Zahara make a similar point about the problem Chakrabarty has with universalizing the human and thinking it against a "stable geologic," both understandings given the lie by the authors' account of the Inuit history of waste.

Unsurprisingly, the essays also engage a variety of feminist theorists, most notably, but not limited to, Donna Haraway, Judith Butler, Elisabeth Grosz, Karen Barad, and Claire Colebrook, whose contribution opens this volume. As already noted, Haraway's "Manifesto for Cyborgs" provides one of the earliest influential formulations of the inseparability of humans and nonhumans in the figure of the cyborg, which she deploys as a means of critiquing mid-1980s variations of naturalizing feminism and Marxism. Her important writing on companion species works to similar purposes, and her very recent coinage, "Chthulucene," appears in Jill Schneiderman's mapping of the Anthropocene naming controversy. Butler and Grosz figure in Lynne Huffer's essay as representatives of the persistence of a shared concept of life or vitality in denaturalizing and renaturalizing feminism, respectively. The work of both of these feminist/queer theorists, along with Karen Barad, appear in several of the essays as examples of different ways in which feminist theory has already been thinking the Anthropocene.

Among the pieces collected in this volume, fellow author Claire Colebrook's recent books on extinction speak most helpfully. Povinelli and Alaimo especially find her linking of the Anthropocene with extinction a generative way to make sense of anthropocene feminism, as do several of the other authors. Colebrook's essay here, "We Have Always Been Post-Anthropocene: The Anthropocene Counterfactual," takes on what she sees as the new human exceptionalism (in its "destructive and inscriptive impact") of current thinking on the Anthropocene. She argues instead, in opposition to this new form of difference, that we should "confront a *new form of indifference*." "An anthropocene feminism," Colebrook asserts, "would not accept the Anthropocene as an epoch, as a line or strata whose significance would not be in dispute. Rather than think of this line as privileged and epochal, we might ask for whom this strata becomes definitive of *the human*." To demonstrate how "we have always been post-Anthropocene," Colebrook offers two counterfactual examples of global human development in relation to questions of gender and sexuality. The aim of these counterfactuals is to ask what might have been different if humans had not been exceptional in disturbing the natural order of the planet. She concludes that the "dream" of a "good Anthropocene" through geoengineering, "a pure ecology in which everything serves to maximize everything else, and in which there is no cost," could "be possible only by way of countless injustices," including prominently those against women. The dream of a good Anthropocene, Colebrook maintains, enacts a logic "that marks all that has stood for humanism, posthumanism, a certain dream of history and of utopian sexual difference," thus demonstrating that the "event of the Anthropocene is exceptional—but not by being extrinsic to what we have come to refer to as nature or humanity."

Like Colebrook, Rosi Braidotti takes up the question of anthropocene feminism in relation to the concept of the posthuman, a concept she has theorized quite extensively. In "Four Theses on Posthuman Feminism," Braidotti thinks through anthropocene feminism as a form of posthuman feminism, beginning with the thesis that "feminism is *not* a humanism." For Braidotti, feminism is resolutely antihumanist and, she adds, anti-Eurocentric. Her second thesis, "Anthropos is off-center," offers a *zoe*-centric relational ontology that decenters humanism not from the outside but "from philosophies of radical immanence, vital materialism, and the feminist politics of locations." Proclaiming *zoe* "the ruling principle," her third thesis urges her fellow feminists "to embrace this humble starting point by acknowledging a life which is not ours—it is *zoe*-driven and geocentered." To do so, she suggests, alluding to Deleuze, could open us "up to possible actualization of virtual forces." Her fourth thesis asserts that "sexuality is a force beyond gender." Treating "sexuality as a human and nonhuman force," Braidotti joins other posthuman feminists in calling for a move away from identity in thinking about sexuality, thereby bringing sexuality as process into full focus. She insists throughout on the importance of maintaining "difference as positivity," which I take as key to her definition of anthropocene feminism as insisting on an ontological relationality.

In "The Three Figures of Geontology," Elizabeth Povinelli offers her own relational ontology in revising Foucault's biopolitics, not for posthumanism but for the age of the Anthropocene. She creates the concept of *geontological power* as an alternative to the concept of biopower, which she sees as both "hiding and revealing this other problematic." Povinelli sets out to articulate "the relationship between *bios* and *geos*" through a theorization of the new forms of thought brought about by the realization that humans might have the planetary force to bring about a sixth extinction. One result she finds in anthropology is "the reappearance of animism and ontology as a mode of destabilizing the dominance of culture and the Anthropos." More broadly, Povinelli claims, "we are witnessing a wild proliferation of new conceptual-theoretical models, figures, and tactics of geontology that are displacing the figures and tactics of the biopolitical." To clarify these proliferating models in relation to Foucault's biopolitics, Povinelli offers three figures: THE DESERT, THE ANIMIST, and THE TERRORIST. Noting that these "three figures of geontology are no different than Foucault's four figures of biopower," she underscores particularly the point that "geontology is not the Other to biontology but a new set of divergences and possibilities." For Povinelli, as for Colebrook, the geontology of the Anthropocene does not mark a break with biontology but rather a revelation of possibilities already inherent in the biopolitical.

Lynne Huffer also finds Foucault's conception of biopower to be helpful in imagining what an anthropocene feminism might look like in "Foucault's Fossils: Life Itself and the Return to Nature in Feminist Philosophy." But where Povinelli relies on Foucault's account of biopower in *History of Sexuality* to speculate on new forms of feminist geopower, Huffer finds a guide to thinking through a new form of anthropocene feminism in Foucault's theorization of fossils and the concept of the archive from *The Order of Things*. More directly than any of the essays in the book, Huffer provides an analysis of what feminism can bring to the Anthropocene, undertaking an archaeological exploration of feminist renaturalization and denaturalization, represented for the purposes of her essay by Grosz and Butler, respectively. Huffer clearly lays out the way in which recent work in feminist new materialism has undertaken a renaturalization of gender and sexuality in opposition to the prevalent modes of denaturalization undertaken at the end of the twentieth century. Despite their different takes on the question of nature and naturalization, Huffer argues that both feminist approaches agree in depending on a theory of life or vitalism. Foucault's discussion of "monsters and fossils" in *The Order of Things* presents, according to Huffer, a more historicized understanding of life's relation to nonlife, a deprivileging of life itself. Much as Colebrook sees the achievement of the Anthropocene as our recognition that one day we, too, will be a sedimentary layer in the lithosphere, so Foucault lets us see that fossilized nonhuman lives appear to us as stone, that fossils show us our own inseparability from the earth, what Povinelli thinks of as geontology.

In "Your Shell on Acid: Material Immersion, Anthropocene Dissolves," Stacy Alaimo invokes the concept of the ecodelic in a way similar to what Povinelli imagines with geontology. Alaimo takes issue with "dominant figurations of the Anthropocene" like those set forth by Chakrabarty and others, which "bracket humans as biological creatures." In place of such figurations, "which abstract the human from the material realm and obscure differentials of responsibility and harm," Alaimo proposes a model of "the Anthropocene subject as immersed and enmeshed in the world." She deploys her own notion of "trans-corporeality" as a way to make sense of a variety of different engagements with the geological, all of which "conceptualize humans as enmeshed with something as rigid as a rock." Like Huffer, Alaimo finds shells and fossils to be powerful figures for an anthropocene feminism, although her archive is the ocean itself and the shell-destroying acidification it has suffered under human intervention. Unlike the spectacular terrestrial impacts of climate change, for example, underwater biochemical changes can only be made legible by imaginative forms of scientific and aesthetic mediation, such as those invoked by Richard Doyle as the "ecodelic insight," the feeling of oneness with the world common both to psychedelic and ecological consciousness. Alaimo's anthropocene feminist version of this insight asks us to embrace "a para-doxical ecodelic expansion and dissolution of the human, an aesthetic incitement to extend and connect with vulnerable creaturely life and with the inhuman, unfathomable expanses of the seas." Only by doing so, she concludes, can we "shift toward a particularly feminist mode of ethical and political engagement" with the Anthropocene.

"The Arctic Wastes," coauthored by Myra J. Hird and Alexander Zahara, exemplifies one example of the new mode of thinking human and geological temporality as one that Alaimo calls for. Hird and Zahara also reject geoengineering precisely for reinstating the separation of humans, *techne,* and nature that the concept of the Anthropocene should work to subvert. Their essay focuses on the history, politics, and environmental impacts of waste in Iqualit, the territorial capital of Nunavut, to document the ways in which nonhuman waste has served as an agent (and even a principal) of colonialism. Reminding Chakrabarty of the uneven distribution of waste across different populations, Hird and Zahara describe how the Euro-Canadian government practiced a kind of "excremental colonialism" through the siting of waste dumps in Nunavut and the disciplining of Inuit populations as generators of modern garbage. The article gives voice to Canadian first peoples from the North to let them testify both to the ways in which they were taught by their southern Canadian government leaders to produce waste and to the need for self-determination in their relationship with their own, and the nation's, waste. Condemning "technomanagerial approaches" to the Anthropocene, Hird and Zahara conclude by describing "the dangerous irony of the Anthropocene": that the solutions to global environmental problems impose a separation of "waste from resource, dirt from clean, and uncivilized from civilized" that the Anthropocene has already shown to be "doomed to failure."

The relationships among indigenous peoples and the contemporary concept of the Anthropocene figure as a starting point for poet-critics Joshua Clover and Juliana Spahr, whose "Gender Abolition and Ecotone War" offers a Marxist poetics of "the character of the Anthropocene" as "the transformation of difference into differential." Clover and Spahr begin with the *Kumulipo,* a more than three-centuries-old poem that was written before contact with the capitalist West and its program-matic distinction between humans and nature. Even while enumerating many differences between humans and nature in its series of poetic lists, the *Kumulipo* never converts them into capitalist "differentials toward the maximized rates of value accumulation." After taking up Italian feminist-materialist critiques of how housework converts gender differences into capitalist differentials, how "gender functions *for capital* not as difference but differential," Clover and Spahr then proceed to re-imagine the Anthropocene not simply as a period but as a set of capitalist forces to "bring together the most cost-effective means of production with the lowest wages," in other words, to rename the Anthropocene as the "Capitalocene." The essay concludes with an articulation of the anthropogenic implications of recent direct actions against California ports, with which both authors have been engaged. Defining the port as a crucially contested ecotone for capitalism's conversion of difference into differential, Clover and Spahr end with a call for "ecotone war," the struggle to conquer and hold those crucial sites for the growth of the Capitalocene.

Many of the authors in the volume address to one degree or another the question of whether our current geological epoch should be renamed the Anthropocene and, if so, where the golden spike should be placed to mark the new epoch's beginning. In "The Anthropocene Controversy," feminist geologist Jill Schneiderman details the naming controversy in terms of the history of geology. Schneiderman situates the question of geological naming in relation to broader taxonomic practices in scientific history, going back to Carl Linnaeus and to the invention of the geological sciences in the eighteenth century. She then explores the role of stratigraphy and its international scholarly societies in adjudicating the naming of the Anthropocene. Schneiderman herself "accepts the idea that there is convincing geological evidence for a new epoch" but is concerned that naming this epoch the Anthropocene "contrasts with earlier discoveries in science, such as the Copernican revolution and Darwin's evolution by natural selection, that have shifted views away from the notion that humanity occupies the center of the universe and the highest rung on a ladder of evolution." She concludes by urging scientists and humanists alike to "remain open to alternative nomenclature."

The volume closes with "Natalie Jeremijenko's New Experimentalism," a conversation between Dehlia Hannah and Jeremijenko, focusing on the latter's series of scientific-like experiments with nature, technology, society, and art. Like Hannah, Jeremijenko conceives of her art as the staging of experiments with nature, experiments which do not depend solely on the human agency of the artist but on "the collaboration of many different people, critters, and nonhuman agents." Together the two take us on a tour of Jeremijenko's experiments. In *Tree Logic,* she planted a mini-forest of trees in the city, hanging upside down from a high truss to learn how the trees will rethink the directionality of their growth. In a post–Super Storm Sandy competition at Rockaway Beach, Jeremijenko "contracted" with the Cross[x]Species Construction Company, setting fish and other aquatic species to work on the beach to reconstruct their environment (or not, in the case of one cichlid, Enrique Peñalosa, who refused to dig as his species is known to do, and as he had done in his previous home in Petco). We hear, too, about the mussel choir, a group of mollusks who, Jeremijenko says, "are instrumented with sensors so as they open and close we can collect data on their gape angle," which can be used both to learn about water quality but in sonified form to generate music, as Jeremijenko did in a Venice lagoon where the mussel choir was arranged to play a cover of "Bicycle Built for Two," which she calls "Bicycle Built for Too Many." Jeremijenko's "small-scale participatory public experimentation" functions as a critique of the expert model of geoengineering a good Anthropocene, offering instead, in the spirit of all of the pieces in the volume, and the broader experiment they are part of, a model of anthropocene feminism in action.

Taken together, then, the contributions to this volume provide a diverse and provocative set of findings in response to the experiment in anthropocene feminism that we undertook beginning in fall 2013. These variegated responses—from feminist theory, geology, anthropology, environmental sociology, philosophy, literary studies, poetry, and art—offer only an initial set of hypotheses and tentative conclusions. In many ways, these essays are the first, not the last, words on the concept of anthropocene feminism. In being so, they have already set out some preliminary parameters for further investigation, and have opened up many more new avenues for exploration than we could ever have imagined. I think I can speak for all of the contributors in saying that we eagerly await the responses—affirmative, contradictory, or otherwise—of our fellow experimenters in the years to come.[6]

NOTES

1. Elizabeth Kolbert, *The Sixth Extinction: An Unnatural History* (New York: Henry Holt, 2014).

2. Donna Haraway, "A Manifesto for Cyborgs: Science, Technology, and Socialist Feminism in the 1980s," *Socialist Review* 2 (March 1985): 65–107.

3. Most recently, advocacy for a "good Anthropocene" has been put forward by the Breakthrough Institute in its "Ecomodernist Manifesto," http://www.ecomodernism.org/manifesto/. An earlier call for a good Anthropocene can be found in Andrew Revkin, "Exploring Academia's Role in Charting Paths to a 'Good' Anthropocene," *New York Times*, June 16, 2014.

4. Growing out of C21's Anthropocene Feminism conference, Dehlia Hannah co-curated an exhibit in 2015 at University of Wisconsin–Milwaukee's INOVA gallery, *Placing the Golden Spike: Landscapes of the Anthropocene*, http://uwm.edu/inova.

5. The ideas in the last few sentences are deeply indebted to Rebekah Sheldon, who also provided valuable input into this introduction as a whole.

6. One of the earliest responses to our experimental provocation will already have been published before this volume sees print, a special issue on "Anthropocene Feminisms" for *philoSOPHIA: A Journal of Continental Feminism*, co-edited by Claire Colebrook and Jami Weinstein, who also presented papers at the C21 conference on Anthropocene Feminism in 2014.

1

We Have Always Been Post-Anthropocene: The Anthropocene Counterfactual

CLAIRE COLEBROOK

The proposed (and close to consecrated) conception of the Anthropocene epoch appears to mark as radical a shift in species awareness as Darwinian evolution effected for the nineteenth century. If the notion of the human species' emergence in time requires new forms of narrative, and imaginative and ethical articulation, then the intensifying sense of the species' *end* makes a similar claim for rethinking "our" processes of self-presentation and self-preservation.[1] Rather than Darwin's timeline of life's grandeur, with a (random but fortuitous) proliferation of difference and complexity, we might have to confront a sudden event of geological impact within an intensively human timeline. Rather than one more event *within time,* not only does the Anthropocene—as did Darwinian evolution—require us to shift our scale of narration away from human generations and history to species' emergence and deep time; it also raises the problem of intersecting scales, combining the human time of historical periods (late capitalism, industrialism, nuclear power) with a geological time of the planet. This, in turn, requires us to open the classically feminist question of the *scale of the personal.*[2] If, as Kate Millett argued, the personal is the political, then this requires us to make some decision as to what counts as the political: is my personal sense of gender meaningful only in terms of the history of the human family, *or* in terms of the narrower history of bourgeois marriage, *or* might we say that the personal is geological and that, to understand the sexed subject, I need to take the emergence of the human species, and the domination of the planet (and other humans), into account?[3]

Bruno Latour has argued that awareness of the Anthropocene closes down the modern conception of the infinite universe, drawing us back once again to the parochial, limited, and exhausted earth.[4] Rather than an open horizon of possibility limited only by the pure laws of logic or universal reason, we are now the "earthbound." Latour draws on the work of Alexandre Koyré, who had defined the modern infinite universe in contrast with the closed world: the *world* is a collection of beings, each defined according to its created kind and each giving the whole its specific and interconnected way of being, as though the cosmos were a grand organism.[5] By contrast, the infinite universe allows for the thought of matter as such, subject to the formal measures of physics; the modern subject, in turn, is a purely formal, rational, and calculative being. Against this modern abstraction of a world of matter opposed to a subject, Latour has argued for contemporary modes of existence defined quite specifically by relation to a singular world lived in its power to affect and to be a matter of concern.[6] The "universe" is no longer a horizon of infinite possibility where we are morally compelled to act "as if" the laws of reason might one day yield a fully rational existence, freed from all pathology.[7] For Latour the detached and objective comportment of modern science will not help us deal with what matters most in a world of climate change. Where once science might have been defined as a practice of logic and truth, pure in its difference from the interests of everyday life, the world that we deal with can no longer be regarded as abstract matter but must be considered as something that has its reality by way of what we do and how we observe. The notion of the earth as bounded, as anything but unlimited, seems to have forced itself upon us. Our potentials and what we can do with ourselves and the planet are not limited by the laws of formal physics or logic but are determined by variables and volatilities that we cannot fully command. As Naomi Oreskes and Eric Conway have argued, one of the contributing factors in the ongoing failure to act on climate change has been a conception of science as an isolated activity *not* bound up with systems of political action and social dynamics.[8] What is required, Latour argues, is a sense of ourselves as *earthbound*—not as observers of matter but as oriented toward matters of concern in which our own being depends on a *world* (a specific world, not an open universe).

If this is so—if we have to abandon the notion that whatever we take the world to be, it might always be otherwise, offering infinite possibilities imagined by way of scientific progress—then it might require us to redefine all those *hyper*-modern proclamations of a posthuman, postfeminist, and postracial future (which rely on refusing forms of intrinsic difference) as *hypo*-modern. We are *not* faced with infinite and open potentiality or becoming; the modern notion of self-definition and a world devoid of any kinds or essences is giving way to differences and distinctions that force themselves upon us; we cannot look back on what we have become and how we have evolved and argue that nothing prevents us from becoming anything we want to be. Nowhere is this shift from indifference to difference more intense than in the problem of feminism. To argue, for example, that sex is an effect of gender, or that we only know life as differentiated *after* the event of human systems of communication, is to refuse matter's resistance and recalcitrance—not its vibrancy or its agency so much as its tendency to remain indifferent.[9] Here I would like to contrast two senses of indifference: the first would be hypermodern and—like Koyré's open universe—exemplified by the notion of a conception of matter as pure quantity without tendencies of its own, subsumable and easily mastered by abstract or formal conceptions of being. Something of this is sustained today in Alain Badiou's conception of being as a *pure* multiplicity; however we determine or quantify being, being is not reducible to the sense we make of it—being *is thinkable only as a void, as what exists after the subtractions of all qualifications.*[10]

Another conception of indifference, and one that I would like to pursue in this chapter, is *hypo*-modern: refusing the disjunction between *either* a closed (fully differentiated) world whose intrinsic sense, difference, and life we need to respect *or* a void that is differentiated or qualified by reason. I would like to propose an indifference that is destructive of inscribed difference, but *not* because there is something like a pure, undifferentiated matter that requires structures of language to render it distinct. There has been a widespread rejection (and revival) of undifferentiated lifeless matter: Jane Bennett insists on matter's own vitality and difference, against the notion of a neutral substrate or a restriction of life and action to organisms.[11] By contrast, Alain Badiou defines Being as a void beyond all predication, but Badiou is perhaps the last in a line of thinkers who want to think of Being as such, and not the difference of Beings. The form of indifference I am charting here would refuse both these notions: neither is the world differentiated by human predication or linguistic structures (being a blank matter before all form), nor does it bear its intrinsic qualities. Indifference is how we might think about an "essentially" rogue or anarchic conception of life that is destructive of boundaries, distinctions, and identifications. To live is to tend toward *indifference,* where tendencies and forces result less in distinct kinds than in complicated, confused, and disordered partial bodies. (One might think here of the human body, whose vital attachment to the earth, food, sex, language, technology, and other humans not only disperses the self across a series of connections but also operates as much to diminish as to intensify stability. The more we attach ourselves to food production and consumption, the more the planet and human bodies suffer from excess and depletion. The more we invest in sexual, commodity, or political desire, the more rigid and elusive networks of pleasure come to be. The more "we" reflect upon "our" mark on the planet, the more we appear to be a single polluting species, while also being more and more divided by the causes and consequences of what has come to be known as the Anthropocene. In short, the more "we" appear to be unified as a species, differentiated from other species, and the more we become defined by the claim of *the* Anthropocene, the more mindful we should become of all the forces and tendencies too minimal to appear as differences.)

Rather than returning to conceptions of the bounded earth as a single living, mutually interdependent organism with its own differences and kinds, we might think of all the differences we make and mark as supervening on a world that does *not* come with its own inscription or difference but is not, for all that, devoid of a complexity that will always exceed any of the differences we read into the world. The Anthropocene has presented itself to many as a nonnegotiable difference: "we" abandon a world that was deemed to be indifferent to our narrow historical periods, and "we" recognize that human history is geologically significant after all and that "we" have made a definitive difference. (There is, once again, a "we" rendered fully present by Anthropocene scarring.) Against this narrative of nonnegotiable and definitive difference, I would suggest that we think about indifference not by referring to a universe devoid of determination (the modern and purely calculable blank matter or substance without qualities that we might come to know disinterestedly). Indifference is the milieu in which we live, always destroying and confusing inscribed differences. This notion of indifference combines *both* Gilles Deleuze's notion that the virtual is more different than the clumsy categories of our differentiated world and Giorgio Agamben's argument that difference emerges from indifference—that difference comes into being and is always haunted by its dissolution.[12] Taking these two very abstract notions seriously would require us to think of the Anthropocene *both* as a difference that emerges from other potential stratifications (a differentiation of a world that might have been more finely or acutely differentiated) *and* as something that prompts the question of the counter-Anthropocene. At what point does a difference make a difference or appear *as different*? Had "we" behaved differently, perhaps we would not have become the species that made a difference; at what point or threshold of our polluting, ecosystem-destroying history did we make a difference? Here indifference does not signal what Daniel Dennett has referred to as the "substrate-neutral" character of evolving life, where the random algorithms of combinations of elements yield complexity.[13] Instead, indifference operates as a counter-Anthropocene provocation. If the Anthropocene is the return of difference—because humans are once again exceptional, but now in their destructive and inscriptive impact—it might be worth asking how such difference is inscribed and on what scale such difference operates. What might it mean to think a counterfactual scenario where humans had *not* inflicted the difference of the Anthropocene on the planet?

At the question of scale, we might ask why it is that a certain geological stratification is privileged as finally confirming human impact and difference, and what possible human existence might have prevented such a scar from occurring. If the Anthropocene is a judgment that constitutes us once again, *as human,* and as different from other species in our impact, then we need to decide at what point planetary impact is deemed to be inscriptive. There are a whole series of thresholds, ranging from sedentary agriculture to colonization, the steam engine, nuclear energy, and capitalism. Not only might we contest just where and at what register differences are inscribed but further political questions might be raised about the convergence of difference. The time of politics and the time of the planet, once deemed to be distinct, are now colliding, but not converging.

Questions of politics were once *of the polity,* so that if we were to think that the "personal is political," then we would look to the history of wages, domestic labor, gender norms, reproductive medicine, education, and cultural production. Today, thinking about the politics of any person (including the very possibility of personhood with rights and freedoms) would also need to be mindful that the capitalism that enabled liberal freedom and personhood relied on favorable conditions that exploited the world's poor and that are almost certainly unsustainable into the future.[14]

The Anthropocene emerges as a dissonant difference; post-Darwinian humans have lived with a sense of the difference of scale between a human time of generations (politics) and the dwarfing times of geological change. To talk about humans *as such* was once deemed to be counterpolitical, with politics being definitively marked in Fredric Jameson's imperative to "always historicize," where history does *not* mean referring to anything as dedifferentiating as "the human condition."[15] In the Anthropocene, these two timelines, in their dissonance and difference, intersect: geological change is occurring within human and humanly experienced time. Human activity—the impact of a single species—has reached such an intensity as to generate geological inscription; this Anthropocene dissonance of difference is privileged precisely because scales that were deemed to be divergent are now converging. Species and geology are now coarticulated; we look at the earth—now—as if, in our future absence, we will be readable as having been. Other forms of human impact—such as pollution or the destruction of ecosystems—have long been acknowledged, but with the claim made for the Anthropocene, a particular difference is deemed to be dramatically different. We do not just make the earth different; we make it different on a different scale. From a modernity in which apparent difference was vanquished—acknowledging only life or matter without intrinsic difference—posthuman claims for being one more aspect of a general "life" have now been vanquished.

The return of "man" opens the last few decades of difference theory up for question. What needs to be rethought are some of the key motifs of what has come to be known as "theory." First, the notion that there is no such thing as the human (either by way of our difference from animals or because of intrahuman differences in culture and history) must give way to a sense of the human as defined by destructive impact. Second, theory (at least in its poststructuralist phase) supposedly placed the real or the material in parentheses, knowable only after the event as that which is made sense of by inscription. But it was precisely at the point that humans regarded the world as an "in itself," known only as it is for us, that "we" were doing damage to the earth itself. Modernity started to destroy the material substrate of its existence at the same time as modernity increasingly denied any reality other than that known and constituted by man. The Anthropocene seems to arrive just as a whole new series of materialisms, vitalisms, realisms, and inhuman turns require "us" to think about what has definite and forceful existence regardless of our sense of world. Not only does the ambivalence of the Anthropocene concern two temporalities (opening us to geological impact while drawing us back to human agency and human historical force); it also pulls in contrary directions with regard to what might be thought of as posthumanity. On one hand, we can no longer afford to think of the world as defined solely through meaning and givenness. As Quentin Meillassoux has argued, "ancestral statements" regarding a time of the planet beyond humans force us to think of a truth beyond our own sense and existence.[16] In this respect, speculative realism might be seen as attuned to an awareness that humans do *not* constitute the world and that there is being beyond human meaning and agency. On the other hand, it is the same Quentin Meillassoux who argues that no natural law (of causality, physics, logic, or mind) can impede the thought of what could with *all logical possibility* defy anything that we might take to be necessary. Meillassoux's influential work, which in many ways inaugurated a whole series of new realisms, is exemplary of a combined chastening of the human—because we no longer assume that the world is reducible to the world *for us*—and a magisterial elevation of thinking: whatever presents itself as natural or necessary is nevertheless given contingently and might always be thought otherwise. I would suggest that, rather than simply say that philosophy, theology, politics, and common sense always have opposing tendencies (though that may be true), the diverging temporalities and humanisms/posthumanisms of the Anthropocene prompt the question of the ways in which human difference and indifference might be thought.

One effect of the Anthropocene has been a new form of difference: it now makes sense to talk of humans as such, both because of the damage "we" cause and because of the myopia that allowed us to think of the world as so much matter or "standing reserve." Humans are, now, different; and whatever the injustices and differences of history and colonization, "we" are now united in being threatened with nonexistence. Alongside the return of the repressed of human exceptionalism and the acceptance that we are now different after all, we might also need to confront a *new form of indifference*. We might need to think beyond the nonnegotiable terrain of sexual difference, where all life emerges from relations and encounters between tendencies. One thing is certain: if there had not been sexual difference in its narrowest sense (man and woman), there could not have been the nuclear family, division of labor, and then industrialism. At the same time, if there had not been industrialism, at least in our world history, women would not have been liberated from domestic labor and granted access to the forms of planet-exploitative luxuries that have generated personhood in its modern Western liberal sense. Life may generate sexual difference as organic life emerges, but there is also a stronger or narrower sense of gendered sexual difference—familial, personal, binary sexual difference—that relies on the same processes of "civilization" that generated the Anthropocene. The family and gendered divisions of labor become crucial for intensified practices of imperialism, militarization, colonization, indentured labor, slavery, and mass production. So we might ask at what point living difference became sexual; at what point organisms relied on sexual difference for the ongoing evolution of life; and at what point that sexual difference became gendered, personal, and productive of the figure of familial "man," who would in turn become destructive of the planet.

For something like human and organic sexual difference and the entire trajectory of feminism and feminist consciousness to emerge, there must have been a longer duration of geological temporality that enabled humanity, its harnessing of the planet's energy, and then (finally) the sexually differentiated person. Again, we come up against the problem of indifferent difference: something like man as such, the human as such, emerges from an inscriptive technological trajectory that does not include all humans, and certainly not all life. How is something differentiated, and what other differences might have been drawn such that "we" might *not* have become the species that was capable of making a geological and destructive difference? If we are claiming that the Anthropocene epoch is a game changer that forces us to rethink a "we" that is given in destructive impact, then we are also prompted to ask about another possible world where what has come to be known as human did not generate such a trace. Why (in the Anthropocene) have we fetishized the differences of our own making, and why are we so sure that we know about the differences that make a difference, or the differences that are readable? Here I would like to make a claim for feminism as a critical labor of difference and indifference. Feminism draws attention to differences that have been deemed not to make a difference, but it has also just as frequently denied what have been declared to be constitutive differences (gender differences, historical differences, religious difference).

This essay was originally delivered at the Center for 21st Century Studies' Anthropocene Feminism conference in April 2014 at the University of Wisconsin–Milwaukee. The center's director, Richard Grusin, opened the conference with a question regarding the possibility of anthropocene feminism (singular) or anthropocene feminisms (plural). I want to suggest that we keep feminism in the singular as one overwhelming problem that generates—inevitably, but in a way that is singular—an impossible multiple. Feminism is always the question of *who*: who speaks, for whom, and whose subjectivity is presupposed in the grammar of the question? Feminism wages a war over difference, either by claiming that woman is *not* subsumable beneath the figure of man or by insisting that women cannot be set apart or excluded from the world of man. Consider Mary Wollstonecraft: when confronted with the claim for the "rights of man," she does not ask to be included but instead asks about *who* this man of rights and reason is. Wollstonecraft argues that "man" is composed as a master in relation to a woman whose reason he does not allow; "woman" is at this stage of history only able to be a "who" by playing the game of submission to male mastery.[17] Just as Wollstonecraft is critical of woman as composed (and politicizes woman by generating a frame of historical difference such that woman might be different from her current historical actuality), so later feminists placed various figures of man or the subject within a specific field, thereby opening the personal to a grander scale. Not only, then, is feminism a contestation of difference and indifference; it is also the opening of a war of scale: rather than accepting a problem as articulated, questions of sexual difference and indifference generate the problem of the composition of articulations. If we talk about "woman" as such, are we referring to the identity that emerges from the history of the family, or is "woman" a figure of Western modernity, comprehensible only with the formation of sexual subjects, *or* do we think of woman not as occurring within the history of humanity but as constituted in a sexual contract that enabled what we are now referring to as the human of the Anthropocene? Now, more than ever, feminism is presented with the question of point of view: there has always been a composed "who" or "we"—which makes any question or discipline possible. In the case of the Anthropocene, we might ask, who is this Anthropos who dates himself at the point of the Industrial Revolution or some other mark of his own making? Does this man of the Anthropocene know what he is saying when he makes a claim for "we" humans: who is he when he talks this way? Does this man of the Anthropos realize what was required to ask the questions he asks and have the desires he expresses? (The very discipline of geology and the conception of historical reflection and global inclusion rely on the same technoindustrial history that generated the Anthropocene scar.) Here I want to suggest that if the personal is political, then it is also geological: this is not to say that geology *as stratified* is the scale that must be deployed to read all other scales but that the figure of "man" in the Anthropocene—industrial man, *Homo faber, Homo economicus,* consumer man, nuclear man—cannot claim to be humanity as such without a prior history of appropriation and stratification.

Anthropocene feminism is therefore multiple, but only in being singular, by always asking, *whose* Anthropocene? When we talk about the planet having been scarred to the point of being geologically readable, what future reader do we imagine, and who is attributing the inscription, and to whom? An anthropocene feminism would not accept the Anthropocene as an epoch, as a line or stratum whose significance would not be in dispute. Rather than think of this line as privileged and epochal, we might ask for whom this stratum becomes definitive of *the human.* The concept of humans considered as a species, or as defined by the "human condition," destroys history at the traditional political level—of the polity located within socioeconomic history—and opens a new political scale, but this scale cannot be simply definitive. Since Marxism at least, political questions have contested historical scale: what you take to be "human," "personal," "sexual," or "natural" needs to be expanded to consider the history from which such timeless notions emerge, but there is no properly political–historical scale. I might consider my sexual identity to be explicable only in terms of mass media conceptions of twenty-first-century subjectivity and lifestyle marketing, *or* I might think that the bourgeois family and oedipal individual are the proper frames of reference, *or* that the family and sexuality emerge from a more intense germinal influx of prepersonal human time, *or* I might think that understanding personal sexuality requires an understanding of an even deeper deep time, focusing on human evolution. The Anthropocene has tended to erase the problem of scale and has done so by fetishizing difference (the privileged difference, of *this* line, readable by this modality of man). The policy implications of the Anthropocene have tended to suspend the typically feminist questions of this "we" that we seek to maintain and has instead led to the return to supposed species solidarity. Worse still, the Anthropocene state of emergency is deemed to be of such severity as to short-circuit deliberation; just as the 2008 global financial crisis allowed the immediate bailout of banks without questions of justice and blame being allowed to delay what was declared to be a necessary response, so the severity of the Anthropocene presents itself as justification in advance for executive actions (such as geoengineering). How is it that geological readability (of a specific scale) has become that which defines the human? Does not this stratum of the Anthropocene and what "we" have done imply another possible form of human life that did not reach the point of this late-technoindustrial mode of readability? Now might be the time to think about pre- or non-Anthropocene humans, beings who did not manage to define themselves as a species by way of climate change. How might "we" have been otherwise? Such a consideration would then open a calculation: given where we are now (with industrialism, technoscience, mass media, globalism, and traditions of liberal justice), there might be a threshold at which we might be prepared to sacrifice the historical "progress" we made for the sake of living better. At what point did we become Anthropocene humans? With the invention of the steam engine, with nuclear energy, or perhaps earlier, with the forms of the sedentary polity that generated the ideas behind these technologies?

What does the Anthropocene tell us? In what ways is it a game changer? Or in what ways does this event within knowledge and human history alter the relation between thought and its outside? We can begin by thinking three implications to do, respectively, with humanity (and posthumanity), temporality (and history), and sexual difference (and gender).

I want to explore these three possible implications while entertaining the Anthropocene counterfactual: let us imagine that all that is named by the Anthropocene (cataclysmic and irreversible human destruction of the planet) had *not* occurred. What would we lose or gain, and would we think and act differently if we could live our time over? The reason why I want to pose this counterfactual is to test an insight from phenomenology and postphenomenology whereby any event that occurs—such as the Anthropocene—should not be seen as external or accidental: *if something is possible, then it should not be deemed to be inessential but should alert us to what it is in the essence that allows for such a possibility.* This is not to confuse a possibility with a necessity, but it *is* to say that if something takes place, then it must be a potentiality that is not extrinsic to the being or life under consideration. Or, put less abstractly, what is life such that it is able to generate a species capable of destroying all life? We already know the answer to that question: extinction is not the opposite of life but is part of life's possibility. (Elizabeth Povinelli has argued that potentiation entails being extinguished: to see something as being able to be otherwise is to see it as living and responsive but also to see it as bound up with the nonliving, as having taken place at the expense of something else.[18])

We might want to say that we can imagine a non-Anthropocene (or even post-Anthropocene) human; what we have come to know as "man" might have evolved differently. Why, then, did human life as it is actualize the capacity to be milieu-destructive: how might we have been otherwise, and would this be the same "we"? We can readily admit that extinction is intrinsic to life. After all, we know that life emerges from catastrophic change and that human life emerged not only after the mass extinction of nonhuman living species but also in a species bifurcation (where we can just as well imagine another world where the Neanderthals became the species who would possibly look back at once-existing humans). Extinction is the way of the world and of life. But the Anthropocene is different, at least intensively; there is not just more extinction but a coming into being and passing away that differ in kind. For hundreds of years, we have read the fossil record and noted the extinction of many species, but if the Anthropocene is true, humans will have become extinct and not just left a fossil here and there but marked out a geological strata. We knew that life was intertwined with extinction, but we did not know that a life-form could have geological impact.

So let us entertain the counterfactual: humans came into being but did not develop technology to the point where the geological impact of the Anthropocene took place. Some evidence of what such a humanity might look like is offered in societies that have not employed the intensive industrialized agriculture that alters the earth's biomass. Not embarking on that route (of industrialized agriculture) avoids intensive resource depletion and carbon emissions. Of course, it is possible (logically at least) that we might have had a world of industrialized agriculture and production that was not dependent on fossil fuels and finite resources. If such a world were possible, is it the world we would choose? I want to consider this counterfactual scenario before looking at what has become of history, humanity, and sexual difference in the actual Anthropocene world that we didn't necessarily choose but that befell us nevertheless.

Counterfactual 1. Humanity could have developed differently, remaining more nomadic and with a sense of history more attuned to the broader rhythms of the earth beyond that of the human agricultural year and its seasons. This possibility is suggested in Nigel Clark's work on the deep historical time and attunement of Aboriginal Australian culture, which not only works with the temporality of nature—including the use of fire to burn back growth that would otherwise fuel larger catastrophic fires—but also has a sense of climatic change far broader than that of the agricultural year of regular and stable seasons.[19] That is, rather than see climate change as an event befalling a stable nature, we might see stable nature as a product of the European imaginary that cannot understand a world that has rhythms and transitions of a complexity greater than the human sense of seasonal change. There's a suggestion in Clark's work that we deconstruct the opposition between climate change denial's claims that major climactic shifts are part of the way of the world and the ecological insistence on the anthropogenic violence done to climate stability: there is no such thing as a natural stability that anthropogenic climate change disturbs in the first instance. "Climate" and "geology" are relational and dynamic composites.

What *is* different about the era of the Anthropocene and anthropogenic climate change on a massive industrialized scale is not that a stable nature has been disturbed but that humans have increasingly stabilized nature to a mechanized and rigid timetable of production based on hyperconsumption, and this in turn has generated volatile and intense change. Climate change in the anthropogenic sense is the consequence of thinking of nature as an unchanging standing reserve. So to think the counterfactual of the Anthropocene would be to imagine that we had not invented nature.[20]

Counterfactual 2. The second possibility is to imagine that the material composition of the world might have been otherwise and that exactly the same technological–industrial complex developed but in a way that drew on a renewable resource that did not pollute the atmosphere (or that humans had managed to find a way, from this planetary composition, to develop solar power or some other technology without costing the earth).

If we entertain the first scenario, how would what we have come to know as humanism/posthumanism, history, and gender be different? One possibility is that there would be no such thing as "*the* human," which relies on a universalizing global imperative that abandons localism and imagines the here and now as being not simply present for me but present for any subject whatever. We might have to think seriously about the move to abstraction, logic, and universalism that occurs with the state form. Civilizations of industrial complexity are not simply knowledge events but rely on the harnessing of human power, but this enslavement is in turn a consequence of the earth offering sufficient resources of excess that would enable the sorts of sedentary cultures that in turn enable hierarchical power structures and the development of what Jared Diamond has referred to as *kleptocracy*.[21] We do not have to buy in to Jared Diamond's specific narrative about how stored energy enables social and political complexity and hierarchy; indeed, it would be important to note again that there would be competition for the point at which differences make a difference. Is it with stored grain, monumental architecture, fire, or some other technology that social units become capable of developing intensive production, capable of producing enough energy to generate "culture" in the highly narrow sense? Only with complex archival inscription and material memory systems such as writing could we have both the expansion of empire and the technological history that generates global hyperconsumption. So we might say that it would be well worth sacrificing Euclid and Newton—if that would be a sacrifice—to avoid embarking on the path to globalism and universal humanism. We would lose human rights, but then we might not require them as much. This is not to say that there would not be human-on-human violence, but there would neither be the industrialized violence of genocide and mass slaughter in warfare, nor would there be the state-forming violence required to develop these potentialities for institutionalized violence. That is, it is only with the appropriation of surplus labor that a culture can develop the symbolic systems required for the organized sacrifice and subjection that mark religion and cultural sublimation, and that in turn enable the collective investment for mass warfare. So, if globalism has been one of the crucial conditions for a sense of the universally human, it is also the case that the ethical demand of the universally human seems imperative in a violent cosmos. Along with human rights, we might happily sacrifice universal suffrage, civil rights, and—of course—women's rights, feminism, and certainly ecofeminism, because perhaps we would not quite need these forms of universalism in a simpler and less rationalized cosmos.

That nonglobal, nonindustrial, nontechnoscientific world would be one counter-Anthropocene scenario. Such a possibility poses this very inconvenient truth: what we know *narrowly* as feminism relies on the hyperconsumption mode of globalism. In its enlightened liberal form, feminism requires (at least initially) a reading elite liberated from domestic labor, capable of thinking about the freedom of thought and reason, blessed with the favorable conditions of possible person-hood, and granted the reflective luxury to use the trope of slavery and its opposite. When Wollstonecraft called for the rights of woman and extended the trope of slavery and abolition to the liberation of women, she was relying on technological developments that allowed the greater freedom of humans precisely because industry was now extracting energy from the earth, in the form of coal and other ultimately polluting and depleting resources. Women could start to demand equality precisely because of an industrial capitalism in a certain portion of the world that extended the leisure time once reserved for the very few. It is true that perhaps such feminist rights would not have been required without what Carole Pateman has referred to as the sexual contract and the ongoing familial form that requires stabilization of the state and mastery of what has become "nature."[22] This thought experiment or imagined scenario of the counter-Anthropocene that did not arrive at rights and universalism lends more weight to Walter Benjamin's claim that every document of civilization is a document of barbarism.[23] This is not just to say that string quartets are written and appreciated in the same world as mass slaughter; it is to say that some violent subjection of humans for the sake of generating surplus production and energy is required to release the time and space of the history of enlightenment. Philosophy, rights, and—I would argue—the constitution of a private self with a definitive sexuality and fulfilling life trajectory are not merely contingently placed alongside planetary and human-on-human violence. Dipesh Chakrabarty has argued that had humans not embarked upon the intense depletion of planetary resources that has resulted in the Anthropocene, human enslavement would have been worse than it has been.[24] Quite crudely, we can locate abolition and suffrage movements at the same time that industrialized economies were able to extract more planetary energy with less hold on human energy.

This counterfactual brings us not so much to another possible world without humanism, and without a single history of human enlightenment and private sexuality, but rather to a threshold: it *is* possible to imagine a counterhistory of minimal impact on the planet that might still allow for many of the things we know to be human—including inscription, morality, language, and technology. It is possible to think that humans could never have "progressed" without some planetary damage or alteration but that such "progress" would not have developed to quite such a suicidal and ecocidal pitch and would not have generated the globalism of humanity in general, a single universal time and a private sexual difference, or recognition of one's self via gender.

Let's explore the second counterfactual and ask if we could have these reparative effects of globalism and humanism without damage to the planet and without the violent extraction of human resources. We would need to imagine another material earth, or another technoscience, that began with renewable and nonpolluting energy. We might imagine that, rather than relying on slavery to generate the *otium* required for philosophical reflection, the ancient Greeks had found a resource that was nonviolent and yet still allowed for the thought of humanity to be generated. Is such a world logically possible?

That question itself is, I would suggest, symptomatic of the logic of the Anthropocene: the idea of a life that could develop to its utmost potentiality without incurring debt or death to itself is both what drives technological–industrial investment *and* generates the delusional idea of a life without expense, loss, or misprision; the notion of generating more (in the final instance) than one initially takes, the dream of a pure ecology in which everything serves to maximize everything else and in which there is no cost: it is *this* logic (or the logic of logic, of the pure counterfactual, or pure *techne* without *physis*) that marks all that has stood for humanism, posthumanism, a certain dream of history and of utopian sexual difference. Nowhere is this more evident than in claims for the good Anthropocene: supposedly if we have the power to transform the planet, then we also have the power to transform the planet for the better. Not only does such a dream not ask the question of *whose* betterment the Anthropocene will intend, and not only does the good Anthropocene consecrate the Anthropos in its current form as a prima facie value, but it sustains the valorization of difference: if we have made a difference, then we can make more of a difference. But all the work on the Anthropocene to date, for all its claims of spikes, cannot agree on *the* difference, and rather than see this as a failure of knowledge, we might ask another question. There are multiple markers or claims for the Anthropocene difference: intensive agriculture, changes in the earth's biomass, nuclear energy, colonization, industrialization, capitalism, and so on. Every one of these markers in turn covers over further differences: can we really charge modernity or capitalism in general? Certainly "man" is too broad an agent if one wants to think about the difference the Anthropocene marks, but rather than more nuanced differences, it might be better to note that any such difference—including the usually targeted capitalism—is achieved by way of indifference (not respecting premodern boundaries, identities, hierarchies, or kinds). To say that we might transform the world by way of geoengineering (make it different and better) might be perceived by many as more of the same. To say that we wish "we" had not made such a difference, and that we should strive to find nature again, is also more of the same. Rather than valorize different forms of a utopian humanity—outside capital, outside industry, beyond humanism—one might say that what has come to be known as the Anthropocene is bound up with a logic of mastering and erasing difference. "Man" can either read the Anthropocene and recognize that there is one humanity after all, different in kind from other organic forms of life, *or* man can mark off capitalism or corporations as the agents of destruction. Any "good" Anthropocene would be possible only by way of countless injustices, just as what we think of as justice has occurred by way of a history of passed and erased thresholds. We perhaps know with some certainty that a world without geometry, physics, biology, and mathematics would not have yielded the degree of destruction "we" have today, but there are no lines of difference that would allow us to clean up and mitigate the past (even in our imagination). If there had been no Plato, no Averroes, no culture of fire, we would not be in this mess, but—then—who would we be?

Where does this leave us? Are we just saying that life is intertwined with death, that all ethical relations to others also negotiate violence, and that feminism is a grubby, queer business that can do so much for so few?

If that is what we were saying, then we would be keeping the counter-Anthropocene ideal in place—yes, that pure world is desirable but never fully achievable. I am arguing something far stronger, I hope, that has implications for how we think about the Anthropocene. All our talk of mitigation and stability maintains a notion of stabilized nature, a nature that is ideally there for us and cyclically compatible with production; it does not confront what the Anthropocene *occludes*. We should not think, at precisely the point at which we posit a geological impact of a certain readable sort, that—had we known this—we would or could have acted in a way that was essentially different or noncontaminating. Or, put another way, the Anthropocene *is* the counter-Anthropocene. We look at the geological scar and remark to ourselves, *as though something has changed*: now, finally, the earth is telling us that we have impact. "My goodness, who would have thought that centuries of slavery, violence, kleptocracy, plundering and then liberation of some humans at the expense of others—who would have thought this was a destructive indictment of 'the human'? Who could possibly have imagined that our species was destructive of its milieu without the definitive evidence of the geological record?"

We are thinking of the Anthropocene as exceptional, as a volatility or destabilization of nature that has been caused, accidentally, by us. But what we know about the political state of exception is this: *if* law can be suspended and lead to a condition of immediate force, without law, then we can experience this lawlessness, this loss of the proper, as always potential, *because there is nothing proper about law.*[25] By analogy, this loss of nature, this exceptional volatility and antihuman hostility *of nature* (where nature is now changing on us, refusing to be stable), is the condition from which what we know as the Anthropocene manufactured a stable nature. What we now call climate change is the reemergence of what made climate possible. Climate was manufactured from climate change.

This event of the Anthropocene is exceptional—but not by being extrinsic to what we have come to refer to as nature or humanity; if, now, we are responding to planetary destruction with surprise, and wondering how we might engineer a future that would *not* cost the earth, then the Anthropocene is hardly an event. It is the continuation of "man" as the being who believes that he can finally be different and who transforms himself to the point where, in his relation to the planet, he no longer makes a difference. And if woman—in the form of ecofeminism—claims that she and she alone can offer a *proper, connected, natural, and attuned* relation to the earth, then we have chosen a gendered sexual difference at the expense of the question of how gendered sexual being emerges from a history that is ecologically bound up with violence and depletion.

NOTES

1. See Gillian Beer, *Darwin's Plots: Evolutionary Narrative in Darwin, George Eliot, and Nineteenth-Century Fiction,* 3rd ed. (Cambridge: Cambridge University Press, 2009).

2. Timothy Clark, "Derangements of Scale," in *Telemorphosis: Theory in the Era of Climate Change,* ed. Tom Cohen (Ann Arbor, Mich.: Open Humanities Press, 2012), 1:148–66.

3. Kate Millett, *Sexual Politics* (New York: Doubleday, 1970).

4. Bruno Latour, "Facing Gaia: Six Lectures on the Political Theology of Nature," Gifford Lectures on Natural Religion, 2013, http://www.bruno-latour.fr.

5. Alexandre Koyré, *From the Closed World to the Infinite Universe* (Baltimore: Johns Hopkins University Press, 1957).

6. Bruno Latour, *What Is the Style of Matters of Concern?* (Amsterdam: Van Gorcum, 2008).

7. Immanuel Kant, *Groundwork of the Metaphysics of Morals,* trans. and ed. Allen W. Wood (New Haven, Conn.: Yale University Press, 2002).

8. Naomi Oreskes and Erik M. Conway, *The Collapse of Western Civilization: A View from the Future* (New York: Columbia University Press, 2014).

9. On sex as an effect of gender, see Judith Butler, *Gender Trouble* (London: Routledge, 1990); Moira Gatens, "A Critique of the Sex/Gender Distinction," in *A Reader in Feminist Knowledge,* ed. Sneja Gunew (London: Routledge, 1991); and Teresa de Lauretis, *Technologies of Gender: Essays on Theory, Film, and Fiction* (Bloomington: Indiana University Press, 1987).

10. Alain Badiou, *Being and Event,* trans. Oliver Feltham (London: Continuum, 2007).

11. Jane Bennett, *Vibrant Matter: A Political Ecology of Things* (Durham, N.C.: Duke University Press, 2010).

12. Gilles Deleuze, *Difference and Repetition,* trans. Paul Patton (New York: Columbia University Press, 1994); Giorgio Agamben, *The Open: Man and Animal* (Stanford, Calif.: Stanford University Press, 2004).

13. Daniel C. Dennett, *Darwin's Dangerous Idea: Evolution and the Meanings of Life* (New York: Simon and Schuster, 1995).

14. Tim Mulgan, *Ethics for a Broken World: Imagining Philosophy after Catastrophe* (Montreal: McGill-Queen's University Press, 2011).

15. Fredric Jameson, *The Political Unconscious: Narrative as a Socially Symbolic Act* (Ithaca, N.Y.: Cornell University Press, 1981).

16. Quentin Meillassoux, *After Finitude: An Essay on the Necessity of Contingency,* trans. Ray Brassier (London: Continuum, 2009).

17. Mary Wollstonecraft, *A Vindication of the Rights of Woman/Mary Wollstonecraft* (New York: Alfred A. Knopf, 1992).

18. Elizabeth A. Povinelli, "After the Last Man: Images and Ethics of Becoming Otherwise," *e-flux Journal* 35 (May 2012), http://www.e-flux.com/.

19. Nigel Clark, "Aboriginal Cosmopolitanism," *International Journal of Urban and Regional Research* 32, no. 3 (2008): 737–44.

20. Timothy Morton, *Ecology without Nature: Rethinking Environmental Aesthetics* (Cambridge, Mass.: Harvard University Press, 2007).

21. Jared Diamond, *Guns, Germs, and Steel: The Fates of Human Societies* (New York: W. W. Norton, 1999).

22. Carole Pateman, *The Sexual Contract* (Stanford, Calif.: Stanford University Press, 1988).

23. Walter Benjamin, "Theses on the Philosophy of History," in *Illuminations: Essays and Reflections,* ed. Hannah Arendt, trans. Harry Zohn, 253–64 (New York: Schocken, 1969).

24. Dipesh Chakrabarty, "The Climate of History: Four Theses," *Critical Inquiry* 35 (Winter 2009): 197–222.

25. Giorgio Agamben, *State of Exception,* trans. Kevin Attell (Stanford, Calif.: Stanford University Press, 2005).

2

Four Theses on Posthuman Feminism

ROSI BRAIDOTTI

This chapter adopts an affirmative stance and provides cartography of the intersections between feminism and the posthuman predicament by arguing the following theses: that feminism is *not* a humanism; that Anthropos has been decentered and so is the emphasis on *bios*; and that, as a result, nonhuman life, *zoe,* is now the ruling concept. Last, but not least, the chapter works out the implications of these shifts of perspective for feminist theory and practice, arguing that sexuality is a force beyond, beneath, and after gender.

FEMINISM IS *NOT* A HUMANISM

There is no underestimating the ties that bind Western feminism, in its liberal as well as socialist variables, to Enlightenment-based humanism. From Mary Wollstonecraft to Simone de Beauvoir, the political case for women's and other minorities' emancipation has been argued along the lines of a notion of equality that assumes an unproblematic belonging to the same category of humanity. This position tended to view the natural order as servitude, violence, and brutality: nature as the naturalization of inequalities. The extent of that sense of belonging to a common idea of the human, however, has come under severe scrutiny from several quarters, especially in the last thirty years.

While the philosophical poststructuralist generation developed its own brand of antihumanism, a radical feminist wave, antiracist critical theory, environmental activists, disability rights advocates, and LGBT theorists have questioned the scope, the founding principles, and the achievements of European humanism and its role in the project of Western modernity. These social and theoretical movements questioned the idea of the human that is implicit in the humanist ideal of "Man" as the alleged "measure of all things." This ideal skillfully combines high standards of physical perfection with intellectual and moral values, turning into a civilizational standard. Michel Foucault—a master of high antihumanism—linked this humanist ideal to a sovereign notion of "reason" that, since the eighteenth century, has provided the basic unit of reference for what counts as human and for everything European culture holds dear.[1] The humanist "Man" claims exclusive access to self-reflexive reason for the human species, thus making it uniquely capable of self-regulating rational judgment. These qualities allegedly qualify our species for the pursuit of both individual and collective self-improvement following scientific and moral criteria of perfectibility. The boundless faith in reason as the motor of human evolution ties in with the teleological prospect of the rational progress of humanity through science and technology.[2]

The "death of Man," announced by Foucault, formalized the epistemological and political crisis of the humanistic habit of placing "Man" at the center of world history.[3] Even Marxism, under the cover of a theory of historical materialism, continued to define the subject of European thought as unitary and hegemonic and to assign him (the gender is no coincidence) a royal place as the motor of social and cultural evolution. Philosophical antihumanism consists in delinking the human agent from this universalistic posture, calling him to task, so to speak, on his concrete actions. Different and sharper analyses of power relations become possible once the obstacle of the dominant subject's delusions of grandeur has been removed. Feminist politics of location, reelaborated through the standpoint of feminist theory and the analysis of the racialized economy of science, produced situated knowledges as the method for grounding micropolitical analyses of power.[4] A more adequate self-understanding emerges once it has become clear that nobody is actually in charge of the course of historical progress.[5] Thanks to feminist and postcolonial analyses, we have come to regard the human standard that was posited in the universal mode of "Man of reason" as inadequate precisely because of its partiality.[6]

This allegedly universal ideal is brought back to his historically contingent roots and exposed as very much a male of the species: it is a *he*.[7] Class, race, and gender never being too far apart from each other, in the intersectional mode pioneered by feminist race theory, *this* particular male is moreover assumed to be white, European, head of a heterosexual family and its children, and able-bodied.[8] In other words, the dominant subject is implicitly assumed to be masculine, white, urbanized, speaking a standard language, heterosexually inscribed in a reproductive unit, and a full citizen of a recognized polity.[9]

Such rational self-assurance has historically played a major role in the construction of a civilizational model that equated Europe with the universalizing powers of reason and progress. This hegemonic cultural model was instrumental to the colonial ideology of European expansion: "white Man's burden" as a tool of imperialist governance assumed that Europe is not just a geopolitical location but also a universal attribute of the human mind that can lend its quality to any suitable objects, provided they comply with the required discipline. Europe as universal consciousness posits the power of reason as its distinctive characteristic and humanistic universalism as its particularity. This makes Eurocentrism into a qualitatively more pervasive trait than a matter of attitude: it is rather a structural element of Europe's self-representation, implemented in both theoretical and institutional practices.

In response to this normative model, feminist, antiracist, and other social movements, notably the environmental and peace movements since the 1970s, developed their own variations of activist antihumanism or radical neohumanism. On this point, the intersections between feminism and race or postcolonial theory are intense and mutually enriching, though not deprived of tensions. Their criticism is focused on two interrelated ideas: the Self–Other dialectics, on one hand, and the notion of difference as pejoration, on the other. They both rest on the assumption that subjectivity as a discursive and material practice is equated with rational, universal consciousness and self-regulating moral behavior, whereas Otherness is defined as its negative opposite. Dialectically redefined as "other than," difference is inscribed on a hierarchical scale that spells inferiority and means "to be worth less than." Such epistemic violence acquires ruthless connotations for real-life people who happen to coincide with categories of negative difference: women, native, and earthly Others. They are the sexualized, racialized, and naturalized "Others" whose social and symbolic existence is disposable and unprotected. Because their history in Europe and elsewhere has been one of lethal exclusions and fatal disqualifications, these "Others" raise crucial issues of power, domination, and exclusion. As Donna Haraway put it, some differences are playful, but others are poles of world-historical systems of domination.[10] Feminist epistemology is about knowing the difference. The antihumanist feminist generation embraced the concept of difference with the explicit aim of making it function differently. Irigaray's provocative question "equal to whom?" is emblematic of this switch away from homologation or reduction to a masculine standard of Sameness.[11]

Feminist critiques of abstract masculinity, triumphant whiteness, and hegemonic able-bodiedness added further criticism on different political grounds.[12] They advocated the need to destabilize this unitary vision of the subject and open it up to the multiple and complex reconfigurations of diversity and multiple belongings, so as to challenge the dominant vision of the "others within" that so far had just confirmed the European subject's self-representation.[13] They also argued that it is impossible to speak in one unified voice about any category, including women, natives, and other marginal subjects. The emphasis falls instead on the internal fractures within each subject-position, or the "difference within." The death of Man paved the way for the deconstruction of Woman and all other categories, in terms of their internal complexities.

Another current of thought that left a significant mark on the humanism–antihumanism debate can be traced back genealogically to the anticolonial phenomenology of Frantz Fanon and of his teacher Aimé Césaire.[14] They take humanism as an unfulfilled project, betrayed by Eurocentric violence, and aim to develop its antiracist and inclusive potential. They are committed to exploring new understandings of humanity after colonialism. Contemporary postcolonial and race theorists continue to pursue this project. They argue the fundamental point that Enlightenment-based ideals of reason, secular tolerance, equality under the Law, and democratic rule need not be, and historically have not been, mutually exclusive with European practices of violent domination, exclusion, and instrumental use of terror. Acknowledging that reason and barbarism are not self-contradictory, nor are Enlightenment and horror, need not result in cultural relativism, or in nihilism, but rather in a radical critique of Western humanism. Edward Said taught us that it is possible to be critical of humanism in the name of humanism and to draw from non-Western sources the inspiration to fulfill the potential of the humanist project.[15] Paul Gilroy's planetary cosmopolitanism pursues this tradition of thinking today and takes critical distance from the posthuman predicament by reiterating that we are simply not all human in the same way or to the same extent.[16]

Another relevant strand of neohumanist discourse emerges within environmental activism, and it combines the critique of the epistemic and physical violence of modernity with that of European colonialism. The ecofeminist and environmental "green politics" asserts the need for both bio- and anthropodiversity.[17] Other examples of this ecological and situated cosmopolitan humanism are Avtar Brah's diasporic ethics and Vandana Shiva's antiglobal neohumanism, and African humanism, or Ubuntu, is receiving more attention, from Patricia Hill Collins to Drucilla Cornell.[18] In a more nomadic vein, Édouard Glissant's poetics of relations inscribed multilingual hybridity and the poetics of relation at the heart of the contemporary posthuman condition.[19]

Thus feminism is resolutely antihumanist to the extent that it rejects Eurocentric humanism in the light of its "methodological nationalism."[20] Contemporary European subjects of knowledge must meet the ethical obligation to be accountable for their past history and the long shadow it casts on their present-day politics, as Edgar Morin, Luisa Passerini, Etienne Balibar, and Zygmunt Bauman have also argued.[21] This postnationalist approach expresses the decline of Eurocentrism as a historical event and calls for a qualitative shift of perspective in our collective sense of identity.[22] Posthuman feminism needs to criticize narrow-minded self-interests, intolerance, and xenophobic rejection of Otherness. Symbolic of the closure of the European mind is the fate of migrants, refugees, and asylum seekers, who bear the brunt of racism in contemporary Europe. A primary task for posthumanist feminist theory therefore is to steer Europe toward a posthumanist project of "becoming-minoritarian" or becoming-nomad, which entails resistance against nationalism, xenophobia, and racism—bad habits of the old imperial Europe, currently replicated in "Fortress Europe."[23]

ANTHROPOS IS OFF-CENTER

The debate on and against humanism, pioneered by feminist, post-colonial, and race theorists, despite its multiple internal fractures and unresolved contradictions, appears as a simpler task than displacing anthropocentrism itself. The Anthropocene entails not only the critique of species supremacy—the rule of Anthropos—but also the parameters that used to define it.[24] "Man" is now called to task as the representative of a hierarchical and violent species whose centrality is challenged by a combination of scientific advances and global economic concerns. Neither "Man" as the universal humanistic measure of all things nor Anthropos as the emblem of an exceptional species can claim the central position in contemporary, technologically mediated knowledge production systems. Brian Massumi refers to this phenomenon as "Ex-Man": "a genetic matrix embedded in the materiality of the human" and as such undergoing significant mutations.[25] This shift marks a sort of "anthropological exodus" from the dominant configurations of the human—a colossal hybridization of the species.[26] The decentering of Anthropos challenges also the separation of *bios,* as exclusively human life, from *zoe,* the life of animals and nonhuman entities. What comes to the fore instead is a human–nonhuman continuum, which is consolidated by pervasive technological mediation.

The political implications of this shift are significant. If the revisions of humanism advanced by feminist, queer, antiracist, ecological, and postcolonial critiques empowered the sexualized and racialized—but still human—"Others," the crisis of Anthropos enlists the naturalized others. Animals, insects, plants, cells, bacteria, in fact the planet and the cosmos, are turned into a political arena.[27] The social constructivist habit of thought that reduces nature to the source of inequalities is revised, in the light of methodological naturalism and neomaterialism. There is, consequently, a meta-discursive level of difficulty in the post-anthropocentric turn, due to the fact that antihumanism is essentially a philosophical, historical, and cultural movement and that the bulk of feminist, queer, and postcolonial theories are based in the humanities and the social sciences, whereas the Anthropocene is in dialogue with the life sciences and information technologies.

There are two interlocked problems: the first is that the humanities are marked by constitutive anthropocentrism, which has historically entailed a complicated relationship to science and technology, as shown by the debate about the "two cultures."[28] The second is a central issue of scale, both temporal and spatial: how can the humanities disciplines— history, literature, philosophy—develop planetary and very long term perspectives in a geocentered and not anthropocentric frame? How will the humanities react to "destroying the artificial but time-honored distinction between natural and human histories"?[29] Is it feasible to contemplate—in a secular and rigorous manner—the idea of human extinction without losing academic credibility?

But things get even more complicated: over the last thirty years, a cluster of radical interdisciplinary fields of enquiry emerged institutionally around the edges of the classical humanities and called themselves "studies." Gender, feminist, queer, race, postcolonial, and subaltern studies, alongside cultural, film, television, and media studies, are the prototypes of the radical epistemologies that have provided a range of new methods and innovative concepts since the 1970s. Institutionally less well funded than the classical disciplines, they have provided new concepts, methods, and insights and have proved to be major sources of inspiration for both the academic world and society. These "studies" areas have targeted the major flaws at the core of the humanities, based on the critiques of humanism I outlined in the previous section, namely, its Eurocentrism, sexism, racism, and methodological nationalism. The point of consensus among the different "studies" areas is that humanist ideals of reason, secularism, tolerance, equality, and democratic rule need to be balanced against the historical reality of European imperialist practices.[30] Acknowledging the compatibility of rationality and violence, however, does not mean that the critical "studies" areas uniformly oppose humanism. It is rather the case, especially for postcolonial studies, that they create alternative visions of the human and of society.

The current postanthropocentric, or posthuman, turn cannot fail to affect the very "studies" areas that, contrary to the field of science and technology studies, may have perfected the critique of humanism but not necessarily relinquished anthropocentrism. A widespread suspicion of the social effects of science and technology seems to pertain to the classical feminist tradition and its Marxist roots. Shulamith Firestone's 1970s technological utopia strikes a rather lonely note in sharp contrast with a rather technophobic attitude in left-wing feminism.[31] The towering work of Donna Haraway in the mid-1980s—in the "Manifesto for Cyborgs"—set an entirely new agenda and established a feminist tradition of politicized science and technology studies integrated with feminist body politics, which changed the rules of the game. Haraway replaced anthropocentrism with a set of relational links to human and nonhuman others, including technological artifacts. She challenged specifically the historical association of females/non-Europeans with nature, stressing the need for feminist and antiracist critiques that rest on a technologically mediated vision of the nature–culture continuum.[32] Donna Haraway offers figurations like the cyborg, oncomouse, companion-species, the modest witness, and other hybrids as figures of radical interspecies relationality.[33] They blur categorical distinctions (human–nonhuman, nature–culture, male–female, oedipal–nonoedipal, European–non-European) in attempting to redefine a program of feminist social justice.

From there on, the collective feminist exit from Anthropos began to gather momentum, and explicit references to the posthuman appear in feminist texts from the 1990s.[34] The postanthropocentric turn takes off as two major issues converge: the first is climate change, which, as Naomi Klein claims, changes everything, including the analytic strategies of feminist and postcolonial studies.[35] The second is information technologies and the high degree of global mediation they entail. These challenges open up new global, ecosophical, posthumanist, and postanthropocentric dimensions of thought. They are expressed by a second generation of critical "studies" areas that are the direct descendants of the first generation of the 1970s critical "studies" areas and pursue the work of critique into new discursive spaces, for instance, cultural studies of science and society, religion studies, disability studies, fat studies, success studies, celebrity studies, and globalization studies, all of which are significant voices of what I have labeled posthuman critical theory. New media is a planet of its own and has spawned several subsections: software studies, Internet studies, game studies, and more. The inhuman(e) aspects of our historical condition—namely, mass migration, wars, terrorism, evictions and expulsions—are addressed by conflict studies and peace research; human rights studies; humanitarian management; human rights–oriented medicine; trauma, memory, and reconciliation studies; security studies; death studies; and suicide studies. And the list is still growing.

Feminist theory is right in the middle of this reconfiguration of knowledge production. The vitality is especially strong in cultural studies and in media and film theory.[36] Building on Haraway's remarkable legacy, feminist science studies goes planetary and displaces the centrality of the human through sophisticated analyses of molecular biology and computational systems.[37] Ecofeminists, who always advocated geocentered perspectives, now expand into animal studies and radical veganism.[38] Feminist theories of non- and posthuman subjectivity embrace nonanthropomorphic animal or technological Others, prompting a posthuman ethical turn.[39] Even feminist interest in Darwin, which had been rare, grows by the end of the millennium.[40]

It follows therefore that, both institutionally and theoretically, the "studies" areas, which historically have been the motor of both critique and creativity, innovative and challenging in equal measure, have an inspirational role to play also in relation to the posthuman context we inhabit. There is a clear intergenerational transition at work within the radical epistemologies expressed by the "studies" areas. Contemporary feminist, gender, queer, postcolonial, and antiracist studies are all the more effective and creative as they have allowed themselves to be affected by the posthuman condition. This turn toward the critical posthumanities marks the end of what Shiva called "monocultures of the mind," and it leads feminist theory to pursue the radical politics of location and the analysis of social forms of exclusion in the current world order of biopiracy, necropolitics, and worldwide dispossession.[41] The posthuman feminist knowing subject is a complex assemblage of human and nonhuman, planetary and cosmic, given and manufactured, which requires major readjustments in our ways of thinking. But she remains committed to social justice and, while acknowledging the fatal attraction of global mediation, is not likely to forget that one-third of the world population has no access to electricity.

Taking critical distance from anthropocentrism, however, raises also a number of affective difficulties: how one reacts to the practice of disloyalty to one's species depends to a large extent on the terms of one's engagement with it, as well as one's assessment of and relationship to contemporary technological developments. In my work, I have always stressed the technophilic dimension and the liberating and even transgressive potential of these technologies against those who attempt to index them to either a predictable conservative profile or a profit-oriented system that fosters and inflates hyperconsumeristic possessive individualism.[42]

The practice of defamiliarization is a key methodological tool to support the postanthropocentric turn. That is a sobering process of disidentification from anthropocentric values, to evolve toward a new frame of reference, which in this case entails becoming relational in a complex and multidirectional manner. Disengagement from dominant models of subject formation has been pioneered in a critical and creative manner by feminist theory in its attempt to disengage from the dominant institutions and representations of femininity and masculinity, also known as the gender system.[43] Postcolonial and race discourse similarly disrupt white privilege and other racialized assumptions about accepted views of what constitutes a human subject.[44]

These disidentifications, however, occur along the axes of difference I outlined earlier—becoming-woman (sexualization) and becoming-other (racialization)—and hence remain within the confines of anthropomorphism. The postanthropocentric turn goes a step further: by challenging the anthropocentric habits of thought, it foregrounds the politics of the "naturalized" nonhuman others and thus requires a more radical break from the assumption of human uniqueness. As a way forward, I have argued for an activist embrace of zoe: nonhuman life. Becoming-earth (geocentered) or becoming-imperceptible (zoe-centered) entails a radical break from established patterns of thought (naturalization) and introduces a radically immanent relational dimension.[45] This break, however, is emotionally demanding at the level of identity, and it can involve a sense of loss and pain. Moreover, disidentification from century-old anthropocentric habits and new relationships to nonhuman others is likely to test the flexibility of the humanities as an established disciplinary field. The "life" sciences, of course, are accomplishing this move away from anthropocentrism with relative ease. It may be worth taking seriously the critical charge that the humanities' development toward complexity is hampered by the anthropocentrism that underscores their institutional practice. In this respect, feminist theory can be relied on to provide original new instruments and concepts, which cannot be dissociated from an ethics of inquiry that demands respect for the complexities of the real-life world we are living in.

Posthuman feminist theory applies a new vision of subjectivity also to the figure of the scientist, which is still caught in the classical and outmoded model of the humanistic "Man of reason" as the quintessential European citizen.[46] Feminism offers an antidote to such androcentric, as well as anthropocentric, attitudes. We need to overcome this "image of thought" and move toward a transdisciplinary approach that affects the very structure of thinking.[47] I would argue strongly for a rhizomatic embrace of conceptual diversity in scholarship, of higher degrees of transdisciplinary hybridization—also at the methodological level—and distance from the flat repetition of the protocols of institutional reason. Zoe-based methodologies can inspire critical theory in the humanities to become the social and cultural branch of complexity theory.

ZOE IS THE RULING PRINCIPLE

All these transformations are not, of course, happening in a vacuum. Advanced capitalism is operating its own opportunistic and exploitative decentering of anthropocentrism, through extensive technoscientific networks. The convergence between different and previously differentiated branches of technology—notably, nanotechnology, biotechnology, information technology, and cognitive sciences—has placed traditional understandings of the human under extreme pressure. The biogenetic structure of contemporary capitalism involves investments in "life" as an informational system; stem cell research and biotechnological intervention upon humans, animals, seeds, cells, and plants pave the way for scientific and economic control and the commodification of all that lives. This context produces a paradoxical and rather opportunistic form of postanthropocentrism on the part of market forces that trade on "life itself."[48] Commercially minded postanthropocentrism treats "life" as both human and nonhuman resource, and a cynical democratization of the value of living organisms is thus enacted.

Informational data are the true capital today, as Patricia Clough points out in in her analysis of the "affective turn."[49] Biogenetic, neural, and mediatic databanks reduce bodies to their informational substrate in terms of energy resources or vital capacities and level out other social differences. The focus is on the accumulation of information itself—its immanent vital qualities and self-organizing capacity. Within the political economy of advanced capitalism, what constitutes capital value is the informational power of living matter itself, a phenomenon that

Melinda Cooper calls "life as surplus."[50] It introduces discursive and material political techniques of population control of a very different order from the administration of demographics that preoccupied Foucault's work on biopolitical governmentality.[51] Today, we are undertaking "risk analyses" not only of entire social and national systems but also of whole sections of the population in the world risk society.[52] The data-mining techniques employed by "cognitive capitalism" to monitor the capacities of "biomediated" bodies—DNA testing, brain fingerprinting, neural imaging, body heat detection, and iris or hand recognition—are also operationalized in systems of surveillance both in civil society and in the wars against terror, according to the necropolitical governmentality that is the trademark of our era.[53]

In response to this system, I would propose species egalitarianism, which opens up productive possibilities of relations, alliances, and mutual specification.[54] This position starts from the pragmatic fact that, as embodied and embedded entities, we are all part of something we used to call "nature," despite transcendental claims made for human consciousness.[55] Resting on a monistic ontology drawn from neo-Spinozist vital materialist philosophy, I have proposed cross-species alliances with the productive and immanent force of *zoe*, or life in its nonhuman aspects.[56] This relational ontology is *zoe*-centered and hence nonanthropocentric, but it does not deny the anthropologically bound structure of the human. Anthropomorphism is our specific embodied and embedded location, and acknowledging its situated nature is the first step toward antianthropocentrism. This shift of perspective toward a *zoe*- or geocentered approach requires a mutation of our shared understanding of what it means to speak and think at all, let alone think critically.

This vitalist approach to living matter displaces the boundary between the portion of life—both organic and discursive—that has traditionally been reserved for Anthropos, that is to say, *bios*, and the wider scope of animal and nonhuman life, also known as *zoe*. The dynamic, self-organizing structure of life as *zoe* stands for generative vitality.[57] It is the transversal force that cuts across and reconnects previously segregated species, categories, and domains. *Zoe*-centered egalitarianism is, for me, the core of the postanthropocentric turn: it is a materialist, secular, grounded, and unsentimental response to the opportunistic transspecies commodification of life that is the logic of advanced capitalism.

The urgent feminist question for me is how to combine the decline of anthropocentrism with issues of social justice. Can an "insurgent postanthropocentrism" come to the rescue of our species?[58] The sense of insurgency in contemporary posthuman scholarship is palpable in the era that Haraway recently labeled the "Capitalocene."[59] Does the posthuman—in its posthumanistic and postanthropocentric inceptions—complicate the issues of human agency and feminist political subjectivity? My argument is that it actually enhances it by offering an expanded relational vision of the self, as a nomadic transversal assemblage engendered by the cumulative effect of multiple relational bonds.[60] The relational capacity of the posthuman subject is not confined within our species, but it includes all nonanthropomorphic elements, starting from the air we breathe. Living matter—including embodied human flesh—is intelligent and self-organizing, but it is so precisely because it is not disconnected from the rest of organic life and connects to the animal and the earth.[61] Nomadic philosophy of radical immanence foregrounds embodiment and embeddedness, not disconnection from the thinking organism. We think with the entire body, or rather, we have to acknowledge the embodiment of the brain and the embrainment of the body.[62] In this respect, vital materialist feminism should strike an alliance with extended mind theories and distributed cognition models inspired by Spinoza and with qualitative neurophilosophies.[63] It is important accordingly not to work completely within the social constructivist method but rather to emphasize process ontologies that reconceptualize the connection to the nonhuman, vital forces, that is, *zoe*.

The case is being argued by a new wave of scholarship: "matter-realist" feminists emphasize "inventive" life and "vibrant matter," while different kinds of neomaterialist feminism are in full swing.[64] There is no question that contemporary feminist theory is productively posthuman, as evidenced by the work of Karen Barad, who coined the terms *posthumanist performativity* and *agential realism* to signify this enlarged and, in my terms, postanthropocentric vision of subjectivity.[65]

Queer science studies is especially keen on a transversal alliance between humans and other species; thus Stacy Alaimo theorizes transcorporeal porous boundaries between human and other species, while Eva Hayward calls for "humanimal relations" and "transspeciated selves."[66] A technoecological, posthuman turn is at work that combines organic autopoiesis with machinic self-organizing powers, as announced by Félix Guattari in his pioneering work on our ecotechnologically mediated universe.[67] The consensus is that there is no "originary humanicity" but only "originary technicity."[68]

Posthumanists of many dispositions are also calling for a transformation of the by now classical radical "studies" areas and to reach out for a new deal with the culture of science and technology.[69] The posthuman turn has gone viral in comparative literature and cultural studies, in new media studies, and in the framework of social theory and neo-Spinozist political theory.[70]

The posthuman feminist subject does yield a new political praxis. It is an empirical project that aims at experimenting with what contemporary, biotechnologically mediated bodies are capable of doing in the radical immanence of their respective locations. Mindful of the structural injustices and massive power differentials at work in the globalized world, I think feminist theory needs to produce more accurate accounts of the multiple political economies of power and subject formation at work in our world. These cartographies actualize the virtual possibilities of an expanded, relational self that functions in a nature–culture continuum and is technologically mediated but still framed by multiple power relations.

The political advantage of this monistic and vital approach is that it provides a more adequate understanding of the fluid and complex workings of power in advanced capitalism and hence can devise more suitable forms of resistance.[71] These explorations of embedded and embodied materialism result not only in a serious reconsideration of what counts as the "matter" for materialist feminist thought. Emphasis on a Spinozist monistic allows us to move toward a dynamic, nonessentialist, and relational brand of materialist vitalism. This results in the dislocation of difference from binaries to rhizomatics, from sex–gender or nature–culture to processes of differing that take life itself, or the vitality of matter, as the main subject.

Neomaterialist feminism has to confront the paradox that matter, including the specific slice of matter that is human embodiment, is intelligent and self-organizing, but this does not in itself resolve or improve the power differences at work in the material world. Feminists may have to embrace this humble starting point by acknowledging a life that is not ours—it is *zoe* driven and geocentered. And yet for us, members of this species, it will always be anthropomorphic, that is to say, embedded and embodied, enfleshed, affective, and relational. It is by embracing resiliently our anthropomorphic frame and the limits and possibilities it entails that we can become creatively *zoe*-centered, opening up to possible actualization of virtual forces. The radical immanence of self-aware anthropomorphism, the politics of that particular location, constitutes the start of a critique of delusional anthropocentrism. We may yet overcome anthropocentrism by becoming anthropomorphic bodies without organs that are still finding out what they are capable of becoming.

SEXUALITY IS A FORCE BEYOND GENDER

As I have argued so far, advanced capitalism as a biogenetic cognitive system of commodification of all that lives reduces organisms to their informational substrate in terms of materiality and vital capacity. By implication, this means that the markers for the organization and distribution of differences are now located in microinstances of vital materiality, such as the cells of living organisms and the genetic codes of entire species. We have come a long way from the gross system that used to mark difference on the basis of visually verifiable anatomical and physiological differences between the empirical sexes, the races, and the species. We have moved from the biopower that Foucault exemplified by comparative anatomy to a society based on the mediated governance of molecular *zoe* power of today. We have equally shifted from disciplinary to control societies, from the political economy of the Panopticon to the informatics of domination.[72] The question of difference and power disparity, however, remains as central as ever.

The technologically mediated world is neither organic–inorganic, male–female, nor especially white. Advanced capitalism is a postgender system capable of accommodating a high degree of androgyny and a significant blurring of the categorical divide between the sexes. It is also a postracial system that no longer classifies people and their cultures on grounds of pigmentation but remains nonetheless profoundly racist.[73] A strong theory of posthuman subjectivity can help us to reappropriate these processes, both theoretically and politically, not only as analytical tools but also as alternative ground for formations of the self.

What are the consequences of the fact that the technological apparatus is no longer sexualized, racialized, or naturalized but rather neutralized as figures of mixity, hybridity, and interconnectiveness, turning transsexuality into a dominant posthuman *topos*?[74] If the machinic apparatus is both self-organizing and transgender, the old organic human body needs to be relocated elsewhere. What and where is the body of the posthuman subject? Some queer theorists, striving to overcome the oedipalized sexual binary system, tend to equate the posthuman with postgender and have taken the leap beyond the flesh.[75] Although the posthuman is not automatically hyperqueer, queering the nonhuman is a popular trend.[76] Ever mindful of Lyotard's warning about the political economy of advanced capitalism, I think we should not trust the blurring effects and states of indeterminacy it engenders.[77] However tempting, it would be misguided to assume that posthuman embodied subjects are beyond sexual or racialized differences. On the contrary, discriminatory differences are more strongly in place than ever, though they have shifted significantly.

In terms of feminist politics, this means we need to rethink sexuality without genders, starting from a vitalist return to the polymorphous and, according to Freud, "perverse" (in the sense of playful and nonreproductive) structure of human sexuality. We also need to reassess the generative powers of female embodiment, which have not been appraised sufficiently by feminists. In this vital neomaterialist feminist approach, gender is just a historically contingent mechanism of capture of the multiple potentialities of the body, including their generative or reproductive capacities. To turn this historically contingent capture apparatus of gender into *the* transhistorical matrix of power, as suggested by queer theory in the linguistic and social constructivist tradition, is quite simply a conceptual error.[78] Sexuality may be caught in the sex–gender binary, but is not reducible to it. The mechanism of capture does not alter the fact that sexuality carries transversal, structural, and vital connotations. As life force, sexuality provides a nonessentialist ontological structure for the organization of human affectivity and desire. By extension, a social constructivist account confines itself to the description of a sociological process of bounded identity formation, missing the point about the in/depth structure of sexuality. The counterargument is that sexuality is both post- and pre-identity, as a constitutive force that is always already present and hence prior to gender, though it intersects with it in constructing functional subjects in the social regime of biopolitical governmentality.

Furthermore, sexuality as a human and nonhuman force pertains to the vital chaos, which is not chaotic but the boundless space of virtual possibilities for pleasure-prone affirmative relations.[79] These intensive forces bypass, underlay, precede, and exceed the normative social apparatus of gender. The vital force par excellence, sexuality gets captured, inscribed, formatted into a sex–gender dichotomy—as a social-symbolic system of attribution of qualities and entitlements—for the purpose of disciplining and punishing the social body.

In other words, for posthuman monistic feminists, gender is a form of governance that has to be disrupted by processes of becoming-minoritarian/becoming-woman/becoming-animal/becoming-imperceptible.[80] They are the transformative counteractualizations of the multiple, always already sexed bodies we may be capable of becoming. In a nomadic vein, I have argued that becoming-woman entails the evacuation or destitution of the socially constituted gendered identities of women (as molar formations), returning them to the virtual multiplicity of chaosmic forces of becoming. This is what I have called the feminist becoming-woman, then the "virtual feminine."[81]

On this point, all vital materialist feminists concur: Grosz refers to it as "a thousand tiny sexes"; Colebrook labels it "queer passive vitalism"; and Patricia MacCormack similarly draws attention to the need to return to sexuality as a polymorphous and complex, visceral force and to disengage it from both identity issues and all dualistic oppositions.[82] Luciana Parisi's innovative adaptation of Guattari's schizoanalysis and Lynn Margulis's concept of "endosymbiosis" produce a schizogenesis of sexual difference as an organic variable of autopoiesis.[83] Posthuman feminists look for subversion not in counteridentity formations but rather in pure dislocations of identities via the disruption of standardized patterns of sexualized, racialized, and naturalized interaction. Feminist posthuman politics is an experiment with intensities beyond binaries that functions by "and–and," not by "either–or."

Posthuman vitalist feminism, resting on a dynamic monistic political ontology, redefines the body as an incorporeal complex assemblage of virtualities that encompasses sexuality as a constitutive element: one is always already sexed. A postanthropocentric feminist approach makes it clear that bodily matter in the human, as in other species, is always already sexed and hence sexually differentiated along the axes of multiplicity and heterogeneity. Sexuality is conceptualized as a generative ontological force that cannot be adequately contained within the dichotomous view of gender defined as the social construction of differences between the sexes but rather is capable of deterritorializing gender identity and institutions.[84]

In other words, we need to experiment with intensity—run with *zoe*—to find out what posthuman sexed bodies can become. Because the gender system captures the complexity of human sexuality in a binary machine that privileges heterosexual family formations and literally steals all other possible bodies from us, we no longer know what our sexed bodies can do. We therefore need to rediscover the notion of the relational complexity that marks sexuality in its human and posthuman forms. These experiments with what sexed bodies can do, however, do not amount to saying that in the social sphere, pejorative differences no longer matter, or that the traditional power relations have been resolved. On the contrary, on a world scale, extreme forms of polarized sexual difference are stronger than ever. They get projected onto geopolitical relations between the West and the rest, creating belligerent gendered visions of a "clash of civilizations" that is allegedly predicated in terms of women's and LGBT people's rights.[85] "Homonationalism" is a pawn in contemporary international relations and a central concern for feminist and queer politics.[86]

These complex developments make it all the more urgent to reassert the concept of difference as both central and nonessentialistic. Difference as the principle of not-One, that is to say, as differing, is constitutive of the posthuman subject and the postanthropocentric forms of ethical accountability that characterize it.[87] In my view, posthuman ethics urges us to endure this principle at the in-depth structures of our subjectivity by acknowledging the ties that bind us to the multiple "Others" in a vital web of complex interrelations.[88] This ethical relational principle breaks up the fantasy of unity, totality, and oneness but also the oedipalized narratives of primordial loss, incommensurable lack, and irreparable separation. What I want to emphasize instead, in a more affirmative vein, is the generative force of the relation and the awareness that difference as positivity entails flows of encounters, interactions, affectivity, and desire. Posthuman feminist theory stresses the productive aspects of vital materialism, that is to say, a generative notion of complexity.

At the beginning, there is always already a relation to an affective, interactive entity endowed with intelligent flesh and an embodied mind: ontological relationality.

Sexuality beyond gender is the epistemological, but also political, side of contemporary vitalist neomaterialism. It consolidates a feminist genealogy that includes creative deterritorializations, intensive and hybrid cross-fertilizations, and generative encounters with multiple human and nonhuman others. The counteractualization of the virtual sexualities—of the bodies without organs that we have not been able to sustain as yet—is a posthuman feminist political praxis.

CONCLUSION: RECOMPOSING HUMANITY

A materialist politics of posthuman differences works by potential becomings that call for actualization. They are enacted through a collectively shared praxis and support the process of recomposition of a missing people. This is the "we" that is evoked and actualized by the postanthropocentric creation of a new pan-humanity. It expresses the affirmative, ethical dimension of becoming-posthuman as a gesture of collective self-styling or mutual specification. It actualizes a community that is not bound negatively by shared vulnerability, the guilt of ancestral communal violence, or the melancholia of unpayable ontological debts but rather by the compassionate acknowledgment of their interdependence with multiple others, most of which, in the age of the Anthropocene, are quite simply not anthropomorphic.

In this respect, posthuman feminist and other critical theorists need to resist the hasty recompositions of cosmopolitan bonds that are currently proposed by corporate and other forms of neohumanism. The global economy is postanthropocentric in unifying all species under the imperative of the market, and its excesses threaten the sustainability of our planet as a whole. But in the era of the Anthropocene, it is also neohumanistic in forging a new pan-human bond made of vulnerability and fear of extinction. The moral overtones of this methodological cosmopolitanism barely conceal its self-interested nature.[89] Feminist, postcolonial, and race theorists have been quick in denouncing the hypocritical nature of such hasty recompositions of a pan-human bond of shared fear of extinction.[90] They have reinscribed power relations at the heart of the climate change and environmental crisis debate and called for more situated and accountable analyses.[91]

This means that the posthuman is not postpolitical but rather recasts political agency in the direction of relational ontology. Feminist posthuman critiques need to focus therefore on the continuing or renewed power differentials, on the structures of domination and exclusion in advanced capitalism. Class, race, gender, and age have moved center stage in the global economy and its necropolitical governmentality. The posthuman is not postwar but rather has inscribed warfare as an extensive logistical operation integrated into its technoscientific apparatus. Environmental issues are inscribed at the intersection of major geopolitical concerns and involve both human and nonhuman agents and forces. Earth-related issues are not immune to social relations of class, race, age, disability, sexual preference and should not be renaturalized.

Starting from philosophies of radical immanence, vital materialism, and the feminist politics of locations, I have argued against taking a flight into an abstract idea of a "new" humanity. What we need instead is embedded and embodied, relational and affective cartographies of the new power relations that are emerging from the current geopolitical order.[92] Class, race, gender and sexual orientations, age and able-bodiedness are more than ever significant markers of human "normality." They are key factors in framing the notion of and policing access to something we may call "humanity." And yet, considering the global reach of the problems we are facing in the Anthropocene today, it is nonetheless the case that "we" are in *this* together. Such awareness must not, however, obscure or flatten out the power differentials that sustain the collective subject ("we") and its endeavor *(this)*. There may well be multiple and potentially contradictory projects at stake in the recomposition of "humanity" right now.

In this respect, the posthuman is not a new generic category but rather a navigational tool—in Deleuze's terms, a "conceptual persona"— that can assist us in coming to terms with the complexities of our times. Like all emerging movements, posthuman feminism is fast moving and already mutating into a number of contemporary discursive events. For instance, a new alliance between environmentally aware "green" politics and traditional "red" politics within the humanities has produced another wave of critical studies areas: postcolonial environmental humanities emerges as a crossover between Native American studies and other indigenous studies areas and the environmental humanities.[93] A similar crossover is occurring with the postcolonial digital humanities, which combine the heritage of postcolonial and indigenous studies and feminist critiques with digital mediation.[94] Confronted by such rich and complex developments, it may be wise for posthuman feminist theory to work toward multiple transversal alliances across communities: many recompositions of the human and new ways of becoming-world together.

NOTES

1. Michel Foucault, *The Order of Things: An Archaeology of Human Sciences* (New York: Pantheon Books, 1970).

2. This notion is upheld today by the transhumanists who defend human enhancement via brain–computer interface and propose such cerebral and neural expansion as a way of fulfilling the potential of rational human evolution. Politically, they remain aligned to the Enlightenment project of social emancipation through scientific progress and the assertion of moral universals. Nick Bostrom, "A History of Transhuman Thought," *Journal of Evolution and Technology* 14, no. 1 (2005): 1–25. This combination of analytic posthumanism and normative neohumanism is challenged by critical posthumanists. Cary Wolfe, *What Is Posthumanism?* (Minneapolis: University of Minnesota Press, 2010); Rosi Braidotti, *The Posthuman* (Cambridge: Polity Press, 2013); Stefan Herbrechter, *Posthumanism: A Critical Analysis* (London: Bloomsbury Academic, 2013).

3. Foucault, *Order of Things.*

4. On feminist politics of location, see Adrienne Rich, *Blood, Bread and Poetry* (London: Virago Press, 1987), and Rich, *Arts of the Possible: Essays and Conversations* (New York: W. W. Norton, 2001). On the analysis of the racialized economy of science, see Sandra Harding, *The Science Question in Feminism* (Ithaca, N.Y.: Cornell University Press, 1986), Harding, *Whose Science? Whose Knowledge?* (Ithaca, N.Y.: Cornell University Press, 1991), and Harding, *The "Racial" Economy of Science* (Bloomington: Indiana University Press, 1993); also Nancy Hartsock, "The Feminist Standpoint: Developing the Ground for a Specifically Feminist Historical Materialism," in *Feminism and Methodology,* ed. Sandra Harding, 157–80 (Bloomington: Indiana University Press, 1987). On situated knowledges, see Donna Haraway, "Situated Knowledges: The Science Question in Feminism as a Site of Discourse on the Privilege of Partial Perspective," *Feminist Studies* 14, no. 3 (1988): 575–99.

5. Rosi Braidotti, *Nomadic Subjects: Embodiment and Sexual Difference in Contemporary Feminist Theory,* 1st ed. (New York: Columbia University Press,

1994), and Braidotti, *Nomadic Subjects: Embodiment and Sexual Difference in Contemporary Feminist Theory,* 2nd ed. (New York: Columbia University Press, 2011).

6. Gayatri Chakravorty Spivak, *A Critique of Postcolonial Reason: Toward a History of the Vanishing Present* (Cambridge, Mass.: Harvard University Press, 1999); Genevieve Lloyd, *The Man of Reason: Male and Female in Western Philosophy* (London: Methuen, 1984).

7. Luce Irigaray, *Speculum of the Other Woman* (Ithaca, N.Y.: Cornell University Press, 1985); Irigaray, *This Sex Which Is Not One* (Ithaca, N.Y.: Cornell University Press, 1985); Helene Cixous and Catherine Clement, *The Newly Born Woman* (Minneapolis: University of Minnesota Press, 1986).

8. Kimberlé Crenshaw, "Mapping the Margins: Intersectionality, Identity Politics, and Violence against Women of Color," in *Critical Race Theory,* ed. Kimberlé Crenshaw, Neil Gotanda, Gary Peller, and Kendall Thomas, 357–83 (New York: New Press, 1995).

9. Irigaray, *This Sex Which Is Not One;* Gilles Deleuze and Félix Guattari, *Anti-Oedipus: Capitalism and Schizophrenia,* vol. 1 (New York: Viking Press, 1977); Deleuze and Guattari, *A Thousand Plateaus: Capitalism and Schizophrenia* (Minneapolis: University of Minnesota Press, 1987).

10. Donna Haraway, "A Manifesto for Cyborgs: Science, Technology, and Socialist Feminism in the 1980s," *Socialist Review* 2 (March 1985): 65–107.

11. Luce Irigaray, "Equal to Whom?," in *The Essential Difference,* ed. Naomi Schor and Elizabeth Weed, trans. Robert L. Mazzola (Bloomington: Indiana University Press, 1994), 80.

12. On feminist critiques of abstract masculinity, see Hartsock, "Feminist Standpoint." On triumphant whiteness, see bell hooks, *Ain't I a Woman* (Boston: South End Press, 1981), and Vron Ware, *Beyond the Pale: White Women, Racism, and History* (London: Verso, 1992). On hegemonic able-bodiedness, see Griet Roets and Rosi Braidotti, "Nomadology and Subjectivity: Deleuze and Critical Disability Studies," in *Disability and Social Theory: New Developments and Directions,* ed. Dan Goodley, Bill Hughes, and Lennard Davis, 161–78 (New York: Palgrave Macmillan, 2012).

13. Julia Kristeva, *Strangers to Ourselves* (New York: Colombia University Press, 1991).

14. Frantz Fanon, *Black Skin, White Masks* (New York: Grove Press, 1967); Aimé Césaire, *Discourse on Colonialism,* trans. Joan Pinkham (1955; repr., New York: Monthly Review Press, 2000).

15. Edward Said, *Humanism and Democratic Criticism* (New York: Columbia University Press, 2004).

16. Paul Gilroy, *Against Race: Imaging Political Culture beyond the Color Line* (Cambridge, Mass.: Harvard University Press, 2000).

17. Maria Mies and Vandana Shiva, *Ecofeminism* (London: Zed Books, 1993).

18. Avtar Brah, *Cartographies of Diaspora-Contesting Identities* (New York: Routledge, 1996); Vandana Shiva, *Biopiracy: The Plunder of Nature and Knowledge*

(Boston: South End Press, 1997); Patricia Hill Collins, *Black Feminist Thought: Knowledge, Consciousness, and the Politics of Empowerment* (New York: Routledge, 1991); Drucilla Cornell, "Exploring Ubuntu: Tentative Reflections," http://www .fehe.org/index.php?id=281.

19. Edouard Glissant, *Poetics of Relation* (Ann Arbor: University of Michigan Press, 1997).

20. Ulrich Beck, "The Cosmopolitan Condition: Why Methodological Nationalism Fails," *Theory, Culture, and Society* 24, no. 7/8 (2007): 286–90.

21. Edgar Morin, *Penser l'Europe* (Paris: Gallimard, 1987); Luisa Passerini, ed., *Identità Culturale Europea: Idee, Sentimenti, Relazioni* (Florence: La Nuova Italia Editrice, 1998); Etienne Balibar, *We, the People of Europe? Reflections on Transnational Citizenship* (Princeton, N.J.: Princeton University Press, 2004); and Zygmunt Bauman, *Europe: An Unfinished Adventure* (Cambridge: Polity Press, 2004).

22. Jurgen Habermas, *The Post-National Constellation* (Cambridge: Polity Press, 2001); Rosi Braidotti, *Transpositions: On Nomadic Ethics* (Cambridge: Polity Press, 2006).

23. Rosi Braidotti, *Nomadic Theory: The Portable Rosi Braidotti* (New York: Columbia University Press, 2011).

24. Paul Rabinow, *Anthropos Today: Reflections on Modern Equipment* (Princeton, N.J.: Princeton University Press, 2003); Roberto Esposito, *Bíos: Biopolitics and Philosophy* (Minneapolis: University of Minnesota Press, 2008).

25. Brian Massumi, "Requiem for Our Prospective Dead (Toward a Participatory Critique of Capitalist Power)," in *Deleuze and Guattari: New Mappings in Politics, Philosophy, and Culture,* ed. Eleanor Kaufman and Kevin John Heller (Minneapolis: University of Minnesota Press, 1998), 60.

26. Michael Hardt and Antonio Negri, *Empire* (Cambridge, Mass.: Harvard University Press, 2000), 215.

27. Braidotti, *Posthuman.*

28. C. P. Snow, *The Two Cultures* (Cambridge: Cambridge University Press, 1998), originally delivered as the Rede Lecture, Cambridge, 1959.

29. Dipesh Chakrabarty, "The Climate of History: Four Theses," *Critical Inquiry* 35 (Winter 2009): 206.

30. Foucault, *Order of Things*; Edward Said, *Orientalism* (Harmondsworth, U.K.: Penguin Books, 1978).

31. Shulamith Firestone, *The Dialectic of Sex* (New York: Bantam Books, 1970).

32. Donna Haraway, *Simians, Cyborgs, and Women* (London: Free Association Press, 1990).

33. Donna Haraway, *Modest_Witness@Second_Millennium. FemaleMan©_Meets_ Oncomouse*™ (London: Routledge, 1997).

34. Braidotti, *Nomadic Subjects,* 1st ed.; Anne Balsamo, *Technologies of the Gendered Body: Reading Cyborg Women* (Durham, N.C.: Duke University Press, 1996); Judith Halberstam and Ira Livingston, eds., *Posthuman Bodies*

(Bloomington: Indiana University Press, 1995); and Katherine Hayles, *How We Became Posthuman: Virtual Bodies in Cybernetics, Literature, and Informatics* (Chicago: University of Chicago Press, 1999).

35. Naomi Klein, *This Changes Everything: Capitalism vs. the Climate* (New York: Simon and Schuster, 2014); Chakrabarty, "Climate of History."

36. In cultural studies, see Maureen McNeil, *Feminist Cultural Studies of Science and Technology* (London: Routledge, 2007). In media and film theory, see Anneke Smelik and Nina Lykke, eds., *Bits of Life: Feminism at the Intersection of Media, Bioscience, and Technology* (Seattle: University of Washington Press, 2008).

37. On feminist science studies going planetary, see Isabelle Stengers, *Power and Invention: Situating Science* (Minneapolis: University of Minnesota Press, 1997), and Sarah Franklin, Celia Lury, and Jackie Stacey, *Global Nature, Global Culture* (London: Sage, 2000). On sophisticated analyses of molecular biology, see Sarah Franklin, *Dolly Mixtures* (Durham, N.C.: Duke University Press, 2007). On sophisticated analyses of computational systems, see Celia Lury, Luciana Parisi, and Tiziana Terranova, "Introduction: The Becoming Topological of Culture," *Theory, Culture, and Society* 29, no. 4–5 (July–September 2012): 3–35.

38. On ecofeminists who advocated geocentered perspectives, see Val Plumwood, *Feminism and the Mastery of Nature* (London: Routledge, 1993), and Plumwood, *Environmental Culture* (London: Routledge, 2003). On ecofeminists who expanded into animal studies and radical veganism, see Patricia MacCormack, *The Animal Catalyst* (London: Bloomsbury, 2014).

39. On feminist theories of non- and posthuman subjectivity embracing nonanthropomorphic animal or technological Others, see Mette Bryld and Nina Lykke, *Cosmodolphins: Feminist Cultural Studies of Technology, Animals, and the Sacred* (London: Zed Books, 2000); Luciana Parisi, *Abstract Sex: Philosophy, Bio-Technology, and the Mutation of Desire* (London: Continuum Press, 2004); Braidotti, *Transpositions*; Braidott, *Posthuman*; Stacey Alaimo, *Bodily Natures: Science, Environment, and the Material Self* (Bloomington: Indiana University Press, 2010); and Myra J. Hird and Celia Roberts, "Introduction: Feminism Theorises the Nonhuman," *Feminist Theory* 12, no. 2 (2011): 109–17. On a posthuman ethical turn, see Braidotti, *Transpositions*, and Patricia MacCormack, *Posthuman Ethics* (London: Ashgate, 2012).

40. On 1980s feminist interest in Darwin, see Gillian Beer, *Darwin's Plots: Evolutionary Narrative in Darwin, George Eliot, and Nineteenth-Century Fiction* (London: Routledge and Kegan Paul, 1983). On growing feminist interest in Darwin by the end of the millennium, see Hilary Rose and Steven Rose, eds., *Alas, Poor Darwin: Arguments against Evolutionary Psychology* (London: Vintage, 2000); Joseph Carroll, *Literary Darwinism: Evolution, Human Nature, and Literature* (London: Routledge, 2004); and Elizabeth Grosz, *Becoming Undone: Darwinian Reflections on Life, Politics, and Art* (Durham, N.C.: Duke University Press, 2011).

41. On the turn toward the critical posthumanities, see Braidotti, *Posthuman*.

The "monocultures of the mind" is from Vandana Shiva, *Monocultures of the Mind: Perspectives on Biodiversity and Biotechnology* (London: Zed Books, 1993). On biopiracy, see Shiva, *Biopiracy.* On necropolitics, see Achille Mbembe, "Necropolitics," trans. Libby Meintjes, *Public Culture* 15, no. 1 (2003): 11–40. On worldwide dispossession, see Saskia Sassen, *Expulsions: Brutality and Complexity in the Global Economy* (Cambridge, Mass.: Harvard University Press, 2014).

42. On the technophilic dimension, see Rosi Braidotti, *Metamorphoses: Towards a Materialist Theory of Becoming* (Cambridge: Polity Press, 2002). On hyperconsumeristic possessive individualism, see Crawford B. MacPherson, *The Theory of Possessive Individualism* (Oxford: Oxford University Press, 1962).

43. Joan Kelly, "The Double-Edged Vision of Feminist Theory," *Feminist Studies* 5, no.1 (1979): 216–27; Judith Butler, *Gender Trouble* (London: Routledge, 1991); Rosi Braidotti, *Patterns of Dissonance* (Cambridge: Polity Press, 1991).

44. Gilroy, *Against Race*; Collins, *Black Feminist Thought.*

45. Braidotti, *Transpositions.*

46. Lloyd, *Man of Reason.*

47. Gilles Deleuze, *Difference and Repetition* (New York: Columbia University Press, 1994).

48. Nikolas Rose, *The Politics of Life Itself* (Princeton, N.J.: Princeton University Press, 2007).

49. Patricia Ticineto Clough, with Jean Halley, eds., *The Affective Turn: Theorizing the Social* (Durham, N.C.: Duke University Press, 2007).

50. Melinda Cooper, *Life as Surplus: Biotechnology and Capitalism in the Neoliberal Era* (Seattle: University of Washington Press, 2008).

51. Michel Foucault, *Society Must Be Defended* (New York: Picador, 2003).

52. Ulrich Beck, *World Risk Society* (Cambridge: Polity Press, 1999).

53. On cognitive capitalism, see Yann Moulier Boutang, *Cognitive Capitalism* (Cambridge: Polity Press, 2012). On necropolitical governmentality, see Mbembe, "Necropolitics," and Braidoitti, *Posthuman.*

54. Keith Ansell Pearson, *Germinal Life: The Difference and Repetition of Deleuze* (London: Routledge, 1999); John Protevi, *Life War Earth* (Minneapolis: University of Minnesota Press, 2013); Braidoitti, *Posthuman.*

55. Genevieve Lloyd, *Part of Nature: Self-Knowledge in Spinoza's Ethic* (Ithaca, N.Y.: Cornell University Press, 1994), and Lloyd, *Spinoza and the Ethics* (London: Routledge, 1996).

56. On neo-Spinozist vital materialist philosophy, see Deleuze and Guattari, *Anti-Oedipus,* and Deleuze and Guattari, *A Thousand Plateaus.* On *zoe,* see Braidotti, *Metamorphoses,* and Braidotti, *Transpositions.*

57. Braidotti, *Transpositions,* and Braidotti, *Nomadic Theory.*

58. Dimitris Papadopoulos, "Insurgent Posthumanism," *Ephemera: Theory and Politics in Organization* 10, no. 2 (2010): 134–51.

59. Donna Haraway, "Anthropocene, Capitalocene, Chthulucene: Staying with the Trouble," *AURA* (Aarhus University Research on the Anthropocene)

(blog), May 9, 2014, http://anthropocene.au.dk; a video of the talk is available at http://vimeo.com/97663518.

60. On a nomadic transversal assemblage, see Braidotti, *Nomadic Subjects,* 1st ed.; Braidotti, *Metamorphoses*; and Braidotti, *Transpositions.* On the cumulative effect of multiple relational bonds, see Braidotti, *Nomadic Subjects,* 2nd ed.

61. Elizabeth Grosz, *The Nick of Time* (Durham, N.C.: Duke University Press, 2004).

62. John Marks, *Gilles Deleuze: Vitalism and Multiplicity* (London: Pluto Press, 1998).

63. On extended mind theories, see Andy Clark, *Being There: Putting Brain, Body, and World Together Again* (Cambridge, Mass.: MIT Press, 1997), and Clark, *Natural-Born Cyborgs: Minds, Technologies, and the Future of Human Intelligence* (Oxford: Oxford University Press, 2003). On distributed cognition models inspired by Spinoza, see Deleuze and Guattari, *A Thousand Plateaus,* and Antonio Damasio, *Looking for Spinoza: Joy, Sorrow, and the Feeling Brain* (Orlando, Fla.: Harcourt, 2003). On qualitative neurophilosophies, see Patricia Churchland, *Braintrust: What Neuroscience Tells Us about Morality* (Princeton, N.J.: Princeton University Press, 2011), and Catherine Malabou, *Changing Difference* (Cambridge: Polity Press, 2011).

64. On "matter-realist" feminists, see Mariam Fraser, Sarah Kember, and Celia Lury, eds., *Inventive Life: Approaches to the New Vitalism* (London: Sage, 2006), and Jane Bennett, *Vibrant Matter: A Political Ecology of Things* (Durham, N.C.: Duke University Press, 2010). On neomaterialist feminism, see Braidotti, *Patterns of Dissonance*; Rick Dolphijn and Iris van der Tuin, eds., *New Materialism: Interviews and Cartographies* (Ann Arbor, Mich.: Open Humanities Press, 2012); Stacy Alaimo and Susan Hekman, *Material Feminism* (Bloomington: Indiana University Press, 2008); Diana Coole and Samantha Frost, *New Materialisms: Ontology, Agency, and Politics* (Durham, N.C.: Duke University Press, 2010); and Vicki Kirby, *Quantum Anthropologies: Life at Large* (Durham, N.C.: Duke University Press, 2011).

65. Karen Barad, "Posthumanist Performativity: Toward an Understanding of How Matter Comes to Matter," *Signs: Journal of Women in Culture and Society* 28, no. 3 (2003): 801–31, and Barad, *Meeting the Universe Halfway* (Durham, N.C.: Duke University Press, 2007).

66. Alaimo, *Bodily Natures*; Eva Hayward, "Sensational Jellyfish: Aquarium Affects and the Matter of Immersion," *differences* 23, no. 3 (2012): 161–96, and Hayward, "More Lessons from a Starfish: Prefixial Flesh and Transspeciated Selves," *Women's Studies Quarterly* 36, no. 3/4 (2008): 64–85.

67. On technoecological turns, see Erich Hörl, "A Thousand Ecologies: The Process of Cyberneticization and General Ecology," in *The Whole Earth: California and the Disappearance of the Outside,* ed. Diedrich Diederichsen and Anselm Franke, 121–30 (Berlin: Sternberg Press, 2013). On organic autopoiesis combined with machinic self-organizing powers, see Humberto Maturana and Francisco J.

Varela, *Autopoiesis and Cognition: The Realization of the Living* (Dordrecht, Netherlands: D. Reidel, 1972); Félix Guattari, *Chaosmosis: An Ethico-Aesthetic Paradigm* (Sydney: Power, 1995); and Félix Guattari, *The Three Ecologies* (London: Athlone Press, 2000).

68. Kirby, *Quantum Anthropologies,* 233; Adrian Mackenzie, *Transductions: Bodies and Machines at Speed* (New York: Continuum, 2002).

69. Parisi, *Abstract Sex*; Bruce Clarke, *Posthuman Metamorphosis: Narrative and Systems* (New York: Fordham University Press, 2008).

70. In comparative literature and cultural studies, see Wolfe, *What Is Post-humanism?*; Herbrechter, *Posthumanism*; Pramod K. Nayar, *Posthumanism* (Cambridge: Polity Press, 2013). In new media studies, see Matthew Fuller, *Media Ecologies: Materialist Energies in Art and Technoculture* (Cambridge, Mass.: MIT Press, 2005), and Jussi Parikka, *Insect Media: An Archaeology of Animals and Technology* (Minneapolis: University of Minnesota Press, 2010). In social theory, see Lury et al., "Becoming Topological of Culture." In neo-Spinozist political theory, see Manuel DeLanda, *A New Philosophy of Society: Assemblage Theory and Social Complexity* (London: Continuum, 2006), and Braidotti, *Posthuman.*

71. Paul Patton, *Deleuze and the Political* (London: Routledge, 2000); Pierre Macherey, *Hegel or Spinoza?* (Minneapolis: University of Minnesota Press, 2011).

72. Haraway, *Simians, Cyborgs, and Women*; Donna Haraway, "The Promises of Monsters: A Regenerative Politics for Inappropriate/d Others," in *Cultural Studies,* ed. Lawrence Grossberg, Cary Nelson, and Paula Treichler, 295–337 (London: Routledge, 1992); and Donna Haraway, *The Companion Species Manifesto: Dogs, People, and Significant Otherness* (Chicago: Prickly Paradigm Press, 2003).

73. Gilroy, *Against Race.*

74. Scott Bukatman, *Terminal Identity: The Virtual Subject in Post-Modern Science Fiction* (Durham, N.C.: Duke University Press, 1993).

75. Balsamo, *Technologies of the Gendered Body*; Halberstam and Livingston, *Posthuman Bodies*; Judith Halberstam, *Gaga Feminism: Sex, Gender, and the End of Normal* (Boston: Beacon Press, 2012); Sarah Kember, "No Humans Allowed? The Alien in/as Feminist Theory," *Feminist Theory* 12, no. 1 (2011): 183–99.

76. Noreen Giffney and Myra Hird, eds., *Queering the Non/Human* (London: Ashgate, 2008); Julie Livingston and Jasbir K. Puar, "Interspecies," *Social Text* 29, no. 1 (2011): 3–14; Claire Colebrook, *Sex after Life* (Ann Arbor, Mich.: Open Humanities Press, 2014).

77. Jean-François Lyotard, *The Inhuman: Reflections on Time* (Oxford: Blackwell, 1989).

78. Butler, *Gender Trouble.*

79. Guattari, *Chaosmosis.*

80. Braidotti, *Transpositions.*

81. On the feminist becoming-woman, see Braidotti, *Patterns of Discourse,* and Braidotti, *Nomadic Subjects,* 1st ed. On the virtual feminine, see Braidotti, *Metamorphoses,* and Braidotti, *Transpositions.*

82. Elizabeth Grosz, "A Thousand Tiny Sexes: Feminism and Rhizomatics," in *Deleuze and Guattari: Critical Assessments of Leading Philosophers,* ed. Gary Genosko, 1440–63 (London: Routledge, 2001); Colebrook, *Sex after Life*; Patricia MacCormack, *Cinesexualities* (London: Ashgate, 2008).

83. Parisi, *Abstract Sex*; Lynn Margulis and Dorion Sagan, *What Is Life?* (Berkeley: University of California Press, 1995).

84. Braidotti, *Nomadic Subjects,* 1st ed.; Braidotti, *Nomadic Subjects,* 2nd ed.; Braidotti, *Nomadic Theory.*

85. Rosi Braidotti, "In Spite of the Times: The Postsecular Turn in Feminism," *Theory, Culture, and Society* 25, no. 6 (2008): 1–24.

86. Jasbir Puar, *Terrorist Assemblages: Homonationalism in Queer Times* (Durham, N.C.: Duke University Press, 2007).

87. Braidotti, *Metamorphoses.*

88. MacCormack, *Posthuman Ethics.*

89. Beck, "Cosmopolitan Condition."

90. Zillah Eisenstein, *Global Obscenities: Patriarchy, Capitalism, and the Lure of Cyberfantasy* (New York: New York University Press, 1998); Shiva, *Biopiracy*; Chakrabarty, "Climate of History."

91. Rob Nixon, *Slow Violence and the Environmentalism of the Poor* (Cambridge, Mass.: Harvard University Press, 2011).

92. John Protevi, *Political Affect* (Minneapolis: University of Minnesota Press, 2009).

93. Graham Huggan and Helen Tiffin, *Postcolonial Ecocriticism: Literature, Animals, Environment,* 2nd ed. (New York: Routledge, 2015); Nixon, *Slow Violence.*

94. Sandra Ponzanesi and Koen Leurs, "On Digital Crossings in Europe," *Crossings: Journal of Migration and Culture* 5, no. 1 (2014): 3–22.

3

The Three Figures of Geontology

ELIZABETH A. POVINELLI

THE FIGURES AND THE TACTICS

For a long time, and perhaps still now, many have believed that Western Europe spawned and then spread globally a regime of power best described as biopolitics. Biopolitics was thought to consist of a "set of mechanisms through which the basic biological features of the human species became the object of a political strategy, of a general strategy of power."[1] Many believe that this regime was inaugurated in the late eighteenth and early nineteenth centuries and consolidated in the 1970s. Prior to this, in the age of European kings, a very different formation of power reigned. Sovereign power was defined by the spectacular, public performance of the right to kill, to subtract life, and, in moments of regal generosity, to let live. It was a regime of sovereign thumbs, up or down, and enacted over the tortured, disemboweled, charred, and hacked human body.[2] Royal power was not merely the claim of an absolute power over life. It was a carnival of death. The crowds gathered, not in reverent silence around the sanctity of the life, but in a boisterous jamboree of killing—hawking wares, playing dice. Its figure, lavishly described at the opening of Michel Foucault's *Discipline and Punish,* was the drawn-and-quartered regicide. How different that formation of power seems to how we legitimate power now; what we ask of it; and, in asking, what it creates. And how different seem the figures through which the contemporary formation entails its power. Not kings and their subjects, not bodies hacked into pieces, but states and their populations, the Malthusian couple, the hysterical woman, the perverse adult, and the masturbating child. Is it such a wonder that some believe a great divide separates the current regime of biopolitics from the ancient order of sovereignty? Or that some think disciplinary power, with its figure of the camps and barracks, and its regularization of life, and biopolitics, with its four figures of sexuality and its normation of life, arch their backs against this savage sovereign *dispositif*? But is this the condition of power that we face today? Do the biopolitical and its figures provide us with the concepts that we need to make sense of what is now all around us but outside our field of vision?

Foucault was hardly the first to notice the transformation of the form and rationale of power in the long history of Western Europe—and, insofar as it shaped the destinies of its imperial and colonial reach, power writ globally. Perhaps most famously, Hannah Arendt, writing nearly twenty years before Foucault would begin his lectures on the biopolitical, bewailed the emergence of the "Social" as the referent and purpose of political activity.[3] Arendt contrasted not the era of European kings and courts to the modern focus on the social body but the latter to the classical Greek division between public and private realms. For Arendt the public was the space of political deliberation and action carved out of and defined by its freedom from and antagonism to the realm of necessity, the private realm, everything having to do with the physical life of the body (labor, reproduction, food, and health)—the so-called animal part of the human, the human as *animal laborans*. Rather than excluding bodily needs, wants, and desires from political thought, the liberal state embraced them; it opened the door and let *Homo economicus* out into the bright light of the public forum. Once the concern for physical life broke free from its enclosure in the dark obscurity of the private realm, the realm of necessity came to be known as the Social, and the Social became the raison d'être of the political. The politics of the liberal state gained its legitimacy insofar as it could demonstrate that it anticipated, protected, and enhanced the biological needs, wants, and desires of its citizens.

But if Foucault was not the first word on the subject of biopolitics, he was also not the last. Jacques Derrida would explore the concept of autoimmunity within the force of liberal law—and Donna Haraway and Roberto Esposito would place the discourse of immunology explicitly within the biopolitics of postmodern bodies.[4] Giorgio Agamben would put Arendt and Foucault in conversation to stretch the emergence of biopower in Greek and Roman law, thus trapping modern politics ever more completely within.[5] And Esposito would counter Agamben's negative reading of the biopolitical by arguing that a positive form of biopower could be found in innovative readings of Heidegger, Canguilhem, and Spinoza.[6] Throughout these debates, other authors have challenged the idea that it is possible to write a history of the biopolitical that starts and ends in European history, *even if* Western Europe was the frame of reference. Achille Mbembe, for instance, argued that the sadistic expressions of German Nazism were genealogically related to the sadisms of European colonialism. And before Mbembe, W. E. B. Du Bois argued that the material and discursive origins of European monumentalism, such as the gleaming boulevards of Brussels, were in the brutal colonial regimes of the Congo. Thus as lighthearted as was Foucault's famous quip that this century would bear the name "Deleuze," he would no doubt have been pleased to see the good race that his concept of the biopolitical has run. Biopower, biopolitics, thanatopolitics, necropolitics, positive and negative forms of biopower, neuropolitics; Foucault, Agamben, Negri, Esposito, Rose, Mbembe, Connolly; anthropology, cultural and literary studies, political theory, critical philosophy, history: Foucault's understanding of biopower has gone viral.[7]

But again, are biopolitics or necropolitics the formation of power in which Late Liberalism now operates? Have we been so entranced by the image of power working through life that we haven't noticed the new problems, figures, strategies, and concepts all around us, suggesting that the emergence of another formation of Late Liberal power is under way? In other words, have we been so focused on exploring each and every wrinkle in the biopolitical fold—biosecurity, biospectrality, thanatopoliticality—that we forgot to notice that the figures of biopower—the hysterical woman, the Malthusian couple, the perverse adult, and the masturbating child; the camps and barracks, the panopticon and solitary confinement—once so central to our understanding of contemporary power, now seem quaint, if not antiquated? How is our allegiance to the concept of biopower hiding and revealing this other problematic—a formation, for want of a better term, I am calling *geontological* power?

LIFE, DEATH, NONLIFE

To begin to see what the biopolitical strains to confine, let me return to Foucault's three formations of power and ask two simple questions, the answers to which might seem long settled: first, are the relations among sovereign power, disciplinary power, and biopower ones of implication, distinction, determination, or set membership? And second, are they intended as a mode of historical periodization, a quasi-transcendent metaphysics of power, or variations within a more encompassing historical and social framework? For all our contemporary certainty that a gulf separates sovereignty from discipline and biopower, Foucault seems unsure of whether he is seeing a concept traversing all three formations or three specific formations each with its own specific conceptual unity. On one hand, he writes that the eighteenth century witnessed "the appearance—one might say the invention—of a new mechanism of power which had very specific procedures, completely new instruments, and very different equipment."[8] And yet Foucault also states that the formations of power do not follow each other like beads on a string. Nor do they conform to a model of Hegelian *Aufhebung*—sovereignty dialectically unfolding into discipline, discipline into biopolitics. Rather, all three formations are always copresent—although they are arranged differently, with different aspects of each emphasized at different points of history.[9] Thus German fascism deployed all three formations of power in its Holocaust: the figure of Hitler exemplifying the right of the sovereign to decide who was enemy or friend and thus could be killed or let live; the gas chambers exemplifying the regularity of discipline power; and the Aryan exemplifying governance through the imaginary of hygiene and population. In the more recent past, Bush–Cheney steadfastly and publicly claimed the right to extrajudicial killing (a right Obama also claims), even though they did not enact their authority in public jamborees where victims were drawn and quartered but rather through secret human- and drone-based special operations or hidden rendition centers. These modern tactics and aesthetics of sovereign power exist alongside what Henry Giroux, building on Angela Davis's crucial work on the prison–industrial complex, has argued are the central features of contemporary U.S. power: biosecurity, with its panoply of ordinary incarceration blocks and severe forms of isolation.[10] Within the disciplinary and biopolitical form of prisons, even explicit sovereign killing—the U.S. death penalty—is heavily orchestrated and of a very different aesthetic and affective order than in the days of kings. This form of state killing has witnesses, but they usually sit behind a glass wall, across which a curtain is drawn while the victim is being prepared to be killed or if "complications" arise. Other evidence floats up in less obvious places—such as in the changing language of Qantas Airways as its planes approach Australia, from a previous announcement that passengers should be aware of the country's strict animal and plant quarantine to the current announcement about the country's strict "biosecurity laws."

What we see, then, are formations of power that seem neither fully genealogically distinct nor fully metaphysically related. They express distinct relations, aesthetics, and tactics toward life and death, but they never fully separate from each other; nor are they simply expressions of a shared transcendental concept. What accounts for this nagging sensation that some common transversal crosses these forms of separation? I am hardly the first to ask this. Alain Badiou has observed that although Foucault was "neither a philosopher nor a historian nor a bastardized combination of the two," nevertheless, according to Badiou, as Foucault moved from an archaeological approach to a genealogical one, "a doctrine of 'fields' substitutes that of sequences (or of epistemical singularities)" in such a way that Foucault was brought back "to the concept and to philosophy."[11] Badiou believes that the concept of power sits at the intersection of his ambivalent philosophy. But if the purpose of philosophy is, to paraphrase Deleuze, to produce concepts that open understanding to what is all around us but not in our field of vision, what concept do we need in order to understand how the awkward relationship between these forms of power reveals the current problem we face? Three observations help provide a backdrop for why I think geontology, geontological power, is an answer.

First, the once unremarkable observation that all three formations of power (sovereign power, disciplinary power, and biopower) work only "insofar as man is a living being" today trips over the *tant que,* the "insofar," the "as long as."[12] This once, perhaps not terribly labored phrasing is now hard to avoid hearing as an epistemological and ontological conditional: as long as we continue to conceptualize humans as *living* things and as long as humans *continue to exist.* Yes, sovereignty, discipline, and biopolitics stage, aestheticize, and publicize the dramas of life and death differently. And, yes, starting from the eighteenth century, the anthropological and physical sciences came to conceptualize humans as a single species subject to a natural law governing life and death. And, yes, these new discourses opened a new relationship between the way that sovereign law organized its powers around life and death and the way biopolitics did. And, yes, Foucault's quick summary of this transformation as a kind of inversion from the right to kill and let live to the power of making live and letting die must be modified by the fact that contemporary states make live, let die, *and* kill. And, yes, all sorts of liberalisms seem to evidence a biopolitical strain from settler colonialism to developmental liberalism.[13] But these transformations and variations can now seem like a sideshow to a much larger drama. The modifying phrase "insofar as" now foregrounds the human, the Anthropos, as just one element in the larger set of "life" subject to the conditions within and of this set—birth, growth, and death, and thus vulnerability and precariousness, as good and bad, normal and disfigured, an expected death and preempted life—and, as Claire Colebrook has noted, subject to a much larger form of death, namely, extinction.[14] It may well be that the concept of mass extinction—the extinction not merely of the human species but of all forms of life—depends on the biopolitical concept of population. But its intensification of the problematic of death has intensified not merely DEATH/EXTINCTION but NONLIFE or *geos,* the inorganic, the inanimate. It is now increasingly clear that the Anthropos remains an element in this set of life only insofar as "life" maintains its distinction from DEATH/EXTINCTION *and* NONLIFE. What presents itself to us now is exactly the awkwardness of these nested epistemological brackets [LIFE(Life{birth, growth, reproduction}Death)NONLIFE]. Certain tokens (human animals, nonhuman animals, plants, rocks and minerals...) of certain types (life, nonlife) no longer seem as self-evidently distinct as they once did. Following the early work of Ian Hacking, we might say that the disclosure of this ontological world is being redisclosed by the emergence of a new condition of knowledge.[15]

This leads to my *second* point, namely, that the disclosure of the artificiality of the double enclosure of life and death and life and nonlife is occurring within, if not strictly because of, contemporary Late Liberal debates about human and planetary extinction. The possibility that humans are responsible for the death of all life *on the planet,* often figured as the death *of the planet,* rather than the letting die or killing of specific human populations, has pulled to the forefront three incommensurate stances on the relationship between *bios* and *geos*: (1) *geos* as a living planetary organism (Gaia), (2) *geos* as that part of the planet defined as nonliving (geology), and (3) *geos* as that part which has but plays no part in contemporary Late Liberal governance.

The name that geologists have given to this new form of thought is the *Anthropocene,* and meteorologists, *climate change.* Since Eugene Stoermer first coined the term *Anthropocene* and Paul Crutzen popularized it, the Anthropocene has meant to mark a geologically defined moment when the forces of human existence began to overwhelm all other biological, geological, and meteorological forms and forces. That is, the Anthropocene marks the moment when human existence became the determinate form of planetary existence—and a malignant form relative to all other forms—rather than merely the fact that humans affect their environment. Geologists have not agreed what criteria will be used to date the start of the Anthropocene. Many criteria and thus many dates have been proposed. Some place it at the beginning of the Neolithic Revolution, when agriculture was invented and the human population exploded. Others date it to the detonation of the atomic bomb that left radioactive sediments in the stratigraphy and helped consolidate a notion of *the Earth* (Gaia) as something that could be destroyed by human action.[16] Hannah Arendt's 1963 reflections on the launching of the Sputnik and the lost contact "between the world of the senses and the appearances and the physical worldview" would be important here, as would be James Lovelock's Gaia hypothesis published two years later.[17] Still others situate the beginning of the Anthropocene in the coal-fueled Industrial Revolution. While the British phrase, "like selling coal to Newcastle," was first recorded in 1538, reminding us of the long history of coal use in Europe, proponents of the Industrial Revolution as the beginning of the Anthropocene point to the eighteenth-century expansion of the Lancashire, Somerset, and Northumberland coalfields as doing three things simultaneously: it uncovered large stratified fossil beds that helped spur the foundation of modern geologic chronology, it created a massive increase in resource extraction, and it released unheard of tons of hydrocarbons into the atmosphere. Karen Pinkus, Alison Bashford, and Rosanne Kennedy have shown the deep entanglements of knowledge, capital, and biological processes that provide conditions for the very idea of the Anthropocene: the concept of the Anthropocene depended on the establishment of a form of knowledge, the geology of fossils and rock stratification, that depended on a form of material production, carbon-fueled capital, that depended on the biogeological possibilities of fossil fuel deposits.[18] Indeed, in a series of essays, Jason Moore has suggested that what we are calling the Anthropocene might be more accurately called the Capitalocene—the last five hundred years of capital's transformation.[19] Dennis Dimick has poetically rephrased the Anthropocene and climate change as Industrial Capitalism's dependence on "ancient sunshine."[20]

However the geologists end up dating the break between the Holocene and the Anthropocene, the idea of the Anthropocene has already had a dramatic impact on the organization of dominant forms of knowledge. The possibility that humans are such an overwhelming malignant force on all other biological forms that life itself faces a planetary extinction has upset a number of traditional human disciplines. We can see the symptoms of the collapse of this practical and conceptual tripartite everywhere, including in the emergent disciplines of the Anthropocene, posthumanism, nonhumanism, and geobiochemistry. Dipesh Chakrabarty has explored, for instance, how the concept of the Anthropocene radically changes the discipline of history insofar as humans, and not merely Europeans, are provincialized.[21] Anthropology's turn toward the Anthropocene has seen a similar seeming disruption: the reappearance of animism and ontology as a mode of destabilizing the dominance of culture and the Anthropos.[22] And Claire Colebrook has argued that the concept of extinction, implicit in the Anthropocene, demands a radical rethinking of the tropes and attachments of sexuality in critical theory—a point made also by Liz Grosz in her explorations of geopower and exemplified by the radical sex advocate TK now performing mountaintop weddings.[23] And of course, the emergence of *geos,* as factor and actor independent of human being, has begun to rattle basic ontology itself. For instance, Eugene Thacker has recently asked why "every ontology of 'life,'" beginning with Aristotle, thinks "of life in terms of something-other-than-life."[24] And Quentin Meillassoux has argued that *arche-fossils* are "not just materials indicating the traces of past life, according to the familiar sense of the term 'fossil,' but materials indicating the existence of an ancestral reality or event; one that is anterior to terrestrial life."[25] For Meillassoux, arche-fossils displace the problematic not merely of life but that of the philosophical concept of *givenness* (consciousness, language, representational life) as such. But perhaps these disciplines are only catching up to a conversation begun elsewhere: with Don Delillo's *White Noise,* and certainly in the literary output of Margaret Atwood, starting with *The Handmaiden's Tale* and continuing through her MaddAddam trilogy.

And this leads to my *third* point. We are witnessing a wild proliferation of new conceptual–theoretical models, figures, and tactics of geontology that are displacing the figures and tactics of the biopolitical. For clarity, I am clustering this proliferation around three figures: THE DESERT, THE ANIMIST, and THE TERRORIST. But to understand the nature of these figures, two points must be kept firmly in mind. First, as the *geontological* comes to play a part in the governance of our thought, it will not merely need to be included in how we have understood life; it will need to be allowed to displace the division of life and nonlife itself. Second, the figures of geontopower are symptomatic *and diagnostic* of the present. Geontology cannot simply be a crisis of life *(bios)* and death *(thanatos)* at a species level (extinction), nor merely between life *(bios)* and nonlife *(geos)*. It must be the door that serves as an exit from both sets of oppositions.

In this way the three figures of geontology are no different than Foucault's four figures of biopower. The hysterical woman (a hystericization of women's bodies), the masturbating child (a pedagogization of children's sex), the perverse adult (a psychiatrization of perverse pleasure), and the Malthusian couple (a socialization of procreative behavior): Foucault cared about these figures of sexuality and gender not because he thought they were the repressed truth of human being but because he thought they were symptomatic and diagnostic of a modern formation of power. In other words, these four figures were expressions of biopower and windows into its operation. Although when presenting his lectures, *Society Must Be Defended,* Foucault discussed the insurrection of subjugated knowledges, understanding these figures as subjugated in the liberal sense of oppressed subjects would, I think, be wrongheaded. The problem was not how these figures and forms of life could be liberated from subjugation but how to understand them as

indicating a possible world beyond or otherwise to their own forms—
to understand them as a stand-in for something else. How might they
become something other than the hysterical woman, the masturbating
child, the Malthusian couple, the perverse adult? And how could they
survive their own emergence, and come to be invested with qualities
and characteristics deemed sensible and compelling, before being extinguished as a monstrosity?[26]

The same can be said of the following figures of geontological power:

THE DESERT and its CENTRAL IMAGINARY, CARBON. THE DESERT
is the figure that stands in for all things denuded of life—or, with
the application of technological expertise, something that could be
made hospitable to life. THE DESERT is, in other words, the space
where life was, is not now, or could be. Thus THE DESERT is found
in the astronomical search for evidence of previous or existing life
on other planets, in the contemporary imaginary of North African
oil fields, and in the fear that all places where fossil fuels are found
will be turned into THE DESERT. THE DESERT is also the geological
category of fossils insofar as we consider these fossils to have once
been charged with life and as providing the condition of life, or at
least our contemporary hypermodern form of life. As Kathryn Yusoff
has argued, fossils create a strange kinship between the living and
the nonliving, traversing their differences even as they threaten the
living with a radical finitude.[27] The specific ways that THE DESERT
is relaying life and nonlife are providing new theoretical movement,
such as in the work of Claire Colebrook on extinction and Eugene
Thacker on nonliving ontologies.[28] And a host of literary, artistic,
and media re-imaginings join them. These cultural texts and objects have a deep history stretching back at least to Edgar Rice Bur-
roughs, through the Mad Max films, and from the science fiction of
Philip K. Dick's *Martian Time-Slip* to the poetics of Juliana Spahr's
Well Then There Now.

THE CARBON IMAGINARY lies at the heart of the figure of THE
DESERT. By *carbon imaginary,* I mean the synthetic space between
the biological thought of metabolic processes and their key events
(birth, growth–reproduction, death) and the ontological thought of
event, conatus, finitude. Indeed, THE CARBON IMAGINARY is the

key to the geontology of Late Liberalism, emphasizing a point that I don't want to be lost as this chapter proceeds, namely, that geontology is not the Other to biontology but a new set of divergences and possibilities being revealed across the terrain of Late Liberalism as biontology is redisclosed.

THE ANIMIST and its CENTRAL IMAGINARY, the INDIGENE. Whereas THE DESERT emphasizes that which is denuded of life or could be made into (the fuel of) life, THE ANIMIST insists that there is no absence of life because everything has a vital force—there is no nonlife because all is life. Certain social and historical populations are charged with long having had this core biontological knowledge and attitude—indigenous and native peoples certainly, but pre-Christian Europeans as well. But THE ANIMIST is also within the contemporary idea that we should all be stewards of the earth. Thus THE ANIMIST includes the recycling contemporary subject and certain ways of portraying and perceiving in a variety of new cognitive subjects. The psychocognitive diagnoses of certain forms of autism and Asperger's are liable to fall within THE ANIMIST. Temple Grandin is an exemplary figure here, not merely for her orientation to cows but also for her defense of alternative cognitions that allow for an orientation to nonhuman and nonlife forms of existence and an understanding of these orientations as the drivers of the highwater marks of human society. THE ANIMIST is, in other words, all those who see an equivalence between all forms of life or who can see life where others would see the lack of life.

The theoretical and political expression of THE ANIMIST is seen in the recent turn toward rethinking the philosophies of vitalism. Some new vitalists have mined Spinoza's principle of conatus (that which exists, whether living or nonliving, strives to persevere in being) to shatter the division of life and nonlife—although others, such as John Carriero, have insisted that Spinoza uncritically accepted that living things are "more advanced" than nonliving things, "that there is more to a cat than to a rock."[29] A similar field of interest and dispute has emerged in the interpretation of the late-nineteenth-century writings of the American pragmatist Charles Sanders Peirce. Can, for instance, Peirce's semiotics of the interpretant be understood as extending into nonliving existents?[30] Whatever Spinoza or Peirce thought, the new vitalism, as Jane Bennett notes, skews forms of vitalism that grounded life in a philosophy of essence. They seek instead to create forms of "ontosympathy" by foregrounding the nature of all existence/existents as precarious assemblages.[31] A touchstone image comes from Deleuze and Guattari's concept of the body-without-organs and, more specifically, the orchid and the wasp as a prototype of existence as assemblage: a way of thinking about existents as coemergent strata within a common assemblage, each dependent in terms of its substantive form, quality, and mode on its relation to the Other. Another touchstone image comes from Donna Haraway's concept of the cyborg. Mel Chen, for instance, understands the intercorporeal as a capital assemblage that constitutes a type of contemporary toxic subjectivity.

Chen's work underlines that this turn to THE ANIMIST is not a mere philosophical rethinking but a political and ethical orientation. And here we come to the second way THE ANIMIST can differ from THE DESERT. The political tactic of THE ANIMIST tends to result in a call for the recognition of the liveliness of the radical Other. In other words, as THE ANIMIST supplants the human as the groundwork of the political and ethical, it maintains a humanist orientation. Take Temple Grandin's claim that "the really social people did not invent the first stone spear. It was probably an Aspie who chipped away at rocks while the other people socialized around the campfire."[32] Is she merely instrumentalizing the human subject's relationship to the rock, or is she substantially leveling the human and nonhuman, life and nonlife, to equal coparticipants in world-making? In other words, THE ANIMIST can result in a more effective engineer of modernity, an existence that does not differentiate among other forms of existence, and a radical antihumanism. All three are currently being explored in literary and cultural expressions of THE ANIMIST. THE ANIMIST isn't merely the exploration of subjectivity of other forms of life, as with the novel *The Hive Mentality,* but is a more open-ended exploration of the transpositional nature of forms of existence, as with the Italian film *Le Quattro Volte* (2010), which moves from human to animal to vegetable to mineral realms as an old goatherd and then a young goat dies, as a fir tree grows, is chopped down to serve as a ritual pole, and then is made into charcoal to light the townspeople's fires. The question THE ANIMIST poses is what happens when we extend one mode of being to all modes of existence.

THE TERRORIST and its CENTRAL IMAGINARY, the VIRUS. THE TERRORIST is the figure of THE DESERT and THE ANIMIST from the perspective of current forms of biontology and biosecurity. THE TERRORIST is all those who seek to disrupt the current biontological organization of state, market, and sociality by opening the political and social to the nonhuman animal, the vegetal, and the geotic. With the dual Late Liberalism crises of post-9/11 and the Great Recession, the terrorist has been associated primarily with fundamentalist Islam.[33] And much of critical thought has focused on the relationship between biopolitics and biosecurity in the wake of these two crises. But, once again, this focus on biosecurity has obscured the systemic reorientation of biosecurity around geosecurity and meteorosecurity: social and ecological effects of climate change.[34] THE TERRORIST is seen in those who insist that the size of the human population must be addressed in the wake of climate change, that a mountain is more important than air-conditioning, that humans are kudzu, that human extinction is desirable. But humans are not the only terrorists. But THE TERRORIST is also the virus and the waste dump, the drug-resistant bacterial infection, and the nuclear fallout. Perhaps most spectacularly, THE TERRORIST is the popular cultural figure of the Zombie—life turned to nonlife and transformed into species war. Thus the difference between THE DESERT and THE TERRORIST has to do with the agency and intentionality of nonhuman life and nonlife. Whereas THE DESERT is a factual assessment of an inert state opened to technological successes or failures, THE TERRORIST is an active antagonistic agent built out of the collective assemblage that is Late Liberalism. Thus THE TERRORIST is also recognition's internal political other operating through the tactics of camouflage and espionage with environmentalists inhabiting the borderlands between activists and terrorists across state borders and interstate surveillance.

Again, these figures and discourses are not the exit from or the answer to biopolitics or biontology. They are not subjugated subjects waiting to be liberated. As with the animist who might or might not smuggle a core human drama back into the vitalized world, all these figures are condensed expressions of the simultaneous continuing grip of the *bios* and *thanatos* and the unraveling of their relevance. They are the strange dreams one has before fully waking. They are the ghosts who exist in between two worlds—the world in which the dependent oppositions of life *(bios)* and death *(thanatos)* and of life *(bios)* and nonlife *(geos)* are sensible and dramatic and the world in which these enclosures are no longer relevant, sensible, or practical.

NOTES

1. Michel Foucault, *Security, Territory, Population: Lectures at the Collège de France, 1977–78,* ed. Michel Senellart, trans. Graham Burchell (New York: Palgrave Macmillan, 2007), 1.

2. But also sometimes of cats. Robert Darnton, *The Great Cat Massacre: And Other Episodes in French Cultural History* (New York: Basic Books, 2009).

3. Hannah Arendt, *On the Human Condition* (Chicago: University of Chicago Press, 1958).

4. Donna J. Haraway, "The Biopolitics of Postmodern Bodies: Determinations of Self in Immune System Discourse," *differences: A Journal of Feminist Cultural Studies* 1, no. 1 (1989): 3–43.

5. See also Andre de Macedo Duarte, "Hannah Arendt, Biopolitics, and the Problem of Violence: From *Animal Laborans* to *Homo sacer,*" in *Hannah Arendt and the Uses of History: Imperialism, Nation, Race, and Genocide,* ed. Richard H. King and Dan Stone, 21–37 (London: Berghahn Books, 2007). Claire Blencowe argues, "Whereas Arendt sees the normalizing force of modern society as being in total opposition to individuality, Foucault posits totalization and individuation as processes of normation, which casts a light upon the relative import they place upon politics and ethics." Blencowe, "Foucault's and Arendt's 'Insider View' of Biopolitics: A Critique of Agamben," *History of the Human Sciences* 23, no. 5 (2010): 113–30.

6. Roberto Esposito, *Bios,* trans. Timothy C. Campbell (Minneapolis: University of Minnesota Press, 2008). See also Campbell, *Improper Life: Technology and Biopolitics from Heidegger to Agamben* (Minneapolis: University of Minnesota Press, 2011).

7. Frederick Rosen, *Life Itself: A Comprehensive Inquiry into the Nature, Origin, and Fabrication of Life* (New York: Columbia University Press, 1991).

8. Michel Foucault, *Society Must Be Defended: Lectures at the Collège de France, 1975–1976,* trans. David Macey (Paris: Éditions de Seuil/Gallimard, 1997), 35. *Apparition* appears as *l'apparition* in the French original.

9. See also Esposito, *Bios,* 57.

10. Henry A. Giroux, *Youth in a Suspect Society: Democracy or Disposability?* (New York: Palgrave Macmillan, 2009), 83. See also Angela Davis, *Abolition Democracy: Beyond Empire, Prisons, and Torture* (New York: Seven Stories Press, 2005).

11. Alain Badiou, *Adventures in French Philosophy* (London: Verso, 2012), 87, 93, 97.

12. Foucault, *Society Must Be Defended,* 239. "Insofar as man is a living being" appears as "une prise de pouvoir sur l'homme en tant qu'être vivant" in the French original.

13. Scott Lauria Morgenson, "The Biopolitics of Settler Colonialism: Right Here, Right Now," *Settler Colonial Studies* 1, no. 1 (2011): 52–76; Sandro Mezzadra, Julian Reid, and Ranabir Samaddar, eds., *The Biopolitics of Development: Reading Michel Foucault in the Postcolonial Present* (New Delhi: Springer India, 2013).

14. Claire Colebrook, *Death of the PostHuman: Essays on Extinction,* vol. 1 (Ann Arbor, Mich.: Open Humanities Press, 2014).

15. Ian Hacking, "Styles of Scientific Reasoning," in *Postanalytic Philosophy,* 145–65 (New York: Columbia University Press, 1985).

16. Richard Monastersky, "First Atomic Blast Proposed as Start of Anthropocene," *Nature,* January 16, 2015, http://www.nature.com/news/first-atomic-blast-proposed-as-start-of-anthropocene-1.16739.

17. Hannah Arendt, "The Conquest of Space and the Stature of Man," *New Atlantis* 18 (Fall 2007): 43–55, originally published in Arendt, *Between Past and Future: Eight Exercises in Political Thought* (New York: Viking, 1963); James E. Lovelock, "A Physical Basis for Life Detection Experiments," *Nature* 207, no. 4997 (1965): 568–70. Many other scholars looked at the function of the "whole earth" in the making of the modern ecological movement, though more recently placing this in the Anthropocene. See, e.g., Elizabeth DeLoughrey, "Satellite Planetarity and the Ends of the Earth," *Public Culture* 26, no. 2 (2014): 257–80.

18. Karen Pinkus, *Fuel: A Speculative Dictionary* (Minneapolis: University of Minnesota Press, 2016); Alison Bashford, "The Anthropocene Is Modern History: Reflections on Climate and Australian Deep Time," *Australian Historical Studies* 44, no. 3 (2013): 341–49; Rosanne Kennedy, "Humanity's Footprint: Reading *Rings of Saturn* and *Palestinian Walks* in an Anthropocene Era," *Biography* 35, no. 1 (2012): 170–89.

19. Jason W. Moore, "The Capitalocene, Part I: On the Nature and Origins of Our Ecological Crisis," March 2014, and Moore, "The Capitalocene, Part II: Abstract Social Nature and the Limits to Capital," March 2014, minor revisions June 2014, *Jason W. Moore* (blog), http://www.jasonwmoore.com/.

20. Joel Achenbach, "Welcome to the Anthropocene," *Achenblog* (blog), *Washington Post,* August 3, 2010, https://www.washingtonpost.com/news/achenblog/. Achenbach is reporting on the talk that *National Geographic*'s Dennis Dimick gave at the Aspen Environmental Forum.

21. Dipesh Chakrabarty, "The Climate of History: Four Theses," *Critical Inquiry* 35 (Winter 2009): 197–222; Chakrabarty, *Provincializing Europe: Postcolonial Thought and Historical Difference* (Princeton, N.J.: Princeton University Press, 2007).

22. Bruno Latour, "Perspectivism: 'Type' or 'Bomb'?," *Anthropology Today* 25, no. 2 (2009): 1–2. In this editorial, Bruno Latour reviews a debate on "Perspectivism and Animism" between Philippe Descola (College of France) and Eduardo Viveiros de Castro (National Museum of Rio de Janeiro) that took place at Maison Suger, Institute of Advanced Studies, Paris, on January 30, 2009.

23. Colebrook, *Death of the PostHuman*; Elizabeth Grosz, *Becoming Undone: Darwinian Reflections on Life, Politics, and Art* (Durham, N.C.: Duke University Press, 2011).

24. Eugene Thacker, *After Life* (Chicago: University of Chicago Press, 2010), x.

25. Quentin Meillassoux, *After Finitude: An Essay of the Necessity of Contingency,* trans. Ray Brassier (London: Bloomsbury, 2009), 10.

26. I elaborate the preceding points in "The Will to Be Otherwise/The Effort of Endurance," *South Atlantic Quarterly* 111, no. 3 (2012): 453–75.

27. Kathryn Yusoff, "Geologic Life: Prehistory, Climate, Futures in the Anthropocene," *Environment and Planning D: Society and Space* 31, no. 5: 779–95.

28. Colebrook, *Death of the PostHuman*; Eugene Thacker, *In the Dust of This Planet* (Alresford Hants, U.K.: Zero Books, 2011).

29. John Carriero, "Conatus and Perfection in Spinoza," *Midwest Studies in Philosophy* 35, no. 1 (2011): 74.

30. Eduardo Kohn, *How Forests Think: Toward an Anthropology beyond the Human* (Berkeley: University of California Press, 2013).

31. Jane Bennett, "A Vitalist Stopover on the Way to a New Materialism," in *New Materialisms: Ontology, Agency, and Politics,* ed. Diana Coole and Samantha Frost, 47–69 (Durham, N.C.: Duke University Press, 2010). See also Arun Saldanha and Hoon Song, eds., *Sexual Difference: Between Psychoanalysis and Vitalism* (London: Routledge, 2014).

32. Temple Grandin, *Thinking in Pictures: My Life with Autism,* expanded ed. (New York: Vintage Books, 2006), 122.

33. Jasbir Puar, *Terrorist Assemblages: Homonationalism in Queer Times* (Durham, N.C.: Duke University Press, 2007).

34. Nafeez Ahmed, "Pentagon Bracing for Public Dissent over Climate and Energy Shocks," *The Guardian,* June 14, 2013, https://www.theguardian.com/environment/earth-insight/2013/jun/14/climate-change-energy-shocks-nsa-prism.

4

Foucault's Fossils: Life Itself and the Return to Nature in Feminist Philosophy

LYNNE HUFFER

> They discerned in fossils an inhuman art, metaphor along
> with materiality, intensification of the world's truths, lithic
> conviviality.
> —Jeffrey Jerome Cohen, Twitter posting

Over the past three decades, feminist philosophers have increasingly turned to the natural sciences to ask new questions about the body, materiality, nonhuman animals, affect, the biosphere, and the forces that animate the physical world. This renaturalizing trend has dramatically shifted the broader landscape of feminist theoretical inquiry away from social constructionism, subjectivity, and epistemology toward ontological and metaphysical concerns about nature, the form–matter relation, the limits of the human, and the question of life itself. Elizabeth Grosz writes in her most recent book, "We need a humanities in which the human is no longer the norm, rule, or object, but instead life itself, in its open multiplicity, comes to provide the object of analysis."[1] Her comment reflects larger interdisciplinary initiatives over the past three decades to link humanistic inquiry with the natural sciences and, especially, the health sciences. These efforts have materialized in the form of bioethics centers; joint faculty positions in health and humanities;

and a proliferation of workshops, institutes, and research incentives designed to integrate what C. P. Snow once called the "two cultures."[2]

In the context of the Anthropocene—the conception of the human as a geomorphic force and the possible mass extinction of multiple forms of life—what are we to make of these posthumanist configurations? More specifically, what happens when we bring a Foucauldian genealogical lens to feminist renaturalization as life philosophy? And what are we to make of the explicitly ethical claims that are grounded in the feminist return to life? If, as Grosz puts it, renaturalization means that we need an "ethics internal to life itself," how can we avoid the dangers of a biopolitics in which, as Foucault puts it, "the life of the species is wagered on its own political strategies"? If we agree with Foucault that modern biopower is characterized by "the entry of life into history" and the bringing of life and its mechanisms "into the realm of explicit calculations," how are we to assess both the value and the danger of the contemporary feminist investment in that life?[3]

Importantly, the new feminist ethics of life is not confined to renaturalizing thinkers. Indeed, the most influential feminist philosopher of *de*-naturalization, Judith Butler, increasingly relies on life as an anchor for the ethical theory she develops in her later work. Both Grosz and Butler—a renaturalizer and a denaturalizer—stake their ethical claims on life itself. But is the vital matter of *life itself* a given? Or might "life itself," like "sex itself," be what Foucault calls an "artificial unity," a fictive ensemble that emerges in our own time as a speculative ideal, "a causal principle, an omnipresent meaning, a secret to be discovered everywhere"?[4] When Jane Bennett writes at the end of *Vibrant Matter*, "I believe in one matter-energy, the maker of things seen and unseen," ought we to wonder about such vitalist creeds for would-be materialists?[5]

I will argue in this essay that "life itself" is a problem of our time and, specifically, of our anthropogenic age: like sex in Foucault, life is "an especially dense transfer point of power" that emerges at a particular historical moment, the contemporary moment of our biopolitical present.[6] Beginning with life as a problem of our time, I explore how a genealogical approach to life itself can open up new questions about the celebration of life in contemporary feminist renaturalizing philosophies. In doing so, I insist on the importance of the epistemic conditions for the possibility of what Foucault calls "games of truth." Theorists like

Grosz assert that it is time to turn away from epistemological questions. I want to make a counterclaim: that to repudiate epistemology, and to call for a new metaphysics and a new ontology of life itself, as Grosz does, evades the paradox of what Foucault calls in *The Order of Things* the historical a priori: that we are both bound and unbound by the temporal contingencies through which epistemes emerge and topple.[7] Focusing specifically on Foucault's description of fossils and monsters in the classical age, I hope to sharpen our sense of the geomorphic aporias that mark today's Anthropocenic discourse, the most acute of which is the emergence of "life itself" in the midst of what many are calling the sixth extinction.[8]

Ultimately, the stakes of my project are ethical. How do we approach the question of ethics in the Anthropocene? My analysis proceeds in three parts. First, I offer a brief overview of the renaturalizing move in feminist philosophy, with a particular focus on the work of Elizabeth Grosz. Second, I examine Butler's work as the Foucauldian, denaturalizing foil for the new feminist return to nature to show that feminist renaturalizers and denaturalizers alike make ethical appeals in the name of life itself. Third, I turn to Foucault to show how genealogy and the historical a priori give us a method and a concept for engaging life as historically contingent. In that turn, I suggest that the genealogical problematization of life we find in Foucault offers a nonvitalist alternative to life philosophy's vitalization of matter. I will argue that asking about the question of ethics in the Anthropocene means problematizing "life itself" as the metaphysical ground of our ethics. Foucault's historically contingent, emergent conception of life forces us to engage with the materiality of the traces of the past through which we construct our present understanding of ourselves, not only as individual disciplinary subjects but, more urgently, in our massification as population and even as a geomorphic force. Those traces include not only the archive of human lives struck down by power but also the fossilized traces of nonhuman lives, what Quentin Meillassoux calls the philosophical problem of "ancestrality."[9] This archival fossilization of matter opens the recoiling movement of ethics as a question.[10] The fractured ground of such a question acquires material form in the figure of the fossil. I read that figure not as the trace of life but as the mark of absence and death: as nature's archive, the fossil record is an archive of extinction.

FEMINIST RENATURALIZATION

The renaturalizing move in contemporary feminist philosophy reflects a broader shift away from feminism's decades-old engagement with questions of epistemology and subjectivity, from standpoint epistemologies to postmodern feminisms of various kinds. The rise of animal studies, posthumanism, critical science and technology studies, object-oriented ontology, and affect theory marks a displacement, if not an outright rejection, of both the sociological foundationalism of standpoint theory and the psycholinguistic antifoundationalism of feminist poststructuralism. As part of this larger shift, feminist renaturalization has mounted an important challenge to the denaturalizing moves that dominated feminist thought in the second half of the twentieth century. The philosophical reprivileging of nature and the biosphere has produced new ways of imagining life, from innovative scientific and phenomenological accounts of corporeality to transspecies political theories to new cosmologies of space and time.

To be sure, the contemporary feminist return to nature is not a return to the kinds of naturalist ontologies that have traditionally been used to justify gender inequality, the marginalization of sexual deviants, or the perpetuation of European colonial conquest and white racial privilege. Today's feminist renaturalization projects challenge those ontologies along with the culture–nature, mind–body dualisms that support them. They tend to rethink binarism itself, reconceptualizing human agency as part of nature or matter rather than in opposition to it. Shifting their focus away from antiessentialist critiques of woman-as-nature, renaturalizers have turned toward animals, the cosmos, subatomic particles and waves, the brain, and the energetic pulse of biological life as objects of feminist concern.

A few salient examples serve to delineate the contours of the renaturalizing move in feminist philosophy. In her influential *Meeting the Universe Halfway,* the theoretical physicist Karen Barad offers an agential realist account of an intra-active matter where meaning and mattering are inextricably connected. New attunements to intra-active matter in all its complexity allow us, Barad says, to "hear nature speak" in the entangled webs of what she calls *spacetimematterings.*[11] Stacy Alaimo picks up on Barad to explore what she calls "trans-corporeality": the "contact zone between human corporeality and more-than-human nature."[12] Along similar lines, the Spinozist philosopher Hasana Sharp elaborates what she calls a "philanthropic posthumanism" for a "new universal," a vital, flourishing assemblage of humans, animals, rocks, and trees whose unity as nature is derived from Spinoza's geometric account of the universe as substance and modes.[13] Finally, in her later work, Elizabeth Grosz develops a Darwinian understanding of nature as dynamic and self-differentiating to articulate what she calls in *Time Travels* "a more politicized, radical, and far-reaching feminist understanding of matter, nature, biology, time and becoming—objects and concepts usually considered outside the direct focus of feminist analysis."[14]

There are obviously important differences among these thinkers, and I do not mean to efface those distinctions: each has her own particular set of methodological and conceptual tools for redressing what she views as a dominant antinaturalism in feminist theory. These examples are offered as broad brush strokes to sketch out a renaturalizing scene. Most crucially, I want to focus on how the feminist return to nature presents itself, on empirical grounds, not only as a more complete and more accurate description of the world than that provided by social constructionists but also as more ethically and politically promising. Karen Barad, for example, devotes the final chapter of her book to questions about our accountability to matter's intra-action; she ends with an ethical call for greater responsibility in our relation to the complexity of matter.[15] Stacy Alaimo concludes her book *Bodily Natures* with the call for "an ethics that is not circumscribed by the human but is instead accountable to a material world that is never merely an external place but always the very substance of our selves and others."[16] Hasana Sharp steers her Spinozist posthumanism toward an ethological ethics that can promote the flourishing of all beings in the biosphere through the cultivation of joyful affects. And in *Becoming Undone,* Grosz expounds on the value of the language of the bees as an "insect ethics" internal to life itself.[17]

Grosz's reflections on life in particular have generated a burgeoning field of exciting and innovative feminist work. Under the banner of new materialisms, feminist science studies, or feminist renaturalization, these contemporary feminist returns to nature provide an important corrective to previous repudiations of scientific data in feminist constructivisms of various kinds. But what are we to make of the posthumanist disregard for the contingent epistemic frames that situate claims about nature and life itself? "Linked to the preeminence of the subject and of concepts of subjectivity," Grosz complains, "is the privileging of the epistemological (questions of discourse, knowledge, truth, and scientificity) over the ontological (questions of the real, of matter, of force, or energy)."[18] Rejecting feminist theory's longstanding obsession with subjectivity and epistemology, Grosz turns toward ontology and even metaphysics as the philosophical ground for her new materialism. "Feminist theory," she writes, "needs to welcome again what epistemologies have left out: the relentless force of the real, a new metaphysics."[19]

From a Foucauldian perspective, Grosz's metaphysical claims presuppose a Darwinian naturalism whose epistemic ground is *specifically* Victorian and therefore historically contingent rather than self-evidently true in all times and places. Indeed, Grosz's Darwinian life is the one "We Other Victorians," as Foucault calls us, take to be the truth of nature.[20] To be sure, Grosz departs from traditional Darwinian humanisms: as a posthumanist, she sees Darwin as a bridge between the "determinism" of "classical science" and "the place of *indetermination* that has been so central to the contemporary, postmodern forms of the humanities."[21] Reading Darwin as "the most original thinker of the link between difference and becoming, between matter and its elaboration as life, between the past and the future," Grosz finds in Darwin an antifoundationalist critique of essentialism and teleology.[22]

Importantly, Grosz highlights sexual difference as central to a Darwinian understanding of life itself. In *Time Travels,* she argues that the three evolutionary principles—individual variation, the proliferation of species, and natural selection—provide an explanation of the "dynamism, growth, and transformability of living systems, the impulse toward a future that is unknown in, and uncontained by, the present and its history" (19). Grosz focuses on the third principle—natural selection—to bring out the crucial role of sexual selection as a subbranch of natural selection. She then rereads Darwinian sexual selection through the Irigarayan lens of sexual difference. Darwin, Grosz argues, confirms "the Irigarayan postulation of the irreducibility, indeed, ineliminability, of sexual difference" (31). Thus sexualization—as Darwinian sexual selection, as Irigarayan sexual difference—constitutes the mechanism of deviation through which other differences are produced. As Grosz explains, sexual selection aesthetically "deviates" natural selection's principle of preservation to form what she calls "an ingenious [Darwinian] temporal machine for the production of the new" (25). Crucially, this ingenious machine produces, in Grosz's view, an ontological equivalence between sexuation and "life itself." Refracting sexual selection through an Irigarayan lens, Grosz thus reclaims sexual difference as "one of the ontological characteristics of life itself, not merely a detail, a feature that will pass.... Sexual difference," Grosz asserts, "is an ineliminable characteristic of life" (31).

In *Becoming Undone*, Grosz expands the Irigarayan–Darwinian frame of *Time Travels* to include the life-affirming philosophies of Deleuze, Bergson, and Simondon. Drawing on Bergson in particular, Grosz describes life as a "fundamental continuum," a "movement of differentiation that elaborates a multiplicity of things according to a unity of impulse or force" (46). Expounding on this Bergsonian conception of life as *élan vital*, Grosz articulates an "ontology of becoming" to be found in the dynamism of things: an "affirmation of the vibratory continuity of the material universe as a whole" (51). This continuity is not only spatial but also temporal. As Grosz puts it, "life... becomes something other than its (species or individual) past while retaining a certain continuity with it" (53). The resulting "symbiosis" between living life and nonliving matter occurs because life contains "virtualities" within itself. As Grosz puts it, "life carries becoming as its core. It is because life is parasitic on matter that life carries within itself the whole that matter expresses" (53).

In *Becoming Undone*, Grosz incorporates sexuality into the same ontological frame that equates sexual difference with life itself. Gayness or straightness, Grosz argues, "is not produced from causes..., nor is it the consequence of a free choice." Rather, it is "the enactment of a freedom," the expression of sexuality as "an open invention" (73). This understanding of sexuality as a self-differentiating force coextensive with life itself has political implications. As Grosz explains, the political problem for sexual beings who have been oppressed or excluded by our sexual order is not the juridical achievement of more recognition, more rights, or more voice; rather, it becomes "how to enable more action, more making and doing, more difference" (73).

Grosz further argues that to facilitate this sexual élan vital of freedom or open invention, feminist theory needs to renaturalize itself: it "needs to turn, or perhaps return, to questions of the real..., questions of the nature and forces of the real, the nature and forces of the world, cosmological forces as well as historical ones" (85). That nod to history notwithstanding, Grosz's arguments are largely transhistorical. Decrying the shortcomings of a feminism obsessed with epistemological questions, Grosz's renaturalizing appeal is a call for a return to metaphysics. Grosz frames this metaphysical turn, like the return to nature, as a return to the new: "a new metaphysics" (85). Again, Grosz finds her most consistent feminist support for this turn in the "new metaphysics" of Luce Irigaray, where she finds "a new account of the forces of the real and the irreducibility of a real that is fundamentally dynamic."[23] For Grosz, that Irigarayan dynamism is driven by the division of being into "two irreducibly different types" (100). "Nature itself," she asserts, "takes on the form of [a] two[ness]" (104) that transcends historical contingency: "whatever historical circumstances are conceivable," Grosz asserts, "there is no overcoming of sexual difference." "The future," she continues, "will always contain and express sexual difference" (111). Indeed, "sexual difference" is "the very measure of creativity itself" (101). Without sexual difference, there would only be "sameness, monosexuality, hermaphroditism, the endless structured (bacterial or microbial) reproduction of the same. . . . Without sexual difference, there could be no life as we know it" (101), "no life on earth" (104). Thus Grosz extracts sexual difference from the epistemic conditions of possibility that allow it to appear as a positivity out of what Foucault calls the contingent site, the "mute ground"[24] or "background"[25] of our knowledge. So doing, she transforms what Irigaray calls "sexual difference" as a problem of "our time" into a transhistorical substance called "life itself."[26]

BUTLER'S ETHICAL TURN TO LIFE

Contemporary feminist philosophers of life often present Judith Butler as the denaturalizing foil to feminist renaturalization. Karen Barad, for example, praises Butler for performatively disrupting feminist social constructionism's unacknowledged conception of sex as a blank, mute, corporeal substance onto which culture makes its mark as gender. But ultimately she finds fault in Butler's insistence on a discursive materiality that cannot account for the nondiscursive aspects of matter. In linking what she views as Butler's flawed humanism to a "failure to theorize the relationship between discursive and nondiscursive practices," Barad articulates a common renaturalizing critique of Butler.[27]

Like Barad, Sharp is critical of the anthropocentric humanism undergirding Butler's work, particularly in its ethical phase. Sharp is especially wary of the death-driven, mournful ethics of sad passions Butler derives from her Hegelian spin on Spinoza. Contra Butler's somewhat heretical Spinozism, Sharp argues for a feminist politics of renaturalization that "begins with the denial of human exceptionalism."[28] Contrasting her own Spinozist "posthumanist view of agency"[29] with Butler's subjectivist, "antinatural concept of the human,"[30] Sharp affirms the value of a "vitalistic" metaphysics—the "conative striving" of "living organisms" as "a desire for life"[31] that exists whether we recognize it or not—as an ethical and political alternative to Butler's melancholy Hegelian project "of perpetual dissatisfaction."[32]

Although Grosz is less concerned than Barad or Sharp with Butler's anthropocentrism, her critiques of Butler are similar in their focus on the problem of Butler's discursive conception of matter. For Grosz, Butler represents "an entire tradition of 'postmodern,' 'constructivist,' or 'performative' feminism in devaluing matter, or in transforming it from noun ('matter') to verb ('mattering') and in the process desubstantializing it."[33] According to Grosz, in Butler "the body itself dissolves, the real always displaces itself by being written on, and matter disappears in the process of mattering, of being valued."[34] And while Grosz applauds Butler's attention to the question of value, she contends that "the process of mattering cannot be cut off from *what matter it is,*" namely, "biological or organic matter."[35] Most important, Grosz grounds her renaturalizing critique of Butler in an ethical claim. Grosz argues that because nature, and not culture alone, is "continually subjected to transformation, to becoming, to unfolding over time, ethics would itself dictate that the natural be owed the debt of culture's emergence, insofar as it is precisely the open-ended incompletion of nature itself that induces the cultural as its complexification and supplement."[36]

Despite their differences, these renaturalizing critiques of Butler all challenge Butler's *discursive* repudiation of what Grosz describes as "what matter is": "biological or organic matter," or "life itself." And indeed, in defending the materiality of the bodies she invoked in *Gender Trouble,* in *Bodies That Matter,* Butler ultimately reinscribes corporeal matter as discursively produced. As Butler puts it, matter is "a process of materialization that stabilizes over time," where materialization is defined as "a forcible reiteration of norms."[37] Not surprisingly, most of Butler's readers have regarded this reiterative, normalizing linkage between matter and intelligibility as an "anti-naturalistic" account of matter. As Pheng Cheah puts it, Butler's synthesis of Foucault and psychoanalysis ends up conflating "an ontogenetic condition of possibility with an empirical cause" to produce a conception of matter as an epistemic object that is always in quotation marks.[38]

In Butler's later work, however, beginning in the late 1990s, those quotation marks give way to a conception of life that seems to evade discourse and legibility. What is this life of *The Psychic Life of Power, Precarious Life, Undoing Gender, Frames of War, Parting Ways*, and *Senses of the Subject*? Like Grosz, Butler tends to use the irreducible term *life* or *life itself* to refer to something that is nondiscursive: an irrepressible force that cannot be contained within meaning's frames. Importantly, Butler's turn to ethics corresponds with her turn to life: life's inherent capacity to contest intelligibility or meaning seems to be one of its key ethical features. In *The Psychic Life of Power*, for example, Butler poses "the ethical as a question" about "life."[39] Here life appears as an enigmatic, psychoanalytically inflected energy, "drive," *Trieb*, or instinct that turns back on itself, tropologically, to produce self-consciousness, conscience, and the psyche according to Hegelian, Nietzschean, and Freudian logics. Loosely aligning the Hegelian body with Nietzschean will and Freudian instinct, Butler suggests that there is something irrepressible about this bodily, instinctive drive or "life" (22, 57).

In *Precarious Life*, life emerges again as a force that is not only insistent and irrepressible but also precarious. In Grosz we saw an ontological equivalence between sexuation and life, and in early Butler we saw the matter of sex as "a regulatory ideal whose materialization is compelled," "an ideal construct which is forcibly materialized through time."[40] But in her turn to ethics, Butler displaces her early ontological questions about sex, gender, and sexuality in favor of a Levinasian preontological ethics of the face that values the vulnerability of nondiscursive human life. To be sure, life's preontological status as human vulnerability differentiates Butler's humanist ethics of life from posthumanist feminist ethics. But it is also worth remembering that Butler's Levinasian humanism is not the same as traditional humanisms: following Levinas, Butler asserts the importance of human relations even as she destabilizes ontological or

metaphysical assumptions about human nature. For Butler, as for Levinas, there's a rift at the origin of the human, and that rift is ethical. This
hardly makes Butler a posthumanist, despite her assertion in *Frames of
War* that there is "no firm way to distinguish in absolute terms the *bios*
of the animal from the *bios* of the human animal."[41] As the title of her
book, *Frames of War,* suggests, Butler continues to insist throughout her
work on the inextricable relation between specifically *human* epistemic
frames and questions of ontology and ethics. "There is no life and no
death," she writes, "without a relation to some frame." "A life," she insists,
"has to be intelligible *as a life,* has to conform to certain conceptions
of what life is, in order to become recognizable" (7). By contrast, Sharp
and Grosz assert that life exists whether we recognize it or not.

Despite this key difference between Butler's new humanism and
renaturalizing posthumanisms, I want to focus on the fact that both
camps invoke life to anchor their ethical claims. As Butler puts it in
Precarious Life, "to respond to the face, to understand its meaning,
means to be awake to what is precarious in another life or, rather, the
precariousness of life itself."[42] And even though, in *Frames of War,*
she hedges on the term "life itself," invoking biopolitics and various
critiques of vitalism, she continues to link the precariousness of life to
something that exceeds the epistemic frame: "precariousness itself," she
writes, "cannot be properly *recognized*" (13). According to Butler, it is
precisely that which exceeds recognition in precariousness that "im-
poses certain kinds of ethical obligations on and among the living" (22).
Importantly, the precarious life Butler invokes here is explicitly linked
to what she calls life's precarity: life's social and political conditioning.
So if, in *Giving an Account of Oneself,* Butler harnessed her ethics of the
Other to a Spinozist desire to persist that "is," she writes, "life itself," in
Frames of War, she rethinks the term "life itself" to include sociality as
life's condition.[43] In doing so, she differentiates her conception of life
from Spinoza's conatus, which she says "can be and is undercut" by our
boundedness to others.[44] Thus she argues in *Frames of War* that if all
lives are precarious, life's conditions make some lives more precarious
than others. Precarity—the politically induced, differential condition of
certain populations to injury, violence, and death—comes to qualify the
precariousness of life itself to which it is nonetheless inextricably connected. In *Parting Ways,* Butler concretizes this ethics of obligation to a
precarious Other as an ethics of dispersion by considering the precarity

of Jewish and Palestinian lives. Such obligation, she writes, constitutes "the condition of a politics of diasporic life."[45] Finally, in a recent book, *Senses of the Subject,* Butler explores the Hegelian understanding that "love must be living to be love," even if it turns out that "life itself can never be contained or exhausted by love." Even in the grief that follows death, there is "something enlivening," the "rustling" movement of "infinity," "evanescent and alive."[46]

As this trajectory suggests, Butler's insistence on the epistemic and sociopolitical frames out of which life emerges ultimately makes her conception of life somewhat different from those of the renaturalizers. And yet, the Levinasian, preontological, consistently "ecstatic"[47] frame of her ethics of the Other requires that Butler implicitly ground her claims in an excess, an ineffable alterity, what Foucault calls in *History of Sexuality Volume One* the "something else and something more" that is sex (153). While Butler articulates that something else and something more as precarious life, Foucault calls that life "'sex' itself" (156): "a causal principle" whose "agency" is not "autonomous" but, rather, "an imaginary point . . . that each individual has to pass in order to have access to his own intelligibility" (154–155). What was once "madness" is now "our intelligibility"; what was once perceived "as an obscure and nameless urge" now gives us "our identity" and "the plenitude of our body" (156) through the distributional, calculative, statistical rationality that characterizes biopower. Many have asked why, in her turn to ethics, Butler turns away from the questions about gender and sexuality that dominated her early work. I want to suggest that in her ethical turn, Butler resignifies sex as life. Genealogy exposes the grid of sexuality that incites, intensifies, and proliferates Butlerian sex as life itself: the precarious life that Butler places at the heart of her ethics.

FOSSIL AND ARCHIVE

Foucault's genealogical approach to biopower, or power over life, brings a genealogical lens to the feminist ethics of life itself in both its renaturalizing and denaturalizing dimensions. Foucault famously argues in *The Order of Things* that life itself was invented in the nineteenth century. If biology was unknown in the eighteenth century, he writes, "there was a very simple reason for it: that life itself did not exist. All that existed was living beings" (127–28). According to Foucault, with the nineteenth-century invention of history, historicity was introduced into nature. The historicity of nature differentiates the mode of being of the modern period from the tabulated, "vegetal values" of the classical age by making the animal being's privileged form.[48] In modernity, being "maintains its existence on the frontiers of life and death" in the form of the animal (277). Historicity introduces life as the "sovereign vanishing point" that replaces the royal sovereign of the previous episteme (277). This shift is reflected in the rise of biology: the *bio-logos,* or science of life, whose focus is the developmental organism with its hidden structures, buried organs, invisible functions, "and that distant force, at the foundation of its being, which keeps it alive" (277). With life comes death, as Foucault puts it: "the animal appears as the bearer of that death to which it is, at the same time, subjected; it contains a perpetual devouring of life by life. . . . Life has left the tabulated space of order and become wild once more" (277). Life becomes "the root of all existence," and the "non-living, nature in its inert form," becomes "merely spent life." "The experience of life is thus posited as the most general law of beings; the revelation of that primitive force on the basis of which they are; it functions as an untamed ontology," and "this ontology discloses not so much what gives beings their foundation as what bears them for an instant towards a precarious form and yet is already secretly sapping them from within in order to destroy them" (278). Crucially, life takes on a central role in the rise of the human sciences over the course of the nineteenth and twentieth centuries: the invention of life and the invention of the human go hand in hand. As Foucault puts it, before the nineteenth century, "man did not exist (any more than life)" (344).

In the 1970s, Foucault reworks this archeological understanding of life and the discourse of the human sciences through genealogies of sexuality in *Abnormal* and *History of Sexuality Volume One.* Here life emerges as sexual instinct: the "dark shimmer of sex"[49] or "fragment of darkness that we carry within us."[50] Bringing together *eros* and *thanatos,* modern power–knowledge transforms the concept of an instinct of life into a drive toward death in a "Faustian pact" that "exchange[s] life in its entirety for sex itself."[51] Picking up on the logic of a "continuous gradation" that *Discipline and Punish* describes as a "great carceral network," *History of Sexuality Volume One* rearticulates that network as a biopolitical *dispositif* of power–knowledge–*pleasure* that, in the late nineteenth century, sexualizes existence as life itself.[52] Pleasure transforms and intensifies the dispositif that, earlier in the century, had invented life as natural, biological, and reproductive. As "the economic principle intrinsic to sexual instinct," pleasure uncouples sexual instinct from fertilization[53] and unhitches sexuality from the procreative kinship system Foucault calls "alliance."[54] Pleasure makes sexual instinct dynamic, self-differentiating, "an open invention," as Grosz might put it.[55] Importantly, pleasure-driven sexual instinct "overflows its natural end"—heterosexual copulation—"and it does so naturally."[56] It therefore becomes "natural for instinct to be abnormal."[57] In Foucault's rendering, the natural deviation that Grosz celebrates in Darwin describes the sexological dispositif of proliferating perversions that incite and implant bourgeois sexuality as life itself. Finally, this pleasure-driven expansion of a gradational ontology of sexual deviation is intensified by the "interplay of truth and sex."[58] The economy of pleasure that defines life as sexual instinct reproduces itself through the invention and intensification of a new pleasure: a "pleasure in the truth of pleasure," the "pleasure of analysis" that is "immanent in this will to knowledge."[59]

Importantly, Foucault further explains in *Abnormal* that this new logic of sexual instinct as the deviant nature of life itself *depathologizes* the abnormal. Although many thinkers have conflated Foucault with Georges Canguilhem's analysis of the normal and the pathological, Foucault departs from Canguilhem by demonstrating a modern shift away from the pathologization of the abnormal.[60] Foucault argues that the invention of sexual instinct and the naturalization of perversion gives rise to psychiatry as "a medicine that purely and simply dispenses with the pathological" (308). This allows psychiatry to become "a medically qualified power that brings under its control a domain of objects that are defined as not being pathological processes" (309). It is the "depathologization" of naturally deviant sexual instinct that allows for the "generalization of psychiatric power" (309); concomitantly, biomedicine expands and intensifies the points of access through which it orders both individuals and populations, shifting its target from mere disease—the pathological—to public health and nonpathological forms of life.[61] This shift is crucial to the logic of biopower and its modes for ordering and intensifying life itself through the measurement, monitoring, and control of populations. The biopolitical norm is internally derived from populations to produce a calculus of distribution that plots variation or deviance as a function not of an externally imposed ideal but of their actual occurrence. This statistical logic of the norm as normal curve reduces the social world with its leaky, dying bodies "to the objective figure of the line, the curve, the histogram's alleged indifference, the purity of number." In the "statistical panopticism" of this scalar method, we as living social beings come to understand ourselves through the "detour" of a "numerical amalgamation of all—a ligature so ontologically alien to the social world that it fails to qualify as a relation at all."[62]

Life itself, then, is the biopolitical product of this shift from disciplinary power–knowledge into an ever-expanding grid of regulatory power–knowledge–pleasure. Like sex itself, the "imaginary element" that is life itself is increasingly constituted by the statistical tracking and manipulation of populations "as something desirable."[63] And again, as Foucault puts it with regard to sex, "it is this desirability" of life "that attaches each one of us to the injunction to know it, to reveal its law and its power."[64]

Foucault's description of the sexualized life of biopower is echoed in Grosz's description of life itself as a vital force at the heart of a new metaphysics and a new feminist ethics of sexual difference. But in Foucault's description of biopower, life is massified as population through a technology of statistics that redistributes life around a norm within a field of gradation. This stochastic, normalizing, massifying technology intensifies life on every scale, from its aggregation as population to the microscopic scale of cells and genomes.[65] Foucault shows how that intensification operates through the interplay of truth and pleasure and how the will to knowledge that drives the disciplinary desire for individual identity and intelligibility also participates in a sexualizing feedback loop of power–knowledge–pleasure whose regulatory pole is the ordering norm of the indifferent histogram.

How, then, might Foucault's genealogical perspective on life itself help us to rethink the return to nature in contemporary feminist thought? Contra the renaturalizers' transhistorical conceptions of life itself, Foucault offers an unstable, contingent conception of life that remains bound to the disintegrating forces of temporal change. Specifically, in Foucault, the evidentiary matter that grounds our belief in something called life itself is, by definition, fragmented, incomplete, and shifting. In bringing our attention to the rift-restoring matter of time's traces, Foucault allows us to rethink life not as a timeless metaphysical substance whose features are derived from modern biology but as a strange, nonhuman writing we might read and "think differently" in shifting interplays of space and time.[66] That rereading involves not structuralism's linguistic abstractions, as so many of Foucault's critics have claimed. As a genealogical epistemology and method, reading and thinking differently requires contact with the materiality of the past. "My object," Foucault says, "is not language but the archive."[67] It is this Foucauldian archival approach to rethinking the material traces of absence or death that can break open the metaphysical frame of life itself that characterizes some feminist renaturalization projects. Specifically, if, as Foucault argues in *The Order of Things,* the spatial ruptures of eighteenth-century European thought transformed natural history into the historicity of nature and, with it, the possibility of life itself, the spatial continuity that defines our contemporary age might be ruptured through a radical rethinking of nature's archives of absence: the fossil record.

To be sure, an obvious posthumanist objection to this turn to the archive for histories of the present that rupture our anthropogenic frame will be that Foucault's archives track human discourse rather than the nondiscursive, nonhuman matter of nature. Does my attempt to trouble the epistemic presuppositions of a concept of life itself rely on a specifically discursive archive, thereby landing me back in our episteme's humanist trap? Or, alternatively, might it be possible to rethink Foucault's archival method as the contact of thinking with a discourse that is other-than-human and other-than-life? Might we reconceive the archive of our histories of the present as a fossilized nature that suspends the human and the life itself to which it is bound? Might we, in other words, rethink the Anthropocene and paleontology through the lens of the Foucauldian archive? Might that suspension of the human and life itself return the fossil to the monstrosity out of which it was extracted?

The Order of Things offers clues for this suspension. In "Monsters and Fossils," at the heart of *The Order of Things,* the fossil emerges against the "background noise" that is "the endless murmur of nature" (155). Like a form from sediment once covered by oceans, Foucault's fossil becomes a figure for the emergence of intelligibility out of the undifferentiated murmur of unintelligibility. *The Order of Things* describes those frames of intelligibility as the epistemic conditions that give rise to the human sciences in the modern age.

But what happens when we read *The Order of Things* through the lens of monstrosity touched by the fossil? What happens when we reread reason's order through the disordering lens of unreason? If the fossil figures the emergence of intelligibility out of unintelligibility's murmur, what happens when we reread paleontology as mad? Let me explain these admittedly bizarre questions by briefly linking *The Order of Things* to Foucault's 1961 book *History of Madness*, a link Foucault himself makes in the preface to *The Order of Things*, where he writes, "The present study is, in a sense, *an echo* of... a history of madness" (xxiv, emphasis added). Can we, reading backward and remembering *History of Madness*, rehear its story about the emergence of the Western subject as an *echo* of life's emergence in *The Order of Things*? In that hearing, might we also rehear *Madness*'s archive as a monstrous echo of the nonhuman fossil record we find in *The Order of Things*?

These questions point to the reverberating repetitions through which Foucault's first book, *History of Madness*, is inverted as the scientific order of the human sciences in *The Order of Things* five years later, in 1966. Importantly for my aim to destabilize the humanist presuppositions that subtend standard conceptions of the archive, I want to highlight here the repeated figure–ground structure that *The Order of Things* and *History of Madness* share. Just as fossils emerge from the murmuring "background noise" (155) of monstrosity in *The Order of Things*, so, too, in *History of Madness*, positivities emerge from the murmuring "background noise" of unreason.[68] Like the books and documents Foucault encounters in his visits to the archives of madness, so, too, these fossil forms bear traces of creatures "who," retrospectively, we understand to have "lived and died."[69] Humanist historians will decipher the archival traces of madness for a positivist project of knowing. So, too, with the "inhuman art"[70] of the fossil record: scientists will read "thousands of forms"[71] through a humanizing lens that translates the imprint of fragments of petrified bone, ammonite, plant matter, and shell as scenes from deep time.[72]

Rereading the fossil record through the lens of *History of Madness* interrupts that human rhythm of reconstituted life in a syncopated relation to the archive of madness. Just as the archive of madness tells the story of the rational subject's emergence through the objectification of madness, so, too, the fossil record tells the story of the emergence of life itself through the objectification of monstrosity in the fossil. Fossils may feel familiar to us in our Victorian thinking—Darwin devoted many pages to them in *On the Origin of Species*[73]—but Foucault makes the fossil strange by rendering it as "the privileged locus of a resemblance" out of sync with the time of its appearance.[74] This out-of-syncness helps us to see it as monstrous, as deeply strange, within the epistemic frame of our own space-time. Like the madman and the poet whose logic of similitude places them "on the outer edge of our culture," Foucault's fossil fractures the now in which lives are made intelligible as biological life.[75] Specifically, as the material record of catastrophic extinction, in Foucault's hands fossils become the strange time-twisting mirrors of "the ends of man," of the face dissolving at the edge of the sea, of life's demise in an anthropogenic age. In that sense, we might read this "lithic conviviality"[76] as a mad paleontology, a "speech after death," to use Foucault's words: the proleptic traces of our own extinction.[77]

In this picture, nature reappears not as a unified substance that contains and propagates life itself but as an abyssal murmur that, like the murmur in *History of Madness,* can only be heard as what Foucault calls "a dull sound from beneath history."[78] As other-than-human forms of "speech after death," Foucault's fossils expose what Foucault calls "the exotic charm of another system of thought" and "the limitation of our own."[79] From the middle of *The Order of Things,* fossils emerge as if from the ocean floor in the shape of "ear, or skull, or sexual parts, like so many plaster statues, fashioned one day and dropped the next," as the cast-off parts of a human; the logic of resemblance peculiar to the fossil recasts those human parts as seashell, bird, or worm (156). Rather than indicating the evolutionary triumph of life in man, Foucault's rendering of this part-animal, part-mineral, fragmented evidence of the spatial disruption of temporal continuity returns evolutionary human parts to another space-time as other-than-human characters in a taxonomic table we cannot fully know. In that return, the background monstrosity of temporal continuity out of which the fossil forms as spatial disruption becomes another kind of nature. Rendered strange as the monstrous materialization of the untimely, Foucault's fossil becomes a haunting figure; like a ghost, it marks what Foucault calls "that uncertain frontier region where one does not know whether one ought to speak of life or not" (161). Thus Foucault leaves us to read the fossil in a dislocated space-time, where the fossil lingers as a strange remnant of something we call life within a frame where that something can no longer be thought.

In its echoing relation to *History of Madness,* the fossil record thus undoes subjectivity and life itself at the site of humanism's heart: the archive. Showing the way, in his 1977 essay "Lives of Infamous Men," Foucault returns to those archives—Charenton, Bicêtre, Salpêtrière—out of which he wrote *History of Madness* in the late 1950s. Like "Monster and Fossil," "Lives of Infamous Men" describes the classical episteme, and like "Monster and Fossil," it traces the emergence of form as the appearance of lives out of a murmuring, monstrous background. If fossilized nonhuman lives appear as stone, Foucault's infamous human lives appear as ashes or dried plants and flowers organized in an herbarium as an "anthology of existences" (157). And just as fossils appear as pictorial poems in the sedimented archive of nature, so, too, archival "poem-lives" appear in asylum registers and police reports to mark the passage of beings: sodomite monks and feeble-minded usurers (159). Furthermore, Foucault tells us, their matter matters: unlike literary characters, he says, these beings "lived and died," appearing to him only in their death, as a fossil would, in the form of petrified insect, fish, or worm (160). To be sure, unlike the fossil, the poem-life appears to us because of an encounter with power that, in striking down a life and turning it to ashes, makes it emerge, like a flash, out of the anonymous murmur of beings who pass without a trace. Foucault's conception of lives in his 1977 essay thus reflects his shift, since *The Order of Things,* where the fossil appears, to a focus on knowing as it is traversed by power. But if we read the fossil in the 1966 text retrospectively, through the lens of "Lives of Infamous Men" and biopower, we can see quite clearly that to "animate" the fragmented remains of the past—the fossilized lives in the archive of nonhuman nature, the poem-lives in the police archive of the human—is to create a biopolitical continuity called "life itself" that fills in the gaps of a discontinuous matter with a transhistorical substance. Indeed, Darwin himself worried about how the "imperfection" of the fossil record destabilized the foundations of his evolutionary theory of life. So, too, with the archive: in Foucault's hands, the poem-lives of madness emerge, like fossils, as the aphoristic remnants—or are they figures of the future?—of an inhuman, monstrous world.

Foucault's genealogical approach to life thus suggests that the return to nature in some contemporary feminist philosophy skirts the danger of universalizing the historically contingent frames of our present world as a new metaphysics of life; in so doing, this new metaphysics draws on assumptions that in fact bind life itself to the human, even as it makes posthumanist claims. We need to take seriously that famous image of the face dissolving at the edge of the sea that closes *The Order of Things*. As Foucault puts it in *Speech after Death*, "I'm speaking over the corpse of others."[80]

Confronted with corpses, positivist historians and biologists alike flirt with fantasies of resuscitation, as in the recent *New York Times Magazine* report on Ben Novak's Revive and Restore deextinction project, a paleogenomic quest to use DNA manipulation to bring back from extinction everything from the passenger pigeon to the wooly mammoth to the Tasmanian tiger.[81] This is what Foucault calls in "Lives of Infamous Men" "the dream to restitute [the] intensity [of those lives] in an analysis" (238). Is the paleogeneticist's dream also the dream of the feminist life philosopher: to resuscitate the dead fossil within the continuum of biopower, to chase the "good feelings of bio-energy"?[82] And isn't this dream of giving life precisely the dream Foucault describes in *History of Sexuality Volume One* as the *ars erotica* of our *scientia sexualis*, where the greatest pleasure is "pleasure in the truth of pleasure" (71) to be wrought from "a great archive of pleasures" (63)? Foucault diagnoses that pleasure as the force of intensification that motivates sexual subjects to play our games of truth in biopower. But in his genealogical thinking, he also enjoins us to problematize life itself along with the humanist subject spawned it its wake. In so doing, he offers us an ethics of something other than life—something other than human—that wanders not from death to life but from death to truth and from truth to death. Foucault's archive, like the fossil in *The Order of Things*, is the *matière* or "stuff" that grounds Foucault's ethical thinking.[83]

That ground is, paradoxically, ungrounding. It breaks our frame: this is what Foucault means by a history of the present. How can we write those monstrous histories of the present in the Anthropocene? Can feminism articulate an ethics that takes seriously the dissolution of the human and life itself that Foucault presents to us: as corpse, as monster, as fossil? What kind of monstrous ethics would that be? Remembering these questions, let me conclude with a quotation from James Baldwin, who, in his 1985 essay "Here Be Dragons," transformed a mythic vision of the human past into the reality of a precarious and violent present:

> Ancient maps of the world—when the world was flat—inform us . . . HERE BE DRAGONS. Dragons may not have been there then, but they are certainly here now, breathing fire, belching smoke.[84]

The mad logic of resemblance of a fossil record that proleptically tracks life's extinction ruptures the grids that make us—and life itself—intelligible. The fossil is an inhuman art, a lithic conviviality, an intensification of the monstrosity of the world's truths. HERE BE DRAGONS: those truths hover, like monsters on old maps, in the murmuring background of an anthropocene feminism that, to quote Foucault, "ought to make us wonder today."[85]

NOTES

1. Elizabeth Grosz, *Becoming Undone: Darwinian Reflections on Life, Politics, and Art* (Durham, N.C.: Duke University Press, 2011), 16.

2. C. P. Snow, *The Two Cultures* (Cambridge: Cambridge University Press, 1998), originally delivered as the Rede Lecture, Cambridge, 1959.

3. Michel Foucault, *History of Sexuality Volume 1: An Introduction*, trans. Robert Hurley (New York: Random House, 1978), 143.

4. Ibid., 154.

5. Jane Bennett, *Vibrant Matter: A Political Ecology of Things* (Durham, N.C.: Duke University Press, 2010), 122.

6. Foucault, *History of Sexuality Volume 1*, 103.

7. Michel Foucault, *The Order of Things: An Archaeology of the Human Sciences* (New York: Random House, 1970), 157.

8. For an overview, see Elizabeth Kolbert, *The Sixth Extinction: An Unnatural History* (New York: Holt, 2014). Kolbert reports current extinction rates as much as forty-five thousand times higher than background rates (for amphibians) (17). The result will be the possible extinction of half of all extant species by 2050 (167). For a philosophical exploration of Anthropocene extinction, see Claire Colebrook, *The Death of the PostHuman: Essays on Extinction,* vol. 1 (Ann Arbor, Mich.: Open Humanities Press, 2014), and Colebrook, *Sex after Life: Essays on Extinction,* vol. 2 (Ann Arbor, Mich.: Open Humanities Press, 2014).

9. Quentin Meillassoux, *After Finitude: An Essay on the Necessity of Contingency,* trans. Ray Brassier (London: Bloomsbury, 2008), 26.

10. Charles Scott, *The Question of Ethics: Nietzsche, Foucault, Heidegger* (Bloomington: Indiana University Press, 1990).

11. Karen Barad, *Meeting the Universe Halfway: Quantum Physics and the Entanglement of Matter and Meaning* (Durham, N.C.: Duke University Press, 2007), 382.

12. Stacy Alaimo, *Bodily Natures: Science, Environment, and the Material Self* (Bloomington: Indiana University Press, 2010), 2.

13. Hasana Sharp, *Spinoza and the Politics of Renaturalization* (Chicago: University of Chicago Press, 2011), 219.

14. Elizabeth Grosz, *Time Travels: Feminism, Nature, Power* (Durham, N.C.: Duke University Press, 2005), 32.

15. Barad, *Meeting the Universe Halfway,* 361.

16. Alaimo, *Bodily Natures,* 158.

17. Grosz, *Becoming Undone,* 22.

18. Ibid., 85.

19. Ibid.

20. Foucault, *History of Sexuality Volume 1.*

21. Grosz, *Time Travels,* 32.

22. Ibid., 18.

23. Grosz, *Becoming Undone,* 100. Although I agree with Grosz that Irigaray is elaborating a new ontology, I disagree that this elaboration is "a new metaphysics," as Grosz claims. Irigaray's explicit indebtedness to Heidegger's dissolution of the metaphysical foundations of ontology is at odds with Grosz's claim.

24. Foucault, *Order of Things,* xvii.

25. Ibid., 105.

26. Luce Irigaray, *An Ethics of Sexual Difference,* trans. Carolyn Burke and Gillian Gill (Ithaca, N.Y.: Cornell University Press, 1993), 3.

27. Barad, *Meeting the Universe Halfway,* 63.

28. Sharp, *Spinoza and the Politics of Renaturalization,* 121.

29. Ibid., 139.

30. Ibid., 153.

31. Ibid., 133.

32. Ibid., 152.

33. Grosz, *Time Travels,* 78.

34. Ibid.

35. Ibid.

36. Ibid., 79.

37. Judith Butler, *Bodies That Matter: On the Discursive Limits of "Sex"* (New York: Routledge, 1993), 9, 2.

38. Pheng Cheah, "Mattering," *Diacritics* 26, no. 1 (1996): 115.

39. Judith Butler, *The Psychic Life of Power: Theories in Subjection* (Stanford, Calif.: Stanford University Press, 1997), 65.

40. Butler, *Bodies That Matter,* 1.

41. Judith Butler, *Frames of War: When Is Life Grievable?* (London: Verso, 2009), 19.

42. Judith Butler, *Precarious Life: The Powers of Mourning and Violence* (London: Verso, 2004), 134.

43. Judith Butler, *Giving an Account of Oneself* (New York: Fordham University Press, 2005), 44.

44. Butler, *Frames,* 30. For an extended version of this argument, see Butler's essay "Spinoza's *Ethics* under Pressure," in *Senses of the Subject,* 63–89 (New York: Fordham University Press, 2015).

45. Judith Butler, *Parting Ways: Jewishness and the Critique of Zionism* (New York: Columbia University Press, 2013), 31.

46. Butler, "Hegel's Early Love," in *Senses of the Subject,* 100, 110–11.

47. Butler, *Parting Ways,* 12.

48. Foucault, *Order of Things,* 277. I have modified the translation of *valeurs végétales* in the French original from "vegetable values" in the published English translation to "vegetal values." For the French original, see Michel Foucault, *Les Mots et les choses: Une archéologie des sciences humaines* (Paris: Gallimard, 1966), 289.

49. Foucault, *History of Sexuality Volume 1,* 157.

50. Ibid., 69.

51. Ibid., 156.

52. Michel Foucault, *Discipline and Punish: Birth of the Prison,* trans. Alan Sheridan (New York: Vintage, 1977), 299, 298.

53. Michel Foucault, *Abnormal: Lectures at the Collège de France, 1974–1975,* trans. Graham Burchell (New York: Picador, 2003), 286–87.

54. Foucault, *History of Sexuality Volume 1,* 106–8.

55. Grosz, *Becoming Undone,* 73.

56. Foucault, *Abnormal,* 278.

57. Ibid., 280.

58. Foucault, *History of Sexuality Volume 1,* 57.

59. Ibid., 71, 73.

60. For a more detailed account of the important differences between Foucault and Canguilhem in the context of sexuality and biopower, see Mary Beth Mader, *Sleights of Reason: Norm, Bisexuality, Development* (Albany: SUNY Press, 2011), 62–65.

61. For an example of how biopolitical health projects and neoliberalism work together by targeting women through reprogenetics, see Ladelle McWhorter, "Darwin's Invisible Hand: Feminism, Reprogenetics, and Foucault's Analysis of Neoliberalism," *Southern Journal of Philosophy* 48 (Spindel Suppl., September 2010): 43–63.

62. Mader, *Sleights of Reason,* 65, 45, 65.

63. Foucault, *History of Sexuality Volume 1,* 156.

64. Ibid., 156–57.

65. Nikolas Rose, *The Politics of Life Itself: Biomedicine, Power, and Subjectivity in the Twenty-First Century* (Princeton, N.J.: Princeton University Press, 2007).

66. Michel Foucault, *The History of Sexuality Volume 2: The Use of Pleasure,* trans. Robert Hurley (New York: Vintage, 1985), 9. Foucault writes that his aim is to "free thought from what it silently thinks, and so enable it to think differently." Rethinking "life itself" can be seen as contributing to that aim.

67. Michel Foucault, "On the Ways of Writing History," in *Essential Works of Foucault, 1954–1984,* vol. 2, *Aesthetics, Method, and Epistemology,* ed. James D. Faubion (New York: New Press, 1998), 293. *Language* appears as *le langage* in the French original.

68. Michel Foucault, *History of Madness,* trans. Jonathan Murphy and Jean Khalfa (London: Routledge, 2006), xxxii.

69. Michel Foucault, "Lives of Infamous Men," in *Essential Works of Foucault, 1954–1984,* vol. 3, *Power,* ed. James D. Faubion (New York: New Press, 2000), 157.

70. Jeffrey Jerome Cohen (jeffreyjcohen), Twitter posting, September 12, 2013: "but they discerned in fossils an inhuman art, metaphor along w materiality, intensification of the world's truths, lithic conviviality."

71. Foucault, *Order of Things,* 156.

72. See Martin J. S. Rudwick, *Scenes from Deep Time: Early Pictorial Representations of the Prehistoric World* (Chicago: University of Chicago Press, 1992).

73. See esp. chapter 9, "On the Imperfection of the Geological Record," and chapter 10, "On the Geological Succession of Organic Beings," in Charles Darwin, *On the Origin of Species,* ed. Gillian Beer (Oxford: Oxford University Press, 2008).

74. Foucault, *Order of Things,* 156.

75. Ibid., 50.

76. Cohen, Twitter posting.

77. Michel Foucault, *Speech Begins after Death,* trans. Robert Bononno (Minneapolis: Minnesota University Press, 2013).

78. Foucault, *History of Madness,* xxxi.

79. Foucault, *Order of Things,* xv.

80. Foucault, *Speech,* 40.

81. See Nathaniel Rich, "The New Origin of the Species," *New York Times Magazine,* March 2, 2014.

82. Foucault, *History of Sexuality Volume 1,* 71.

83. In this sense, we might say, as Foucault does in a different context, that the archive is the ground for thinking "the freedom of the subject and its relationship to others—which constitutes the very stuff [*matière*] of ethics." See Michel Foucault, "The Ethics of the Concern for Self as a Practice of Freedom," in *Essential Works of Foucault, 1954–1984: Ethics: Subjectivity and Truth,* ed. Paul Rabinow (New York: New Press, 1997), 300.

84. James Baldwin, "Here Be Dragons," in *The Price of the Ticket: Collected Nonfiction, 1948–1985* (New York: St. Martin's Press, 1985), 679.

85. Foucault, *History of Sexuality Volume 1,* 159.

5

Your Shell on Acid: Material Immersion, Anthropocene Dissolves

STACY ALAIMO

Who is the "anthro" of the "Anthropocene"? In its ostensible universality, does the prefix suggest a subject position that anyone could inhabit? While the term *Anthropocene* would seem to interpellate humans into a disorienting expanse of epochal species identity, some accounts of the Anthropocene reinstall rather familiar versions of man. Feminist theory, long critical of "man," the disembodied, rational subject, and material feminisms, which stress inter- or intra-actions between humans and the wider physical world, provide alternatives to accounts that reiterate man as a bounded being endowed with unilateral agency. And while the geological origins of the term *Anthropocene* have spawned stark terrestrial figurations of man and rock in which other life-forms and biological processes are strangely absent, the acidifying seas, the liquid index of the Anthropocene, are disregarded, even as billions of tiny shelled creatures will meet their end in a catastrophic dissolve, reverberating through the food webs of the ocean. Thinking with these aquatic creatures provokes an "ecodelic,"[1] scale-shifting dis/identification, which insists that whatever the "anthro" of the "Anthropocene" was, is, or will be, the Anthropocene must be thought with the multitude of creatures that will not be reconstituted, will not be safely ensconced, but will, instead, dissolve.

ANTHROPOCENE VISION

As *Anthropocene* joins *climate change* and *sustainability* as a pivotal term in public environmental discourse, it may be useful to consider how the novel category becomes enlisted in all too familiar formulations, epistemologies, and defensive maneuvers—modes of knowing and being that are utterly incapable of adequately responding to the complexities of the Anthropocene itself. Feminist theory, especially material feminisms and posthumanist feminisms, offer cautionary tales, counterpoints, and alternative figurations for thinking the Anthropocene subject in immersive onto-epistemologies. Whereas a critical posthumanism contests the human as a conceptual apparatus that underwrites ordinary practices of exploitation, the concept of the Anthropocene testifies that *Homo sapiens* has "achieved" an exceptional feat, that of epoch-making planetary alteration. Take the title of Will Stefan, Paul J. Crutzen, and John R. McNeill's article "The Anthropocene: Are Humans Now Overwhelming the Great Forces of Nature?," which concludes that "humankind will remain a major geological force for many millennia, maybe millions of years, to come."[2] The hand-wringing confessions of human culpability appear coated with a veneer of species pride. To think of the human species as having had a colossal impact, an impact that will have been unthinkably vast in duration, on something we externalize as "the planet" removes us from the scene and ignores the extent to which human agencies are entangled with those of nonhuman creatures and inhuman substances and systems.

As the capitalist rapacity of the few and the subsistence needs of the many result, unintentionally, in the vast obliteration of ecosystems and the extinction of species, modes of acting within economic, technological, and environmental systems, such as quotidian acts of consumption, seem worlds apart from the aesthetically rendered scenes that deliver a spectacular view of manufactured geographies to spectators positioned outside the action. The epistemological position of the "God's-eye view" that Donna Haraway critiqued in "Situated Knowledges" dominates many of the theoretical, scientific, and artistic portrayals of the Anthropocene. Ironically, at the very moment that the catastrophes of the Anthropocene should make it clear that what used to be known as nature is never somewhere else (even the bottom of the sea has been altered by human practices), the "conquering gaze from nowhere," the "view of infinite vision," the "God trick" of an unmarked, disembodied perspective reasserts itself.[3] Yet the ostensibly infinite perspective excludes so much. Claire Colebrook, in *Death of the PostHuman*, argues that the "very eye that has opened up a world to the human species, has also allowed the human species to fold the world around its own, increasingly myopic, point of view."[4] Strangely, this humanist myopia may manifest as visual tropes that view the world at sanitized distances. And "the world" in these images is an eerily lifeless entity, devoid of other species, as if the sixth great extinction had already concluded.

Prevalent visual depictions of the Anthropocene emphasize the colossal scale of anthropogenic impact by zooming out—up and away from the planet. Andrew Revkin's essay in the *New York Times*, "Confronting the Anthropocene," begins with a photo of a glowing spider-shaped blob of gold against darkness, with the following caption: "Donald R. Petitt, an astronaut, took this photograph of London while living in the International Space Station."[5] *National Geographic*'s story "Age of Man," written by Elizabeth Kolbert, begins with a rather dystopian aerial photo of Dubai, in which the vivid aqua waterway only highlights the otherwise utterly brown, bleak cityscape.[6] The *Encyclopedia of Earth* begins its entry on "Anthropocene" with a cylindrical map (flat and rectangular), showing "the earth at night, demonstrating the global extent of human influence."[7] The blog *The Anthropocene Journal* sets out a stark, but at least nongendered, cluster of terms in its subtitle: "People. Rock. The Geology of Humanity."[8] Despite the subtitle "The Geology of Humanity," with its ambiguous "of," which could intermingle humanity and geology, the images shown on the "State of the Art" posting, for example, detach the spectator from the scene. Moreover, the blog's banner image features a globe, as if seen from space, showing North America lit up in yellow and blue capillary-like lights. Félix Pharand-Deschênes, listed as an "anthropologist and data visualizer," created this image as well as other similar images that appear on his Globaïa website.[9] Scrolling down his "Cartography of the Anthropocene" page, one encounters a series of globes, each with patterns formed by lines marking roads, cities, railways, transmission lines, and underwater cables.[10] The patterns of bright blue or shimmering gold lines that span the planet demonstrate the expansiveness of human habitation, commerce, and transportation networks, marking human travel, transport, and activity against a solid background that obscures winds, tides, currents, and the travels of birds, cetaceans, or other creatures. Nonhuman agencies and trajectories are absent.

Where is the map showing the overlapping patterns of whale migrations with shipping and military routes? Or the sonic patterns of military and industrial noise as it reverberates through areas populated by cetaceans? Or established bird migration routes, many of which have been rendered inhospitable to avian life? The movements, the activities, the liveliness of all creatures, except for the human, vanish.[11] And, once again, in the dominant visual apparatus of the Anthropocene, the viewer enjoys a comfortable position outside the systems depicted.[12] The already iconic images of the Anthropocene ask nothing from the human spectator; they make no claim; they neither involve nor implore. The images make risk, harm, and suffering undetectable, as toxic and radioactive regions do not appear, nor do the movements of climate refugees. The geographies of the sixth great extinction are not evident. The perspective is predictable and reassuring, despite its claim to novelty and cataclysm.

David Thomas Smith's photography is introduced on the ArtStormer site with an epigraph by A. Revkin: "We are entering an age that might someday be referred to as, say, the Anthropocene. After all, it is a geological age of our own making."[13] The singular human agency, as well as the possessive phrase "our own," is notable. What sort of subject could have produced a geological age? Betsy Wills introduces the photographs, which, unlike the images of the globe, depict merely a particularly processed portion of the earth, using highly mediated data: "Composited from thousands of digital files drawn from aerial views taken from internet satellite images, this work reflects upon the complex structures that make up the centres of global capitalism, transforming the aerial landscapes of sites associated with industries such as oil, precious metals, consumer culture information and excess. Thousands of seemingly insignificant coded pieces of information are sown together like knots in a rug to reveal a grander spectacle."[14] These constructions are grand spectacles indeed. The swirling baroque designs captivate. They urge viewers to shift scales and recognize how small alterations of the landscape may be multiplied into geographical immensity (Figure 5.1). This immensity, however, is safely viewed from a rather transcendent, incorporeal perspective, not from a creaturely immersion in the world.

FIGURE 5.1. David Thomas Smith, 1000 Chrysler Drive, Auburn Hills, Michigan, United States, 2009–10. Image courtesy of David Thomas Smith. Copyright David Thomas Smith.

Moreover, although trees are visible, for the most part these landscapes are devoid of life; they depict hard, flat surfaces, planetary puzzle pieces. The aesthetic is one of order and symmetry within complexity, suggesting the possibility of and desire for exquisite, intricate manipulations. Despite the scaling up, these are, to contradict Mina Loy, tame things despite their immensity,[15] as the world is rendered into a kaleidoscopic vision you may hold in your mind like a toy in your hand. The super-symmetrical structure of Smith's photos, however, with double mirror images, in which everything in the top half is repeated in the bottom half and everything on the left is repeated on the right, presents an implicit critique of the scale of human transformation of the earth by dramatizing a claustrophobic enclosure in a world that, in its predictable repetitions, becomes all too human, all too structured. Smith's work encapsulates the problematic of the Anthropocene, as its aesthetic seduces with its precise symmetries and the prospect of mastery, but ultimately confines the viewer in a place devoid of surprises. Brilliantly, its aesthetic pleasures are the selfsame as its critique, as its visual delights repeat in solipsistic symmetries. It may be fitting to invite Patricia Johanson, an environmental artist, into this discussion: "I believe human beings are increasingly threatened and impoverished by the relentless conversion of every scrap of territory for our own limited and temporary uses."[16]

ABSTRACT FORCE

The concept of the Anthropocene, with its geological reference and its undifferentiated "anthro," retreats to a simple equation of "man" and "rock," an oddly stark rendition when one considers that current biophysical realities can only be approached through scientific captures of a multitude of intersecting biological and chemical, as well geological, transformations, which intermesh human and natural histories. Even though the concept of the Anthropocene muddles the opposition between nature and culture, the focus on geology, rather than, say, chemistry or biology, may segregate the human from the anthropogenic alterations of the planet by focusing on an externalized and inhuman sense of materiality.[17] Dipesh Chakrabarty's momentous essay "The Climate of History" raises essential questions about the nature of the human, some of which, in my view, turn on the conception of species identity, corporeality, and agency. Chakrabarty's first thesis in this essay is "Anthropogenic Explanations of Climate Change Spell the Collapse of the Age-Old Humanist Distinction between Natural History and Human History."[18] Despite the collapse of distinctions, Chakrabarty brackets humans as biological creatures—our own corporeality as living beings becomes eclipsed by the enormity of our collective geological alterations. He writes, "Human beings are biological agents, both collectively and as individuals. They have always been so. There was no point in human history when humans were not biological agents. But we can become geological agents only historically and collectively, that is when we have reached numbers and invented technologies that are on a scale large enough to have an impact on the planet itself."[19] While we could read the phrase "biological agents" as meaning that humans *are* biological *and* act on the biological, the phrase "geological agents," which follows, delimits the first phrase to imply that humans have had an effect on biological entities—not that we are ourselves interwoven into living and nonliving trans-corporeal networks. Moreover, the distinction between biological and geological agency is not tenable, because biological and chemical transformations flow through the world in multiple and messy ways. And, of course, the origin of so many Anthropocenic alterations—the colossal output of carbon—is a matter of chemistry and, on epochal time scales, biology, as fossil fuels issue from decomposed organisms. The essay "The New World of the Anthropocene," published in *Environmental Science and Technology* by Jan Zalasiewicz and colleagues, states that "far more profound" than the "plainly visible effects . . . on the landscape" "are the chemical and biological effects of global human activity," including the rise of CO_2 levels, the sea level rise, the acidification of the oceans, and the sixth great extinction.[20] Attending solely to the lithic imports delusions of separation and control that have no place in the global biological, chemical, and geophysical intra-actions of the Anthropocene. Yet Chakrabarty subordinates "man's" interactions with "nature" to a new paradigm in which humans become a geological force when he asserts, "For it is no longer a question simply of man having an interactive relation with nature. This humans have always had, or at least that is how man has been imagined in a large part of what is generally called the Western tradition. Now it is being claimed that humans are a force of nature in the geological sense."[21] While the idea that humans have become a "force of nature in the geological sense" may seem to merge humans with something called "nature," the abstract formulation of the "force" reinstalls "man" as a disembodied potency, outside the nature he would alter. Thinking human as "force" represents a retreat from the radical risk, uncertainty, and vulnerability of the flesh, as humans are rendered strangely immaterial. This immateriality, then, also creates an impasse for thinking in terms of species identity.

Chakrabarty's fourth thesis results in an impasse: "The Cross-Hatching of Species History and the History of Capital Is a Process of Probing the Limits of Historical Understanding."[22] Drawing on Gadamer, Chakrabarty contrasts "historical consciousness" as a "mode of self-knowledge" with what he claims would be an impossible achievement, "self-understanding as a species":

Who is the we? We humans never experience ourselves as a species. We can only intellectually comprehend or infer the existence of the human species but never experience it as such. There could be no phenomenology of us as a species. Even if we were to emotionally identify with a word like *mankind,* we would not know what being a species is, for, in species history, humans are only an instance of the concept species as indeed would be any other life form. But one never experiences being a concept.[23]

I would like to address this question rather indirectly by shifting from Gadamer and broadening the framework to include a range of theories and perspectives on species-being. While the question of "who is the we" is always at play, and will become more complicated, to say humans have never experienced themselves as a species seems mistaken. It is hard to imagine that indigenous peoples would not have elaborated, within their cultures and traditional ecological knowledges, a sense of what it is to be human within a multispecies world. Elizabeth DeLoughrey in "Ordinary Futures: Interspecies Worldings in the Anthropocene" draws on Maori models of epistemology, for example, to offer an "alternative mode of understanding climate change than Dipesh Chakrabarty's argument that our awareness of ourselves as geological agents cannot be understood ontologically." In the Maori mode that she describes, the subject is incorporated "into planetary networks of kinship" in which "knowing and being are constitutive and interrelated."[24] In the

West, Darwin's *Descent of Man* intensified a species consciousness even as it intermingled the human with other creatures as progenitors and kin. Even those who deny evolution proclaim a particularly *human* exceptionalism, which could itself be understood as a form of species identification, albeit with religious rather than scientific origins. Furthermore, contemporary environmental discourses address humans as one species among other species, seeking to ignite an ethical or political sense of being part of a community of descent that is only intensified by the recognition of human culpability so readily available in the Anthropocene. More quotidian relations with other species could also be said to characterize phenomenologies embroidered with species recognition. Species is certainly a concept, but it is a concept that is as substantial and as close at hand as one's own morphology. One does not need to read Darwin to notice the ways in which one's body is similar to and different from the bodies of other living creatures. Natural history museums, zoos, television programs, or face-to-face encounters with wild or domestic animals spark a sense of species identity that is not singular but is generated from a sense of species in relation. Exhibit A may well be that of people comparing their own hands to the fins of whale or dolphin skeletons displayed at a natural history museum— kinship inscribed in the bones. Donna Haraway's work, from *Primate Visions* to *The Companion Species Manifesto* to *When Species Meet,* attests to multiple modes of cross-species encounters, relationships, and phenomenologies that can be understood as modes of species consciousness, in which humans are both embodied creatures dwelling in their own present moments and creatures able to imagine vast historical narratives such as the coevolution of humans and canines. As Haraway states, "the temporalities of companion species comprehend all the possibilities activated in becoming with, including the heterogeneous scales of evolutionary time for everybody but also the many other rhythms of conjoined process."[25]

Chakrabarty's assertion that no one ever "experiences being a concept" is also strange, given the body of scholarship focusing on how those who inhabit marked identities and subjectivities, those who have been cast outside the Western conception of "man" or "the human," have negotiated, resisted, and transformed identity categories and subject positions. Feminist theory, postcolonial theory, critical race studies, and cultural studies offer numerous accounts of the relation between subjects, identity categories, and other concepts such as "woman," for example, from Monique Wittig's claim that lesbians are not women because woman is a structural relation to man to Gayatri Spivak's notion of strategic essentialism. The vertiginous intellectual work required to "be a concept" is evidenced by W. E. B. Du Bois's theory of "double consciousness," Frantz Fanon and Homi Bhabha's conceptions of mimicry, the feminist practice of "consciousness-raising," and Judith Butler's notion of "gender trouble."[26] A Lacanian theorist may contend that one always experiences oneself as something akin to a concept, in that the mirror stage testifies to the fundamental misrecognition of self as coherent whole, despite gaps and contradictions. These are, for the most part, politicized modes of knowing and being, not "pure" or abstract species consciousness, to be sure. Rory Rowan puts it quite well: "Anthropos can be understood not as a pre-constituted identity but rather as the object of political contestation in the struggle to define the terms of future human existence on the planet."[27] Rowan's sense of the "Anthropos" as concept within the terrain of political struggle places the term where it belongs, in the messy space where science, history, cultural identities, and politics coincide. Ultimately, whatever it may mean to think oneself as a species will be inextricably bound up with other, more local identities and cultural conceptions rather than separate from them. The Anthropos, despite the predominant visualizations that obscure local contexts, could provoke a sense of species identity quite different from the lofty Western, capitalist humanism, with the recognition that every member of the species is at once part of long evolutionary processes, a member of a species that has had a staggering impact on the planet, and an inhabitant of a particular geographic, social, economic, and political matrix, with attendant and differential environmental vulnerabilities, culpabilities, and responsibilities.

One of Chakrabarty's most significant provocations is that thinking the human species as geophysical force—more on that later—precludes attention to social justice. Ian Baucom notes Chakrabarty's "quite stunning turn to the concept of species; to a new thinking of freedom for human life in its biological totality; to a mode of universalism apparently antithetical both to his preceding philosophy of history; and to what Gayatri Spivak has called the practice of postcolonial reason." He adds, "Confronted with the arriving and coming catastrophes of climate change, freedom can no longer be conceived of as the freedom of difference against the power of the globalizing same."[28] Baucom captures the crux of the matter here, as the enormity of global environmental crises would seem to call for human collectivity that trumps all other differences. Jamie Lorimer notes that as a "growing body of critical work makes clear, scientific invocations of a planet-shaping Anthropos summon forth a responsible species—or at least an aggregation of its male representatives. A common 'us' legitimates a biopolitics that masks differential human responsibilities for and exposures to planetary change."[29]

This should give us pause, especially because scientific discourse gains legitimacy precisely through its free-floating "objectivity." Scientific neutrality lends itself to a mode of popularization that cleanses the term *Anthropocene* from any entanglement with political genealogies, specificities, and identities. Indeed, the visual depictions of the Anthropocene discussed earlier do just that by scaling up so that human poverty, drought, flooding, or displacement is obscured from sight and the viewer is not implicated, nor is someone potentially affected by climate disasters or slow violence.[30] Sylvia Wynter's work, although too complex to be adequately discussed here, is nonetheless invaluable for this debate. In the discussion between Wynter and Katherine McKittrick, titled "Unparalleled Catastrophe for Our Species? Or to Give Humanness a Different Future: Conversations," Wynter states, commenting not on Chakrabarty's question about who the "we" is but instead on Jacques Derrida's 1968 talk "The Ends of Man," which concluded with the same question:

> The *referent-we* of man and of its ends, he implies, *is not* the *referent-we* of the human species itself. Yet, he says, French philosophers have assumed that, as middle-class philosophers, their *referent-we* (that of Man2) is isomorphic with the *referent-we* in the *horizon of humanity.* I am saying here that the above is the single issue with which global warming and climate instability now confronts us and that we have to replace the ends of the *referent-we* of liberal monohumanist Man2 with the ecumenically human ends of the *referent-we in the horizon of humanity.*[31]

Wynter contends that to deal with climate change requires "a far-reaching transformation of knowledge," which includes the very definition of the human as such,[32] which she herself offers throughout her dazzlingly original theoretical work. Alexander G. Weheliye states,

"Wynter's large-scale intellectual project, which she has been pursuing in one form or another for the last thirty years, disentangles Man from the human in order to use the space of subjects placed beyond the grasp of this domain as a vital point from which to invent hitherto unavailable genres of the human."[33] Wynter's project, disentangling man from the human, may address the quandary of the Anthropocene in that it suggests that multiple "genres" of the human may be inhabited, which means that the term *Anthropocene* does not require a new sort of univocal "man." Environmentalisms; movements for environmental justice, climate justice, and social and economic justice; along with struggles for indigenous sovereignty will no doubt emerge from particular, local formulations of the human, which may or may not be linked with the Anthropocene. In *Friction: An Ethnography of Global Connection*, Anna Lowenhaupt Tsing argues that "universals are effective within particular historical conjunctures that give them content and force. We might specify this conjunctural feature of universals in practice by speaking of engagement. Engaged universals travel across difference and are charged and changed by their travels. Through friction, universals become practically effective."[34] As an engaged universal, the species identity of the Anthropocene would not be free floating but instead conjunctural. How will the Anthropocene travel, and what sort of friction will those travels entail? Will the politically forged and conjuncturally specific conception of the Anthropos enable new modes of struggle for social justice, environmental justice, climate justice, biodiversity, and environmentalisms?

One of the most intriguing concerns that Chakrabarty puts forth is the idea that the Anthropocene means reckoning with humans as a "force." Some of his concerns, I would suggest, could be addressed by a more material conception of the human and a less unilateral sense of agency. He writes,

> But if we, collectively, have also become a geophysical force, then we also have a collective mode of existence that is justice-blind. Call that mode of being a "species" or something else, but it has no ontology, it is beyond biology, and it acts as a limit to what we also are in the ontological mode.
>
> This is why the need arises to view the human simultaneously on contradictory registers: as a geophysical force and as a political

agent, as a bearer of rights and as author of actions; subject to both the stochastic forces of nature (being itself one such force collectively) and open to the contingency of individual human experience; belonging at once to differently-scaled histories of the planet, of life and species, and of human societies.[35]

The shift from the abstract "geophysical force" to "species" is jarring, given that species—a biological category—is said to have "no ontology" and to exist "beyond biology." I agree that the human must be apprehended "simultaneously on contradictory registers" and scales; indeed, this is something that my conception of trans-corporeality, which is grounded in environmental justice and environmental health movements, seeks to do. And as Rowan suggests, stressing the Anthropos as an object of political contestation, rather than as an already fossilized term, allows for differentiation of particular groups of humans, along the lines of culpability and exploitation, distinguishing, say, indigenous Amazonian peoples whose lands have been destroyed by oil companies from those who benefit from oil company revenues, or middle-class U.S. citizens driving automobiles from the citizens of Pacific islands being driven from their homes by rising sea levels. Thinking the human as a species does not preclude analysis and critique of economic systems, environmental devastation, and social injustice. In fact, if we shift from the sense of humans as an abstract force that acts but is not acted on to a trans-corporeal conception of the human as that which is always generated through and entangled in differing scales and sorts of biological, technological, economic, social, political, and other systems, then that sort of human—always material, always the stuff of the world—becomes the site for social justice and environmental praxis.

In "Brute Force," Chakrabarty writes, "But to say that humans have become a 'geophysical force' on this planet is to get out of the subject/object dichotomy altogether. A force is neither a subject nor an object. It is simply the capacity to do things."[36] Feminist theory, science studies, and environmental theory have long critiqued the subject–object dualism, often by underscoring the strange agencies of the entities considered inert objects. New materialisms emphasize materiality as agential, stressing the entanglements and interactions between humans and the nonhuman world. Interactive material agencies may be dispersed and nearly impossible to trace, delimit, or scientifically capture, but that does not mean they evaporate. Claiming that a force is neither subject nor object, however, seems to dematerialize said force when, in fact, the Anthropocene results from innumerable human activities, activities that humans have engaged in as ordinary embodied creatures and as rapacious capitalists and colonialists. The force is not as abstract as it would seem, because the activities, the processes, and the results are not at all immaterial and not at all mysterious. Humans are not gravity.[37] Perhaps the term "force" leads us astray. Chakrabarty notes, "A force is the capacity to move things. It is pure, nonontological agency."[38] Just because the scale of humans as a "geological force" is so immense, nearly unthinkable from the minuscule moments of everyday life, does not mean that it is an entirely different entity. It is a matter of scale, not a difference of kind. Human beings, who eat, who heat and cool their homes, who plug in their electronic devices, who transport themselves and their goods, who use fossil fuels in their everyday lives, and who may or may not reckon with an environmental consciousness, are, ultimately, part of this supposedly "nonontological agency." Moreover, other accounts of the Anthropocene, such as that of Zalasiewicz and colleagues, cited earlier, stress its biological and chemical dimensions—which are even more difficult to conceive as an abstract or pure force, apart from the messy interactions of material beings and the stuff of the world.

The Anthropocene suggests that agency must be rethought in terms of interconnected entanglements rather than as a unilateral "authoring" of actions. Jessi Lehman and Sara Nelson argue in "After the Anthropocene," for example, that "humanity's agency as a geological force confronts us not as a product of our supposedly unique capacity as humans for intentional action (as described by Marx, 1867, in his comparison of the architect and the bee), but as an unintended consequence of our entanglements with myriad non-human forces—chief among them fossil fuels. The Anthropocene therefore simultaneously expands and radically undermines conventional notions of agency and intentionality."[39] Similarly, Derek Woods in "Scale Critique for the Anthropocene" contends that "assemblage theory is necessary to move beyond the notion that the 'species' is a geologic force," proposing that the "scale-critical subject of the Anthropocene is not 'our species' but the sum of terraforming assemblages composed of humans, nonhuman species, and technics."[40] Woods's argument is convincing, especially in that it addresses one of the ironies or paradoxes of the Anthropocene: "The present is a moment of human disempowerment in relation to terra-forming assemblages."[41] That is certainly the case, as processes have been set in motion that will have devastating effects for thousands of years. And yet, in the face of this shattering disempowerment, some groups of humans will, nonetheless, persist in attempting to do something. Modes of thinking, being, and acting may arise from a political recognition of being immersed in the material world, as they contend with the conceptual challenges of shifting time scales and traversing geocapitalist expanses where one's own small domain of activity is inextricably bound up with networks of harm, risk, survival, injustice, and exploitation. Some activist practices, such as personal carbon footprint analysis and other "micro-practices of everyday life,"[42] already exemplify the attempt to understand the human as a geophysical "force," through politicized modes of knowing and acting that are immersed and contingent rather than disembodied.

IMMERSED, ENMESHED SUBJECTS

To counter the dominant figurations of the Anthropocene, which abstract the human from the material realm and obscure differentials of responsibility and harm, I propose that we think the Anthropocene subject as immersed and enmeshed in the world. In contrast to Globaïa's "Cartography of the Anthropocene" maps discussed earlier, Nicole Starosielski's multimedia project Surfacing, for example, portrays undersea fiber-optic cable systems in such a way that "the user becomes the signal and traverses the network."[43] The user is immersed in technologies, marine spaces, geographies, landscapes, and histories: "You begin on the coast, carried ashore by undersea cable. From your landing point, you can traverse the Pacific Ocean by hopping between network nodes. You might surface at cable stations where signal traffic is monitored, on remote islands that were once network hubs, and aboard giant ships that lay submarine systems."[44] The design deliberately frustrates attempts to gain a bird's-eye view or to escape, as the user is always positioned, always inside the system. And many of the photographs of particular places where the user surfaces, such as Vung Tau, Vietnam, or Papenoo, Tahiti, reflect a human scale, the ordinary perspective of a person with a camera. The photo of Pacific City, Oregon, places the viewer behind a worker operating heavy machinery and only slightly above the muck of the drilling site. While this beautifully designed project is not explicitly about the Anthropocene, it nonetheless encourages its users to experience the sort of built, global systems that have become emblematic of the Anthropocene—but in an immersed, never omniscient position. The project does not simply scale up into representations that afford transcendence but instead demands scale shifting and imaginative encounters with human and nonhuman agencies. Similarly, describing her book, Starosielski writes, "Rather than envisioning undersea cable systems as a set of vectors that overcome space, *The Undersea Network* places our networks undersea: it locates them in this complex set of circulatory practices, charting their interconnections with a dynamic and fluid external environment."[45] By doing so, it offers "what might be an unfamiliar view of global network infrastructure," which brings "geographies back into the picture" and reintroduces, perhaps, an "environmental consciousness, to the study of digital systems."[46]

The immersed subject of trans-corporeality reckons with the Anthropocene as an intermingling of biological, chemical, and climatic processes, which are certainly neither simply "natural" nor managed by human intention.[47] The trans-corporeal subject emerges from environmental health and environmental justice movements, including the citizen-scientists who must discern, track, and negotiate the unruly substances that move across bodies and places. Thinking the subject as a material being, subject to the agencies of the compromised, entangled world, enacts an environmental posthumanism, insisting that what we are as bodies and minds is inextricably interlinked with circulating substances, materialities, and forces. Rhonda Zwillinger's photographic volume *The Dispossessed* could be read as an example of trans-corporeal inhabitations of the Anthropocene.[48] Zwillinger documents how people with multiple chemical sensitivity (MCS) attempt to fashion less toxic living spaces, portraying the human as coextensive with the built landscape of consumerism, where everyday objects, the domestic, and the desert landscape become scrambled and menacing. In one photo a woman sits under her carport, surrounded by the stuff that should be within a home—her bed, computer, and so forth—cluttering the space, which is neither indoors nor outdoors but a hybrid zone. This stuff, the ordinary things of late-twentieth-century human habitats, has unexpected, injurious agencies for those with

MCS; they penetrate the person, harming physical and mental health. Zwillinger's photos offer an intimate, tangible, and everyday—rather than philosophically abstract—sense of Anthropocene scale shifting, as they ask us to imagine the domestic as linked to toxic networks of industrial production, consumer use, and disposal. They call the viewer to trace the invisible, interactive material agencies that cross through bodies and places rather than removing the human from the scene. Set in the vast desert landscape, the makeshift and often confining living arrangements of those with MCS radiate outward in all directions, linking human homes to undomesticated but nonetheless contaminated landscapes. Zwillinger depicts the toxic Anthropocene as unnervingly commonplace.

In Colebrook's brilliant and disturbing essay "Not Symbiosis, Not Now: Why Anthropogenic Climate Change Is Not Really Human," she contends, "The figural and critical truth of the Anthropocene is that just as there is no pure earth [that] might be reclaimed, so there is no thought that is not already contaminated and made possible by the very logic of man that ecology might seek to overcome."[49] Specifically, Colebrook points to recent theoretical turns that coincide with material feminisms and feminist posthumanisms, "these turns 'back' to bodies, matters, historicity, ecology and the lived," calling them "reaction formations or last gasps."[50] She asks, "What if all the current counter-Cartesian, post-Cartesian or anti-Cartesian figures of living systems (along with a living order that is one interconnected and complex mesh) were a way of avoiding the extent to which man is a theoretical animal, a myopically and malevolently self-enclosed machine whose world he will always view as present for his own edification?"[51] Since my conception of trans-corporeality qualifies as an anti-Cartesian figure of "living systems" as a "complex mesh," Colebrook's contention stings. And yet I wonder whether, as a feminist theorist, her use of "man" here intentionally allows for the possibility that feminist theories may somehow depart from the modes of thought produced by man as a "myopically and malevolently self-enclosed machine," even as they function within "already contaminated" thought. Although this is not the sort of contamination she had in mind, I would pose the trans-corporeal onto-epistemologies of those with MCS as an alternative to the self-enclosed theories of the world, as people with MCS register material agencies of substances that can never be imagined as external and that demand both an experiential and theoretical grappling with the precise ways in which self and world are intermeshed.

While it is one thing to conceptualize how toxins circulate through bodies and environments, it is another for humanities scholars and artists to conceptualize humans as enmeshed with something as rigid as a rock. Some scholarly and artistic engagements with the geologic shift scale in ways that are intimate and generative. In *Stories of Stone: An Ecology of the Inhuman,* for example, Jeffrey J. Cohen writes, "This book is something of a thought experiment, attempting to discern in the most mundane of substances a liveliness. Despite relegation to a trope for the cold, the indifferent and the inert, stone discloses a queer vivacity, a perilous tender of mineral amity." Cohen posits a "human–lithic enmeshment" as he analyzes the ecomaterialisms of the Middle Ages and contemporary theory, noting that stones "erode the boundary that keeps biological and mineral realms discrete."[52] The editors of the beautiful collection *Making the Geologic Now: Responses to Material Conditions of Contemporary Life* define their concept of the "geologic turn" with reference to practices that involve "exposure and visceral response to actual event-ness, or to change or forces."[53] Making "a geologic turn," they say, entails recalibrating "infrastructures, communities, and imaginations to a new scale—the scale of deep time, force, and materiality.... We do not simply observe [the geologic] as landscape or panorama. We inhabit the geologic."[54] And the geologic inhabits us. Ilana Halperin, an artist described as having "deep love of geology," writes in her essay "Autobiographical Trace Fossils" how the "boundary between the biological and geological can begin to blur."[55] Referring to "body stones," such as gall- and kidney stones, she states, "In the body, each stone is a biological entity, and once out of the body it belongs to the realm of geology."[56] Kathryn Yusoff argues for a "'geological turn' that takes seriously not just our biological (or biopolitical) life, but our geological (or geopolitical) life, as crucial to modes of subjectification in the Anthropocene." She investigates what she terms "geologic life," "a mineralogical dimension of human composition that remains currently undertheorized in social thought."[57] Stephanie LeMenager in *Living Oil: Petroleum Culture in the American Century* explores museums, photography, literature, and other cultural productions as she documents an immersed, intimate, and unsanitized sense of dwelling in the Anthropocene: "We experience ourselves, as moderns and most especially as modern Americans, every day in oil, living within oil, breathing it and registering it with our senses. The relationship is, without question, ultradeep."[58] As different as these projects are, none of them extracts the human from the world; instead, they conceptualize the human as intermingled with the lithic and the inhuman—the energy, matter, and temporalities of the geologic.

YOUR SHELL ON ACID: ANTHROPOCENE DISSOLVES

Notwithstanding the lively and generative thinking with stones, geologic life, and petrocultures, by Cohen, Yusoff, LeMenager, and others, I would like to contribute another sort of figuration of the Anthropocene that is aquatic rather than terrestrial. It is vital to contemplate the Anthropocene seas, not only because marine ecosystems are gravely imperiled but also because the synchronic depth and breadth of the oceans present a kind of incomprehensible immensity that parallels the diachronic scale of anthropogenic effects.[59] The deep seas, once thought to house "living fossils" that terrestrial time left behind, are in fact home to sea creatures who live at a slower pace, within the cold, dark, and heavy waters. Oceanic depths, especially, resist the sort of flat mapping of the globe that assumes a "God's-eye view." The view of the earth from space reveals merely the surface of the seas, a vast horizontal expanse that is rendered utterly negligible when one considers the unfathomable depths and three-dimensional volume of the rest of the ocean. To begin to glimpse the seas, one must descend rather than transcend,[60] be immersed in highly mediated environments that suggest the entanglements of knowledge, science, economics, and power. Whereas the human alterations of the geophysical landmasses of the planet can be portrayed as a spectacle, the warming and acidifying oceans, like the atmospheric levels of CO_2, cannot be directly portrayed in images but must be scientifically captured and creatively depicted. The depths of the ocean resist flat terrestrial maps that position humans as disengaged spectators. Marine scientists must, through modes of mediation, become submerged, even as persistent Western models of objectivity and mastery pull in the opposite direction.[61] The substance of the water itself insists on submersion, not separation. Even in the sunlit, clear, shallow waters that divers explore, visibility is never taken

for granted, nor does distance grant optimal vision. The oceans prof-
fer a sense of the planet as a place where multiple species live as part
of their material environs. As human activities change the chemical
composition, the temperature, and the alkalinity of the waters, marine
creatures also change.

Lesley Evans Ogden in "Marine Life on Acid," published in *BioScience* in 2013, explains that the term *ocean acidification* was coined only
in 2003, yet this problem has already become known as "climate change's
evil twin."[62] She explains what is happening:

> The ocean is a massive carbon sink estimated to have absorbed one-
> third of all the CO_2 produced by human activities. The tracking of
> carbon concentrations in the ocean, which began in the mid-1980s,
> has indicated that concentrations of CO_2 are increasing in parallel
> with the growing amount of this gas in the atmosphere. Short-
> term and long-term cycles continually exchange carbon among
> the atmosphere, the ocean, and land. CO_2 reacts with seawater to
> form carbonic acid, but as a weak acid, carbonic acid almost im-
> mediately dissociates to form bicarbonate ions and hydrogen ions.
> The increasing concentration of hydrogen ions makes seawater
> more acidic.[63]

Ogden notes that the ocean is "now nearly 30 percent more acidic
than it was at the beginning of the industrial era" and that finding "a
comparable acidification event" entails "going back 55 million years."[64]
Research on how the shift in alkalinity affects sea life and ecosystems
is only just beginning, but already a strange array of effects have been
captured. Acidification makes the eggs of the red sea urchin not as quick
as they need to be in blocking out a second sperm, resulting in inviable
embryos; the tiny plankton *Ostreococcus tauri,* which is normally one
micrometer, enlarges to one and a half micrometers with increased
CO_2, which means that some creatures dependent on it for food may no
longer be able to eat it.[65] The alteration of ocean alkalinity even causes
confusion and destructive behavior in fishes—which is fascinating in
its scrambling of biosemiotics with pH levels. Even more dramatically,
the increasingly acidic seas are dissolving the shells of sea animals.
Nina Bednaršek has documented the thin, partially dissolved shells of
pteropods, tiny marine snails, which are "important as food for other

zooplankton, fish, and marine mammals."[66] Many marine species, from krill to whales, depend on the pteropods, or sea butterflies, for food. If pteropods disappear from the polar and subpolar regions (to focus on just two regions), "their predators will be affected immediately": "For instance, gymnosomes are zooplankton that feed exclusively on shelled pteropods. Pteropods also contribute to the diet of diverse carnivorous zooplankton, myctophid and nototheniid fishes, North Pacific salmon, mackerel, herring, cod and baleen whales."[67] Pteropods are also important "biogeochemically," as part of the carbon cycle, when their shells sink to the ocean floor after their demise.[68] Considering how these creatures are crucial not only for the food web that sustains a multitude of other marine species but also as a carbon sink underscores the swirling, intimate interrelations between matters of biology, ecology, geology, and chemistry.

Whereas increasingly acidic seawater is itself difficult to represent in compelling ways, aesthetically entrancing images of dissolving shells of marine animals may enlist concern for ocean acidification. Nina Bednaršek's beautiful micrographs of two pteropod shells, one intact and one in the process of dissolving, appear in Ogden's article "Marine Life on Acid," but they also appear in the National Resource Defense Council's online magazine *On Earth,* the National Climate Assessment report, and the online technology publication *Ars Technica.*[69] Time-lapsed videos or photographs set in a series depict these dissolves in palpable manners. One striking panel of five images showing the pteropod shell dissolving at zero, fifteen, thirty, and forty-five days, by David Littschwager, which *National Geographic* owns the rights to as a stock image, appears on the National Oceanic and Atmospheric Administration website and on many other sites, including that of the Ukrainian Science Club.[70] Interestingly, in these images, the actual fleshy creature that inhabits the shell is absent. The empty shells suggest that the animals did not survive, but they also may invite viewers to imagine taking up residence there, within the precarious abodes. The design of the shells, the spirals that swirl with a continual, smooth transformation between what is inside and what is outside, suggest the contemplation of our own bodies as intertwined with our surroundings.

Video depictions of dissolving shells are even more irresistible than the photographs. Julia Whitty includes Tim Senden's video of an X-ray micro–computed tomography (CT) of a shelled pteropod *Limacina helicina antarctica* in her essay "Snails Are Dissolving in Acidic Ocean Waters," published in *Mother Jones* (Figure 5.2). The silent, twenty-two-second black-and-white video, which depicts a spinning, spiral, white shell, its edges dissolving into a transparent cloud, is rather entrancing, inviting a kind of mind-altering contemplation.[71] The beauty and fragility of the rotating shell are difficult to abandon. The brief black-and-white video is addictive. Highly mediated, depicting the shells of creatures rather than their fleshy bodies, these images nonetheless make claims on their viewers, seducing us to mobilize concern in scale-shifting modes.

The Tasmanian artist Melissa Smith, who creates art about the effects of climate change, has made several works featuring the pteropod within her Dissolve and Dissolve II series, including *Dispel,* a stunning 2:30 video animated by the same Tim Senden who produced the black-and-white video discussed in the previous paragraph. The name *Dispel* suggesting both dispersion and vanishing, the video shows a milky and translucent shell against a vibrant red background. Smith describes the video: "This work is emotively charged both visually and aurally. The cascading image of an X-ray micro-CT scanned pteropod shell, rotates and reveals its beauty before falling away to its demise. The soundtrack extends the viewer's perception of the visual to evoke an even deeper sense of loss."[72] The video begins with the shell gently falling into the frame of the camera and slowly, hypnotically rolling across the screen. Then it gets closer to the viewer, both encompassing the viewer, pulling her gaze in and through the spiral, but also allowing her to see through the transparency. The shell's extraordinary fragility is accompanied by mournful cello and piano music. In the end, revolving still, it disappears, white vanishing into red, as the shell spirals into smaller dimensions. The red background, signaling urgency, collides with the somber music and slow, mesmerizing rotations. The viewer's experience shifts from being a spectator to being ensconced to being part of the dissolve, left hovering within the red.

These shells, bereft of their fleshy creatures, without a face, nonetheless evoke concern, connection, empathy. While a gory scene depicting the living creature meeting its demise would separate the human spectator from this already distant form of marine life by sensationalizing it or rendering it abject, the elegant minimalist aesthetic of the shell lures us into a pleasurable encounter that nonetheless gestures toward

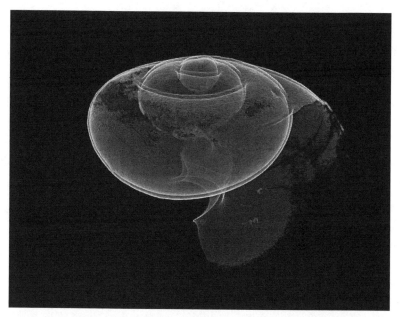

FIGURE 5.2. Video still from an X-ray micro-CT of a shelled pteropod *Limacina helicina antarctica*. Image courtesy of Tim Senden and the Australian National University CT Lab.

the apocalyptic. Within the contemporary digital landscape in which ocean creatures are posed in highly aesthetic ways, by environmental organizations, scientists, and popular media, the shells take up their place in the virtual gallery of aesthetic marine pleasures, haunted by the missing fleshy life.[73] To say they call us to contemplate our own "shells"—or bodily and psychic boundaries—on acid suggests something akin to a psychedelic experience. The spiral shells, especially when they are spinning around in the video versions, do, in fact, suggest the spiral as the icon of altered states. This mode of engagement, this type of attention, often involves a "dissolution between" the human and the "outside world," as Wikipedia tells us: "Some psychological effects may include an experience of radiant colors, objects and surfaces appearing to ripple or 'breath,' colored patterns behind the closed eyelids (eidetic imagery), an altered sense of time (time seems to be stretching, repeating itself, changing speed or stopping), crawling geometric patterns overlaying walls and other objects, morphing objects, a sense that one's thoughts are spiraling into themselves, loss of a sense of identity or the ego (known as 'ego death'), and other powerful psycho-physical reactions. Many users experience a dissolution between themselves and the 'outside world.'"[74] Intrepid viewers may dis/identify in the dissolve, simultaneously identifying with the shelled creature and contemplating the dissolution of boundaries that shore up human exceptionalism, imagining this particular creature's life and how extinction will ripple through the seas.

This dissolution between the human self and the world suggests what Richard M. Doyle, in *Darwin's Pharmacy: Sex, Plants, and the Evolution of the Noösphere,* defines as an "ecodelic insight," "the sudden and absolute conviction that the psychonaut is involved in a densely interconnected ecosystem for which contemporary tactics of human identity are insufficient."[75] Although Doyle is not writing about the question of scale in terms of the Anthropocene, his conception of the ecodelic may be useful for forging environmentally oriented conceptions of the Anthropos, not as a bounded entity, nor as an abstract force, but as manifestation: "And in awe we forget ourselves, becoming aware of our context at much larger—and qualitatively distinct—scales of space and time. And over and over again we can read in ecodelic testimony that these encounters with immanence render the ego into a non sequitur, the self becoming tangibly a gift manifested by a much larger dissipative structure—the planet, the galaxy, the cosmos."[76] I am interested in how the ecodelic erodes the outlines of the individual self in "encounters with immanence" that provoke alluring modes of scale shifting. The problem here, however, is that contemplative or psychedelic practices have an association, in Western culture at least, with a navel-gazing, spiritual transcendence—the exact opposite of the sort of materially immersed subjectivity I think is necessary for environmentalism. Recasting Doyle's scenario by imagining the anthropogenically altered, acidified seas, rather than the perfect, ethereal expanses of the cosmos (descending rather than transcending), may provoke a recognition of life as always immersed in substances and chemistries that are, within the Anthropocene especially, neither solid nor eternal. More difficult to contend with, however, is that the ecodelic figuration of the dissolve may be useless in terms of social justice and climate justice, in that it does not provoke consideration of differential human culpabilities and vulnerabilities. And yet, as a vivid image of slow violence, it could be taken up as a mode of dis/identification and alliance for particular groups of people who are contending with other sorts of invisible environmental harm. In her essay on the New Zealand Maori writer Kerri Hulme, Elizabeth DeLoughrey states that Hulme's stories "suggest that experience of embodied thought allows for merger with other species." DeLoughrey argues against apocalyptic fiction, however, and the figuration of the dissolve is rather apocalyptic. But other similarities resonate, such as her reading of Hulme's "narrative merger with fossils (and later the sea)" as "an encounter with deep planetary time that renders an interspecies relationship."[77]

As one figuration of the Anthropocene among many others that are possible, the exquisite photos and videos of dissolving shells may perform cultural work, portraying the shift in alkalinity as a vivid threat to delicate yet essential living creatures. Whereas the predominant sense of the Anthropocene subject, en masse, is that of a safely abstracted force, the call to contemplate your shell on acid cultivates a fleshy posthumanist vulnerability that denies the possibility of any living creature existing in a state of separation from its environs. The image of the diminutive creature, with its delicate shell dissolving, provokes an intimacy, a desire to hold and protect, even as we recognize that such beings hover as part of the unfathomable seas. The scene of the dissolve demands an engaged, even fearsome activity of scale shifting from the tiny creature to the vast seas. In *The Posthuman,* Rosi Braidotti challenges us to imagine a vital notion of death: "The experiment of de-familiarization consists in trying to think to infinity, against the horror of the void, in the wilderness of non-human mental landscapes, with the shadow of death dangling in front of our eyes."[78] Arguing not for transcendence but instead for "radical empirical immanence," she contends that "what we humans truly yearn for is to disappear by merging into this generative flow of becoming, the precondition for which is the loss, disappearance and disruption of the atomized, individual self."[79] Envisioning the dissolve, then, can be an immanent, inhuman or posthuman practice.

In the era of the sixth great extinction, it is not difficult to discern the shadow of death. Marine life faces many other threats in addition to acidification, including warming waters and the ravages of mining, drilling, ghost nets, shark finning, and industrial overfishing. Marine habitats are riddled with radioactive waste, toxic chemicals, plastics, and microplastics, all of which become part of the sea creatures that, not unlike Beck's citizen in risk society, lack the means to discern danger and the impermeability that would exclude it. Contemplating your shell on acid is a mode of posthumanist trans-corporeality that insists that all creatures of the Anthropocene dwell at the crossroads of body and place, where nothing is natural or safe or contained. To ignore the invisible threats of acidity or toxins or radioactivity is to imagine that we are less permeable than we are and to take refuge in an epistemological and ontological zone that is somehow outside the time and space of the Anthropocene. Those humans most responsible for carbon emissions, extraction, and pollution must contemplate our shells on acid. This is a call for scale shifting that is intrepidly—even psychedelically—empathetic rather than safely ensconced. Contemplating your shell on acid dissolves individualist, consumerist subjectivity in which the world consists primarily of externalized entities, objects for human consumption. It means dwelling in the dissolve, a dangerous pleasure, a paradoxical ecodelic expansion and dissolution of the human, an aesthetic incitement to extend and connect with vulnerable creaturely life and with the inhuman, unfathomable expanses of the seas. It is to expose oneself as a political act, to shift toward a particularly feminist mode of ethical and political engagement.

NOTES

Many thanks to John C. Blum at C21 for his keen editorial eye and to Richard Grusin, Emily Clark, and Dehlia Hannah for the invitation to speak at the C21 Anthropocene Feminism conference, which asserted the significance of feminist thought for the proposed epoch. This essay benefited from lively interchanges at the conference. It also benefited from rich conversations with Stephanie LeMenager about the Anthropocene, climate change, and politics and from her generous reading. All shortcomings are, as ever, my own.

1. Richard Doyle, *Darwin's Pharmacy: Sex, Plants, and the Evolution of the Noösphere* (Seattle: University of Washington Press, 2011).

2. Will Stefan, Paul J. Crutzen, and John R. McNeill, "The Anthropocene: Are Humans Now Overwhelming the Great Forces of Nature?," *AMBIO: A Journal of the Human Environment* 36, no. 8 (2007): 618.

3. Donna J. Haraway, "Situated Knowledges: The Science Question in Feminism and the Privilege of Partial Perspective," in *Simians, Cyborgs, Women: The Reinvention of Nature* (New York: Routledge, 1991), 188, 189.

4. Claire Colebrook, *Death of the PostHuman: Essays on Extinction,* vol. 1 (Ann Arbor, Mich.: Open Humanities Press, 2014), 22. This passing reference to

Colebrook's work should by no means imply that it can be readily encapsulated. Indeed, I think her extensive, bold, and often disconcerting work on the concepts of extinction and the Anthropocene makes her the preeminent philosopher of these emerging fields of thought.

5. Andrew Revkin, "Confronting the Anthropocene," *New York Times,* May 11, 2011, http://dotearth.blogs.nytimes.com/2011/05/11/confronting-the-anthropocene/?_php=true&_type=blogs&_r=0.

6. Elizabeth Kolbert, "Age of Man," *National Geographic,* March 2011, http://ngm.nationalgeographic.com/2011/03/age-of-man/kolbert-text.

7. "Anthropocene," *Encyclopedia of Earth,* September 3, 2013, http://www.eoearth.org/view/article/150125/.

8. Owen Gaffney, "State of the Art," *Anthropocene Journal,* October 1, 2013.

9. Ibid. The posting shows artwork and data visualizations by Félix Pharand-Deschênes, David Thomas Smith, Stephen Walter, Jason deCaires Taylor, Radhika Gupta, John Stockton, and NASA's Landsat program.

10. "Cartography of the Anthropocene," 2013, http://globaia.org/portfolio/cartography-of-the-anthropocene/.

11. Jamie Lorimer makes a similar argument, calling for attention to what he terms "nonhuman mobilities": "Tracing networks maps the geographies of intersecting lines through which landscapes are to be reanimated and by which their difference is threatened. . . . An attention to animals' geographies—thinking like an elephant, an insect, or even a molecule—can help attune to the diverse ways in which nonhuman life inhabits the novel ecosystems of an Anthropocene planet." See Lorimer, *Wildlife in the Anthropocene: Conservation after Nature* (Minneapolis: University of Minnesota Press, 2015), 177, 176.

12. Take, by contrast, Nicole Starosielski's multimedia project *Surfacing,* a digital map of underwater cable systems in which "the user becomes the signal and traverses the network." See Starosielski, "Surfacing: A Digital Mapping of Submarine Systems," *Suboptic,* 2013, 3. *Surfacing* will be discussed later.

13. Betsy Wills, "'Anthropocene': Aerial Photography by David Thomas Smith," March 15, 2013, http://artstormer.com/2013/03/15/anthropocene-aerial-photography-by-david-thomas-smith/.

14. Ibid.

15. "There is no Space or Time / Only intensity, / And tame things / Have no immensity." Mina Loy, "There Is No Life or Death," in *The Lost Lunar Baedeker: Poems of Mina Loy,* ed. Roger L. Conover (New York: Farrar, Strauss and Giroux, 1997), 3.

16. Patricia Johanson, quoted in Xin Wu, *Patricia Johanson and the Reinvention of Public Environmental Art, 1958–2010* (Surrey, U.K.: Ashgate, 2013), 155.

17. One of the sections to follow will discuss remarkable exceptions that enmesh the human with the lithic.

18. Dipesh Chakrabarty, "The Climate of History," *Critical Inquiry* 35 (Winter 2009): 201.

19. Ibid., 206–7.

20. Jan Zalasiewicz, Mark Williams, Will Steffen, and Paul Crutzen, "The New World of the Anthropocene," *Environmental Science and Technology Viewpoint* 44, no. 7 (2010): 2229.

21. Chakrabarty, "Climate of History," 207.

22. Ibid., 220.

23. Ibid.

24. Elizabeth DeLoughrey, "Ordinary Futures: Interspecies Worlding in the Anthropocene," in *Global Ecologies and the Environmental Humanities: Postcolonial Approaches,* ed. Elizabeth DeLoughrey, Jill Didur, and Anthony Carrigan (New York: Routledge, 2015), 354.

25. Donna J. Haraway, *When Species Meet* (Minneapolis: University of Minnesota Press, 2007), 25.

26. W. E. B. Du Bois, *The Souls of Black Folk* (Mineola, N.Y.: Dover, 1994); Frantz Fanon, *Black Skin, White Masks* (New York: Grove Press, 1967); Homi Bhabha, *The Location of Culture* (New York: Routledge, 2004); Judith Butler, *Gender Trouble: Feminism and the Subversion of Identity* (New York: Routledge, 1999).

27. Rory Rowan, "Notes on Politics after the Anthropocene," *Progress in Human Geography* 38, no. 3 (2014): 449.

28. Ian Baucom, "The Human Shore: Postcolonial Studies in an Age of Natural Science," *History of the Present: A Journal of Critical History* 2, no. 1 (2012): 4. Many thanks to Sangeeta Ray for sending me this essay.

29. Lorimer, *Wildlife in the Anthropocene,* 3.

30. "Slow violence" is of course Rob Nixon's term from *Slow Violence and the Environmentalism of the Poor* (Cambridge, Mass.: Harvard University Press, 2011). Nixon points out the painfully ironic timing of the "the grand species narrative of the Anthropocene," which is "gaining credence at a time when, in society after society, the idea of the human is breaking apart economically, as the distance between affluence and abandonment is increasing." He asks, "How can we counter the centripetal force of that dominant story with centrifugal stories that acknowledge immense disparities in human agency, impacts, and vulnerability?" See "The Great Acceleration and the Great Divergence: Vulnerability in the Anthropocene," *Profession,* March 19, 2014, https://profession.commons.mla.org/2014/03/19/the-great-acceleration-and-the-great-divergence-vulnerability-in-the-anthropocene/.

31. Sylvia Wynter and Katherine McKittrick, "Unparalleled Catastrophe for Our Species? Or to Give Humanness a Different Future: Conversations," in *Sylvia Wynter: On Being Human as Praxis,* ed. McKittrick (Durham, N.C.: Duke University Press, 2015), 24. I should note that this brief inclusion of Wynter's brilliant work does not address the many ways in which its original conceptions clash with other models of environmental and feminist science studies and material feminisms in this book, for example, her idiosyncratic definition of the "biocentric" and her use of Darwin. Wynter critiques the idea that humans are "purely biological beings," arguing instead that humans are hybrid creatures of

both "mythoi and bios" (34, 31). Critical posthumanist and animal studies scholars, including myself, would not agree with this human exceptionalist argument that denies nonhuman beings their own modes of culture. Wynter plainly states, for example, "As far as eusocial insects like bees are concerned, their roles are genetically *preprescribed* for them. Ours are not" (34). Such rigid distinctions are problematic not only for posthumanists but also for new materialists, in that it is problematic to draw a sharp line between biological embodiment and culture, given their many intra-actions. Even genetics can no longer be seen as encapsulated within the "biological" because epigenetics means that social, political, and environmental factors alter bodies. See, e.g., Shannon Sullivan, *The Physiology of Sexist and Racist Oppression* (Oxford: Oxford University, 2015).

32. Wynter and McKittrick, "Unparalleled Catastrophe for Our Species?"

33. Alexander G. Weheliye, *Habeas Viscus: Racializing Assemblages, Biopolitics, and Black Feminist Theories of the Human* (Durham, N.C.: Duke University Press, 2014), 24.

34. Anna Lowenhaupt Tsing, *Friction: An Ethnography of Global Connection* (Princeton, N.J.: Princeton University Press, 2005), 8.

35. Chakrabarty, "Climate of History," 14.

36. Dipesh Chakrabarty, "Brute Force," *Eurozine*, October 7, 2010, http://www.eurozine.com/articles/2010-10-07-chakrabarty-en.html.

37. I am grateful to Karen Barad's critique of this sentence, during the October 2014 SLSA conference, and her suggestion that I consider the (hypothetical) graviton particle. The graviton has confused me, however, because, if the graviton does exist, it would be a particle but would have no mass. So by saying that "humans are not gravity," I intend to critique Chakrabarty's mystification of humans as an abstract force. Reading a bit of physics, including Barad's work, does not leave me with the sense that even gravity is not gravity in that it may not be an immaterial force but instead remains a bit of a mystery. Barad states, "Constructing a quantum theory of gravity means understanding how to apply quantum theory to the general theory of relativity. This has proved exceedingly difficult." By contrast, it is not so difficult to demonstrate the many ways, from agriculture to automobiles to acidification, that humans have brought about the Anthropocene. Karen Barad, *Meeting the Universe Halfway* (Durham, N.C.: Duke University Press, 2007), 350. There is a very good chance that my thin understanding of physics caused me to misunderstand Barad's critique.

38. Dipesh Chakrabarty, "Postcolonial Studies and the Challenge of Climate Change," *New Literary History* 43, no. 1 (2012): 13.

39. Jessi Lehman and Sara Nelson, "After the Anthropocene: Politics and Geographic Inquiry for a New Epoch," *Progress in Human Geography* 38, no. 3 (2014): 444.

40. Derek Woods, "Scale Critique for the Anthropocene," *Minnesota Review* 83 (2014): 134.

41. Ibid., 140.

42. Rosi Braidotti, *Transpositions* (Cambridge: Polity, 2006), 278.

43. Starosielski, "Surfacing," 3.

44. Nicole Starosielski, Erik Loyer, and Shane Brennan, "Surfacing," http://www.surfacing.in/. Starosielski's book is *The Undersea Network* (Durham, N.C.: Duke University Press, 2015).

45. Starosielski, *Undersea Network,* 2.

46. Ibid., 2–3.

47. Stacy Alaimo, *Bodily Natures: Science, Environment, and the Material Self* (Bloomington: Indiana University Press, 2010).

48. See ibid., 119–25, and Rhonda Zwillinger, *The Dispossessed: Living with Multiple Chemical Sensitivities* (Paulden, Ariz.: Dispossessed Project, 1998).

49. Claire Colebrook, "Not Symbiosis, Not Now: Why Anthropogenic Climate Change Is Not Really Human," *Oxford Literary Review* 34, no. 2 (2012): 198–99.

50. Ibid., 193.

51. Ibid.

52. Jeffrey J. Cohen, *Stories of Stone: An Ecology of the Inhuman* (Minneapolis: University of Minnesota Press, 2015), 6, 62.

53. Elizabeth Ellsworth and Jamie Kruse, eds., *Making the Geologic Now: Responses to Material Conditions of Contemporary Life* (Brooklyn, N.Y.: Punctum Books, 2013), 152.

54. Ibid., 25.

55. Ilana Halperin, "Autobiographical Trace Fossils," in Ellsworth and Kruse, *Making the Geologic Now,* 156.

56. Ibid.

57. Kathryn Yusoff, "Geologic Life: Prehistory, Climate, Futures in the Anthropocene," *Environment and Planning D: Society and Space* 31, no. 5 (2013): 780.

58. Stephanie LeMenager, *Living Oil: Petroleum Culture in the American Century* (New York: Oxford University Press, 2014), 6.

59. For another figuration of the Anthropocene ocean, see DeLoughrey's "Ordinary Futures," which reads New Zealand Maori author Keri Hulme's speculative fiction by way of deep seabed mining, proposing that "we might read Hulme's oceanic imaginary in line with a cultural politics that destabilizes the state claims of the Foreshore and Seabed Act (and the Marine and Coastal Area Bill), a way of narrratively imagining a relationship to the oceanic through ordinary modes of merger and submersion—an adaptive, interspecies hermeneutics for the rising tides of the anthropocene" (367).

60. See Stacy Alaimo, "New Materialisms, Old Humanisms; or, Following the Submersible," *NORA: Nordic Journal of Feminist and Gender Research* 19, no. 4 (2011): 280–84.

61. Take, for example, James Cameron's *Aliens of the Deep* (2005), a documentary about deep-sea exploration that repeatedly supplants the seas with the planets. The deep seas are cast as the perfect practice arena for space explorers, marine biology is said to be a good starting point for astrobiology, and the samples from

the ocean are the "next best thing" for the planetary scientist to examine. The ethereal trumps the aqueous; the transcendent transcends the immanent. Marine biologist Dijanna Figuero's compelling and informative discussion of symbiosis in riftia (giant tube worms), for example, is followed by a cut to Cameron telling a scientist, "The real question is, can you imagine a colony of these on [Jupiter's moon] Europa?" Stacy Alaimo, "Dispersing Disaster: The Deepwater Horizon, Ocean Conservation, and the Immateriality of Aliens," in *Disasters, Environmentalism, and Knowledge,* ed. Sylvia Mayer and Christof Mauch, 175–92 (Heidelberg, Germany: Universitätsverlag, 2012).

62. Lesley Evans Ogden, "Marine Life on Acid," *BioScience* 63, no. 5 (2013): 322.

63. Ibid.

64. Ibid., 328.

65. Ibid.

66. Ibid., 323.

67. James C. Orr et al., "Anthropogenic Ocean Acidification over the Twenty-First Century and Its Importance to Calcifying Organisms," *Nature,* September 29, 2005, 685.

68. Ogden, "Marine Life," 323.

69. Jason Bidel, "Our Climate Change, Ourselves," *On Earth* (blog), May 6, 2014, http://www.onearth.org/articles/2014/05/national-climate-assessment; National Climate Assessment report, U.S. Global Change Research, 2014, http://nca2014.globalchange.gov/downloads; Scott K. Johnson, "Sea Butterflies Already Feeling the Sting of Ocean Acidification?," *Ars Technica,* November 27, 2013, http://arstechnica.com/science/2012/11/sea-butterflies-already-feeling-the-sting-of-ocean-acidification/.

70. NOAA, "What Is Ocean Acidification?," http://www.pmel.noaa.gov/co2/story/What+is+Ocean+Acidification%3F; Richard A. Kerr, "Ocean Acidification: Unprecedented, Unsettling," 2010, http://nauka.in.ua/en, originally published in *Science,* June 18, 2010, 1500–1501.

71. Julia Whitty, "Snails Are Dissolving in Acidic Ocean Waters," *Mother Jones,* November 2012, http://www.motherjones.com/blue-marble/2012/11/first-evidence-marine-snails-dissolving-acidic-waters-antarctica. Tim Senden of the Department of Applied Maths at the Research School of Physics and Engineering, Australian National University, produced this video, which is available on YouTube at https://www.youtube.com/watch?v=48qrlTFqelc. Information about complex technologies and procedures of the X-Ray CT Lab is available at http://www.anu.edu.au/CSEM/machines/CTlab.htm.

72. Melissa Smith, "Climate Change as Art," *Australian Antarctic Magazine* 25 (December 2013), http://www.antarctica.gov.au/about-us/publications/australian-antarctic-magazine/2011-2015/issue-25-december-2013/art/climate-change-as-art.

73. Jellyfish and other gelatinous creatures, for example, have been portrayed as "art" in museum exhibits, coffee table books, videos for relaxation, and scientific

and popular websites. See Stacy Alaimo, "Jellyfish Science, Jellyfish Aesthetics: Posthuman Reconfigurations of the Sensible," in *Thinking with Water,* ed. Janine MacLeod, Cecilia Chen, and Astrida Neimanis, 139–64 (Kingston, Ont.: McGill-Queen's University Press, 2013).

74. Wikipedia, "Lysergic Acid Diethylamide," http://en.wikipedia.org/wiki/Lysergic_acid_diethylamide.

75. Doyle, *Darwin's Pharmacy,* 20.

76. Ibid., 21.

77. DeLoughrey, "Ordinary Futures," 365.

78. Rosi Braidotti, *The Posthuman* (Cambridge: Polity, 2013), 134.

79. Ibid., 136.

6

The Arctic Wastes

MYRA J. HIRD AND ALEXANDER ZAHARA

NUNAVUT'S WASTE

In the Eastern Canadian Arctic city of Iqaluit (population approximately seven thousand), a four-story pile of waste, known locally as the West 40 Landfill, rests atop a peninsula that extends well into Nunavut's Frobisher Bay.[1] To say that the dump "rests," however, is perhaps misleading: for the fourth time in just over a year, the dumpsite spontaneously caught fire in 2014.[2] For more than three months, the fire burned continuously, leading to a variety of responses from stakeholders: publics filed numerous formal and informal complaints to the city regarding the smell of dump smoke; a territorial health department advisory warned that children, women of childbearing years, pregnant women, the elderly, and those with respiratory issues should avoid breathing in dump smoke entirely (presumably, the healthy, postmenopausal, preelderly woman was safe); the local elementary school shut down twice because of children complaining of headaches; and several major community events were postponed, including the city's annual spring cleanup.[3] All of this culminated in the federal and territorial governments' reassurances that the public's exposure to dump smoke was safe for human health. Or, at least it *should* have been safe, if standing at a distance of seventy meters from the dump. Meanwhile, a hired landfill consultant explained to the Iqaluit City Council that their waste management operations "virtually guaranteed this problem would happen."[4] Without technical intervention, the consultant assured the city council, the fire would burn for at least another year. Putting out the dump fire cost the city nearly C$2.75 million and took more than two weeks to complete.[5] Unlike the modern landfills of Canada's other capital cities, Iqaluit's municipal solid waste site is (noticeably) in constant exchange with air, land, and sea: what Euro-Canadians typically refer to as "the environment."

The dump is just one of the many waste sites located near or within the city of Iqaluit. In January 2013, a 1995 map of the city's contaminated waste sites resurfaced in the local Nunavut newspaper. In the article, federal and territorial politicians were asked for help in cleaning up the community's six remaining waste sites; although most (if not all) of these sites are left over from federal government military and resource development initiatives, the responsibility for these sites is largely unknown. And in the nearly two decades since the map was originally commissioned as part of the Department of Indian and Northern Affairs' Arctic Waste response program, only one site—Iqaluit's "Upper Base," a 1950s-era Pinetree Line radar station—has been fully remediated.[6] The remaining sites, which persist despite being known sources of contaminant exposure, are unavoidable features of the landscape.[7] A more than half-century old metal dump is located in the nearby Territory Park, right next to the city's most popular campsite; three other waste sites, including the city's dump, are located at Causeway, the city's main launch point for those seeking to go out on the land to hunt and/ or camp; and two others (a metal dump and the contaminated North 40 site) are located centrally between an under-construction airport, a college residence, and the territorial penitentiary. These sites, as the councilor who wrote the article explained, "pose a threat to that [Inuit] way of life" because of their desorption into local "country" foods, such as berries and aquatic wildlife (i.e., seal, arctic char, and shellfish).[8] More than just colonial reminders, we argue, these waste sites are colonial in and of themselves.

In this chapter, we examine waste within the wider context of colonialism as well as contemporary neoliberal governance practices to argue that waste is part of the colonial context within which Inuit and other aboriginal peoples in northern Canada continue to live: waste, in other words, has become a particular neocolonial symptom.[9] Neocolonial governance leads to the configuration of waste as capitalism's fallout—its unanticipated supplement—which can be managed as a technological issue (bigger and better waste facilities) and individual responsibility for diversion (primarily recycling).[10] Perhaps the failure of waste in Canada's northern communities to conform to Euro-Canadian governance may be understood as a living-with the historical colonial legacy that continues to indelibly shape the northern landscape and its people.

Waste is a particularly provocative material concept with which to think about neocoloniality because of the important part this concept has played, and continues to play, in "excluding certain groups of people from specific social, political, and physical spaces."[11] The long-standing association of waste, dirt, and disease with racialized and colonized peoples as a justification for practices of subjugation certainly offers insights into waste as a cultural signifier, but in the context of the Anthropocene, waste takes on, we argue, a distinct hue.[12] The Anthropocene captures an emerging recognition of, and interest in, the simultaneous operation of human-created infrastructures and global politicoeconomic practices characteristic of industrial capitalism and geological processes stretching back through deep time. Whether in the form of mining, nuclear, industrial, hazardous, sewage, or municipal, and whether it is dumped, landfilled, incinerated, or buried deep underground, waste constitutes perhaps the most abundant and enduring trace of the human for epochs to come. While stratigraphers debate the appropriate geographic coordinates for the next golden spike, the real provocation of the Anthropocene is not that we are leaving a message for some imagined future humanity to decipher but that we are bequeathing a particular futurity through a projected responsibility. In this chapter, we want to take up the challenge posed by Dipesh Chakrabarty to conceptualize the neocolonial subject within the context of the Anthropocene.[13] The Anthropocene, Chakrabarty argues, recharacterizes the neocolonial subject as both the colonized and a geological force, wherein humans may "no longer" think themselves separate from nature. We will explore this as a provocation to better understand the human species' precarious relationship with earth but also as a caution that it not subsume violent neocolonial legacies within a universal discourse about humanity.

The history of waste in Canada's North, we argue, is inseparable from its colonial legacy, as U.S. and Canadian military, as well as American and Canadian prospectors, industry, and settlers, both introduced waste to the North and—for the most part—abandoned it there. This past, together with waste's future promise—the fallout of increased oil, gas, and mineral extraction; military installations; shipping; and the tourist trade to the health of humans and nonhumans—projects a responsibility to present and future generations to resolve. And while the Anthropocene speaks of a universal human species that impacts the planet, we emphasize the uneven distribution of both the causes of anthropogenic change and of the *effects* of this waste landscape— capitalism's implicit dividend—that are differentially experienced and lived by Inuit in Canada's North.

TEACHING IQALUMMIUT TO WASTE

Much of Iqaluit's short history involves Euro-Canadians and Euro-Americans teaching Inuit how to waste.[14] Prior to the settlement of Qallunaat (non-Inuit) in Nunavut, the Inuit of Baffin Island (what is known as Nunavut's Qikiqtani Region) were seminomadic and relied solely on the land for sustenance. One or two Inuit families together hunted a variety of seasonal animals (e.g., caribou, seal, ptarmigan, muskox, and polar bear) for food, clothing, tools, and other necessities. In the summer, caribou skin was used to make summer tents, and in the winter, snow and ice were used to make iglu, and sod was used to make houses called qammaq.[15] Given the presence of middens across the Arctic, claims that Inuit produced little to no waste prior to colonization are likely made as political statements regarding the profoundly different volume and kind of waste that colonization brought to the Arctic. They also suggest that garbage itself might be a colonizing force—one that is configured through settler ontology, a point we return to later in the chapter.[16]

Inuit visited the area of Iqaluit to fish, hunt, and trade; however, it wasn't until the American military selected the region as a World War II airbase that Inuit began moving into year-round settlements.[17] Although many Inuit settled near Iqaluit temporarily to work for the American military, by the early 1950s, only fifty Inuit lived in Iqaluit permanently.[18] In the late 1950s, when the Canadian government constructed the Distant Early Warning (DEW) Line as a strategic defense against Soviet invasion during the Cold War, Inuit began to settle in earnest.[19] This shift to a sedentary lifestyle, which was both driven by and reliant on government subsidies and a Euro-Canadian-style labor-based economy, resulted in deep social and cultural changes that transformed the relationship among Inuit, land, family and community practices, food, health, education, and waste.

In general brushstroke, the history of colonization in Canada's North resembles that of colonization in Canada's South—though, significantly, it occurred more than a century later.[20] Early explorers depended on Inuit to survive what Europeans experienced as the harsh northern climate. The Hudson Bay Company and other outfitters organized hunting around capital and profit. Like First Nations and other aboriginal peoples in southern parts of Canada, Inuit in the North were rapidly and purposefully assimilated into mainstream Canadian culture. Anthropological reports from the mid-twentieth century describe Iqaluit (then Frobisher Bay) as a town where "sophisticated southern populations," "rugged old-timer Northern whites," and a "shadowy social world of metis and natives" lived together in close proximity.[21] Whereas most government workers lived in "Southern Canadian type 'suburbias,'"[22] many Inuit lived in self-made, one- or two-room shacks.[23] Since the Canadian military did not provide housing for Inuit casual laborers, Inuit used the military's own discarded materials. An unnamed American military official described the "ingenuity and cleverness" of his Inuk laborer in preventing waste materials from being produced—a characteristic that was not readily shared by his American counterparts.[24]

The line between resourceful and dirty was (and is) largely dictated by normative assumptions about cleanliness and waste. As Marie Lathers notes, "management of the abject" (i.e., of feces, dirt, or waste) was central to the American (and we would argue Canadian) colonial project of the early twentieth century. The particularities of this project developed through a discourse of "excremental colonialism" wherein the "brown person" became disempowered (and dehumanized) through his association with the abject.[25] Indeed, one government official noted with disgust that when Inuit began wearing Euro-Canadian cotton materials, the clothing was worn "until . . . it fairly rots off."[26] Here, as Warwick Anderson puts it, waste was used to delineate "the polar opposites of white and brown, retentive and promiscuous, imperforate and open, pure and polluting, civilized and infantile."[27] Though many Inuit fondly recall scavenging for food and other materials left to them regularly, in dumps, by the American military, the Canadian government was less inclined to do so.[28] All government employees were enjoined to "assist"

Inuit people's (inevitable) transition to modernity by "insist[ing] upon the maintenance of cleanliness and sanitation amongst the Eskimo employees and their famil[ies]."[29] By 1960, for example, scavenging for household materials was banned in Resolute Bay. In Iqaluit, at least one Inuk reported fear of being caught by military officials for scavenging for wood and mattresses at an abandoned dump site.[30] Government reports from the mid-twentieth century discussed the difficulty Inuit had in adapting to Euro-Canadian standards of waste management.[31] Ironically, Inuit were hired for the Euro-Canadian residents' laundry operations, sewage disposal, waste collection, and cleaning, suggesting that although unclean themselves, Inuit were entrusted to unburden white people from the toil of their own cleaning.[32]

The shifting Inuit way of life toward wage labor and a market-based economy was reinforced by several directed government initiatives. Examining the development of Iqaluit, Matthew Farish and P. Whitney Lackenbauer note that by the mid-1950s, Euro-Canadian bureaucrats had taken a "high modernist" approach to development in the Arctic.[33] The explicit goal was to build "a nation in the northern half of this continent truly patterned on our [southern] way of life."[34] More than this, the North American Arctic was meant to become a "*safe* space for development projects."[35] As more and more Inuit were assimilated into the market economy, Inuit across Nunavut began to rent government-subsidized housing. These houses were often described as unfit for the climate, and most relied on electricity for heating that was turned off if tenants did not make their rent payments.[36]

Similar to American colonialists in the Philippines, who, as Anderson points out, quite literally examined slides of indigenous people's feces, Canadian federal government employees were sent to inspect the cleanliness of Inuit houses.[37] It was noted by government officials that Inuit women's housekeeping "lacks organization." Federal government officials recorded Inuit diet ("almost all the food was bought from the store"), patterns of food preparation ("soups are heated but do not always have water added to them"), shopping ("men make most of the purchases"), and cleanliness ("toilet bowls are allowed to fill before they are removed ... washing clothes is still a problem in many homes"). In the late 1960s, adult education classes were provided to Inuit women whose housekeeping did not "measure up to the standards set by white women."[38]

The Canadian government's particular mode of paternal governance was reinforced well into the mid-twentieth century. Government officials, military, and southern industry personnel justified Inuit assimilation on the grounds that it was necessary not only for northern development initiatives but for Inuit people's survival. Colonization, it appears, had been so successful that the traditional Inuit way of life, as well as the people themselves, were considered to be in danger of extinction. In 1964, the Department of Northern Affairs and National Resources created *Q-Book: Qaujivallaalirutissat,* a guidebook written in both English and Inuktitut that was designed to help Inuit "when they are faced with the many new things which are happening in the North."[39] Here the government explicitly recognized the reliance of Inuit on the market-based economy, stating that "[the working Eskimo] can no longer hunt with bow and arrow like in the old days. . . . Some of them would die if they were not helped by the white man." The guidebook advised that educating Inuit children with a Euro-Canadian curriculum was a vital factor in achieving Inuit assimilation:

> Eskimo children know a lot about the animals birds and flowers around them. In school they can learn about the habits and usefulness of many things in nature. At school he also learns about mines, machines and factories in which many people work. He will learn how useful these things are to all men.[40]

Many thousands of aboriginal children throughout Canada—including Inuit—were removed from their families and forced to live in residential schools.[41] In Canada's North, Inuit children were placed in communities throughout the other provinces and territories. Many Inuit believed (accurately or otherwise) that their family allowances would be taken away if they did not send their children to residential schools—this would have meant a loss of crucial food or housing needed to support small children and elderly relatives.[42] Educating Inuit youth (particularly young girls) in other communities was thought to have the added bonus of influencing Inuit women to become better at household chores. Women, who were traditionally the dominant figure in the tent household, and whose "authority seems to have been usurped" by settlement, often found the furnished adult education classes to be both boring and demeaning. One government official, at least, recognized that Inuit women's decision-making roles in families and communities had changed. His solution was to recommend involving Inuit men in the household, mainly as a way of enforcing Euro-Canadian gender roles: "the influence of men on purchasing, cooking, and home care should be realized and exploited . . . since women have been excluded from some of their traditional decision making situations."[43] Within the Canadian federal government's patriarchal tradition, colonialism and waste were inextricable.

In 1999, through the political struggle of numerous Inuit activists (who themselves had been educated in Canada's residential school systems), the Nunavut Land Claims Agreement was made into law. The result was the creation of the largest land claim in Canada's history and Inuit self-governance over the newly formed Nunavut Territory.[44] Inuit were no longer the "eaters of raw meat," nor were they the numerical ID given to them by federal government officials.[45] Now Inuit were to be considered "real human beings" with final decision-making authority over the territory's government and development.[46]

Since its colonization, both Iqaluit's population and the amount of waste it produces have grown rapidly. In 1989, when Iqaluit's population reached nearly three thousand people, the city was producing approximately fifteen thousand cubic meters of waste annually. Plastics, which made up only 4.2 percent of the waste stream in 1974 (compared to 10.1 percent in the rest of Canada), increased to 13.3 percent of the waste stream by 1989.[47] In 2011, with a population of just over seventy-four hundred, annual waste production was calculated at 82,805 cubic meters.[48] As Inuit activist and writer Zebedee Nungak wryly notes, "now, our garbage is as 'civilized' as anybody else's."[49]

AND THEN SOME

The municipal solid waste openly dumped in northern communities is a small fraction of Canada's northern waste portfolio.

There are approximately—no one knows the exact figure—twenty-seven thousand abandoned or "orphaned" mines in Canada, most of which are in Canada's northern regions. The Giant Mine, located on the Ingraham Trail close to Yellowknife, was abandoned in 2005, leaving responsibility to the Ministry of Indian Affairs and Northern Development and the taxpayer for the cost and cleanup of some one hundred onsite buildings, eight open pits, contaminated soils, and waste rock around the mine and some 237,000 tons of arsenic trioxide dust.[50]

In January 1978, the Soviet satellite Cosmos 954 exploded through the atmosphere over the Northwest Territories, spreading some sixty-five kilograms of fissionable uranium 235 over an area of 124,000 square kilometers.[51]

The grasshopper effect is a term used to explain how persistent organic pollutants (POPs) from all over the world end up in polar regions. Many POPs are industrial waste by-products that are transported to the Arctic via air currents from southern communities. Contaminants evaporate in warm temperatures and condense in cold climates, where they accumulate on the land and in country food. As a result, women who eat country food have higher contaminant loads in their breast milk than those who do not.[52]

When the U.S. Army stopped work on the pipeline from Norman Wells to Whitehorse, it abandoned hundreds of trucks, graders, and construction equipment as well as some 60,476 barrels of oil in the pipe and some 108,857 barrels that are presumed to have spilled into the landscape.[53]

The DEW Line, set up in northern Canada during the Cold War to detect incoming Soviet bombers and sea–land invasion, left in its wake sixty-three abandoned sites contaminated with various toxic chemicals that have had to be removed—square inch by square inch—to southern Canada for treatment. The numerous military stations littered across the northern landscape also present various waste issues, from abandoned equipment to leaking chemical containers and brownfields.

Disposal of sewage and gray water at sea is regulated in all Canadian waters, except for the Arctic Ocean, where "any ship and any person on a ship may deposit in arctic waters such sewage as may be generated."[54] Thousands of vessels have traveled the Arctic since 1990, the vast majority of them tourism, research, and federal government military support vessels.[55]

A new study reveals that concentrations of microplastics (plastic debris that is less than five millimeters in diameter) in high Arctic sea ice is over two orders of magnitude greater than what is found in all other ocean surface waters, including the so-called Great Pacific Garbage Patch. The research concludes that the Arctic is a global sink for microplastic debris—one that will result in a substantial release of plastic particles into the ocean upon human-induced sea ice melt.[56]

TRUE NORTH STRONG AND FREE

In a contemporary refrain of Canada's national anthem, Prime Minister Stephen Harper stated at the 2009 G-20 Summit that Canada has "no history of colonialism."[57] Harper reiterated the government's stance that Canada is a nation whose resources and opportunities are shared equally by all citizens. As well as denying hundreds of years of Old World dependence on Canadian resources, and of prospectors' and settlers' dependence on aboriginal peoples for survival, navigation, hunting, and labor—all of which inspired the material and cultural subjugation of Canada's original peoples—Harper's statement exemplifies the liberal state that Michel Foucault identified as one that "justifies its jurisdiction on a type of origin myth."[58] Faced with the long and deep history of aboriginal peoples in what became Canada, anthropologist Michael Asch argues that Europeans chose to identify colonial settlement as sovereignty's historical starting point. The Crown declared Canada a terra nullius before colonization—an absurdum recently reiterated by the Supreme Court of Canada.[59]

Embedded in the colonial imagination of sovereignty is the messy juxtaposition of the Arctic as simultaneously (1) the "True North strong and free"[60]—a remote and pristine landscape whose innocent history embodies an aesthetic of uncontained and uncontaminated wilderness—(2) the North as Canada's largest and most diverse emerging resource for industrial extraction—a vital piece of the circumpolar pie[61]—and, increasingly, (3) the North as anthropogenic trace and therefore "a symbolic pinnacle for global sustainable development."[62]

The dramatic increase in demand for northern natural resources over the past twenty years has only intensified with the prospect of climate change making these resources more accessible.[63] According to Aboriginal Affairs and Northern Development Canada, the North contains approximately 25 percent of Canada's remaining discovered recoverable crude oil and natural gas and approximately 40 percent of Canada's projected future discoveries.[64] This means more people and equipment moving temporarily from South to North, much more drilling and extraction, and, inevitably, more waste.

A technocratic language of environmental management is increasingly eclipsing debates about Inuit control over land and sea, a discourse that includes the interests not only of scientists and conservationists in land stewardship, climate regulation, and biodiversity but of oil, gas, and mineral mining, tourist, and other Euro-Canadian and international corporates. Once again, Inuit rights are being fused with resources into a single issue. Inuit rights over northern development in areas of oil and gas exploration, hunting, and fishing are now advanced on the grounds of thousands of years of successful Inuit stewardship. This stewardship, however, is formulated within terms that assume resource development as a given and, moreover, as Jessica Shadian argues, within a discourse that corroborates Canada's Western neoliberal ideology.[65] In other words, Inuit have rights because of their status as Canadians, and the needs of Canadians as a whole (e.g., resource extraction, profit, global corporate investment, and employment) are what define the terms of sustainable development in the North. As the Canadian government's "Northern Strategy" states,

> Canada's North is a fundamental part of Canada—it is part of our heritage, our future and our identity as a country. The Government has a vision for a new North and is taking action to ensure that vision comes to life—*for the benefit of all Canadians.*[66]

As such, "indigenous people have in effect been engaged in a massive program of foreign aid to the urban populations of the industrialized North" for the past several hundred years.[67] Thus, through contemporary interests in development, Inuit communities are being assimilated into greatly expanding industrial corporate interests in the North through casual resource extraction labor, capacity-building training, and the tourist trade.[68] Inuit communities are themselves caught up in often fraught internal struggles as they negotiate access to development on the land and in the sea.[69]

For Inuit, the North is a place of complicated histories of violence, subjugation, collective memory, landscape, survival, tradition, and more. Researchers continue to identify the multitudinous human health and environmental risks that attend northern development, such as living with contamination.[70] The strategic interest in the North, first as a military defense site in the 1940s and then as a site for resource extraction and development that has been accelerating since the oil crisis in the early 1970s, continues to promise the spoils of Western civilization to

Inuit peoples: more jobs, more training, more money, and greater investment. But as one advocate for Inuit rights challenging the Canadian polar gas pipeline project points out,

> initiatives such as the pipeline have too often been proposed together with promises that it will shepherd native people into the twentieth century.... [Instead] too often it serves only to dislocate and disorient native peoples and leaves them unequipped for the twentieth century, stripped of their lands and waters and the ability to follow their traditional pursuits once it has passed them by.[71]

Thus, among whatever dividends Inuit may or may not actually accrue—and numerous studies demonstrate that many are peripheral and temporary, problems associated with what is known as the "staples trap" or "resource curse"[72]—northern development ultimately leaves substantial waste in its wake:

> Today, the greatest and certainly the most direct threat to the security of Arctic residents stems from damage to the environment. The Arctic, in effect, has been treated as a dumping ground by government, military establishments and industries concerned only with the needs of southern societies.[73]

Whether or not environmental degradation is the most direct threat, there is no doubt that it adjoins poverty, suicide, a lack of safe and affordable housing, food security, substance abuse, and a host of other profound and pressing issues facing Inuit people.

SELF-DETERMINATION

This is not to say that Inuit do not act, know, or care about waste management. In Iqaluit, as with other Arctic communities, there exists a multiplicity of perspectives on waste and other issues. Rather than rehearsing a familiar colonial discourse that defines (and thus confines) indigeneity to local or traditional practices and epistemologies, we argue that Inuit perspectives are embedded in (whether deeply aware of, occurring in response to, or independent of) Nunavut's recent and ongoing colonial history.[74]

Many Inuit, for example, consider community and resource development as a necessary and even desirable way forward in the context of Nunavut's myriad social issues—many of which stem from decades of colonial violence[75] and "chronic underfunding" from Canada's federal government.[76] Inuit living in Nunavut have among the lowest household incomes in the country,[77] and the difference in average income between Inuit and Qallunaat is striking: In 2005, the average income for non-Inuit Nunavut residents was C$70,000 per year, while Inuit residents earned just under C$22,000.[78] Nearly 60 percent of those living in Nunavut smoke, ranking it the highest territory or province per capita in the country.[79] Residents also have high levels of diabetes, heart disease, and other diet-related illnesses, and Nunavut households experience food insecurity at a rate seven times higher than the Canadian average.[80] In the city's two grocery stores, food comes highly packaged and/or nearing its expiration date. Violence against women is a major issue, and the single women's shelter struggles to meet the overwhelming need. Substance abuse is a major problem, and alcohol can only be purchased in restaurants and hotels. Suicide rates are ten times higher in Nunavut than in the rest of Canada.[81] In September 2014, an eleven-year-old boy committed suicide in Cape Dorset, the territory's second child suicide in just over a year.[82]

For many Euro-Canadians, the dump fire was simply a by-product of poor leadership on the part of the city. Years of improperly managed waste—the mixing of plastics, paper, cardboard, food waste, batteries, and even human sewage at the dump—have produced what the landfill engineer emphatically described as "one of [the] worst landfills in North America."[83] Yet for many of those living in Iqaluit (both Inuit and Qallunaat), the dump fire was indicative of something more—a double standard experienced by those living in Canada's North. In Iqaluit, musings of "this would never happen in Toronto" were not uncommon. Common, too, were responses from Euro-Canadians who consider living in the Arctic "to be a choice," one that is inherently unsustainable due to high government subsidies.[84] These comments contrast what Inuit activist Sheila Watt-Cloutier refers to as "the right to be cold": the right for indigenous populations to live on traditional lands and not

be forced to move or otherwise act or live in ways that are prescribed
to them by Euro-Canadians. As such, when the territorial and federal
governments refused to provide funds toward the dump fire's projected
C$7 million extinguishing fee, many Inuit protested.[85] Inuit and others
advocating for improved waste technology and for the Iqaluit dump to
be extinguished were doing so not necessarily out of a desire to expand
consumption and capitalism but as a way of addressing long-standing
issues of inequity.

Through our discussions of waste with Iqaluit community members,
current and historical relationships with the federal government were
frequently brought to the fore. For example, Iqalummiut complained
of the yearly military exercise Operation Nanook, which spends millions of dollars "defending Arctic sovereignty" rather than addressing
"a real emergency," such as the Iqaluit dump fire.[86] Similarly, one long-
term Qallunaat resident lamented that the federal government did not
understand "northern sovereignty," which, according to her, necessarily
requires "women and children, communities, clam diggers, and fisher-
man, and berry pickers" to exist. It is perhaps not surprising, then, that
in a region where sovereignty is configured through *interactions with* nature rather than ownership over it, issues of waste are frequently related
to the mid-twentieth-century colonial period—when (as we discussed
earlier in this chapter) settler framings of humans dominating nature
were enforced.[87] One Inuk man, for example, explained how waste and
consumption practices emerged as the result of government initiatives.
In doing so, he resituated current waste problems within the context of
the federal government's "high modernist" project in the Arctic:

> It's a catch-22 kind of thing. . . . Because we didn't need television,
> we didn't need rifles, we didn't need snowmobiles. We were living
> just fine the way we were. And this white man comes, "oh you need
> shelter, oh you need furniture to get status in your life. Oh you need
> pots and pans." But we didn't. We were fine the way we were. . . . As
> soon as the white man said, "you need to be in communities" . . .
> we were all scattered all over the place, and then the government
> said we got used to money. And the government said "if you want
> more money you gotta send your kids to school [in the South]."
> And that's how the communities formed.[88]

Our respondents' characterizations of federal government relationships, as they relate to personal experiences of colonialism, are important. They are materially constitutive of how Inuit and other Iqalummiut participate politically as activists, politicians, industrial negotiators, disengaged citizens, and so on. As another respondent remarked,

> even on the land—you know, we put them [garbage] in the boats, our tents, [when] we go on the land. Garbage. Garbage. We eat, eat, eat. Garbage. Put it in the garbage bag. Right after, if we are going to leave from the campsite, we are going to take the gar-bages too. Because you have to respect the land. It's just the land and the nature. I know nature gets mad all the time. We cannot handle it. Right? Human beings. Humans, us humans, cannot [pauses] like [pauses] control the nature. Right? We live in the richest land of Canada and of the Universe. We have sapphires, we have crystals, and animals. . . . There's a lot of beautiful lakes, you can catch some fish. Red fish, arctic char, you know? Other stuff. Salmons. We've got all of them almost. Arctic cods. You can go like five minutes and go find cod, and go make some fish and chips for ourselves. . . . That's the way. We don't deal with garbage. We [Inuit] don't want them [the garbage] to be in the lakes, or on the river, or on the sea, because we have to eat it [and] be re-sponsible for everything. . . . I know they [the federal government] come and say, "yeah, I'm just a number" and blah blah blah. They don't consider us as human beings. I know it. . . . They [the federal government] think they found us, but no. Been there for centuries and stuff. . . . They [my ancestors] lived environmentally free. It was strong stuff. Healthy. You never seen garbage. Nothing.[89]

This statement was made in the context of Inuit struggles for self-determination: it points to a Western cosmology that separates humans from their environment as the cause of anthropogenic "mega-problems," including climate change and other waste-related issues. Our respondent's use of the term "environmentally free" problematizes the very *im-material* construction of "environment" as a concept—of a nature that is placed "outside of" human existence. And the focus on garbage as not having existed prior to colonial contact underscores this point, because any materials that *were* wasted *could not* have been "out-of-place" in that the very definition of materials as "out-of-place" is derivative of a settler cosmology.[90] Moreover, his assertion that we cannot "control" or "handle" nature counters Western understandings of sovereignty wherein a mastery over people and nature is implicit. Read this way, this is less an aesthetic statement than it is a naming of the very relationship that the Anthropocene has just now discovered—that human–nature relations are inextricable.

CONCLUSIONS

If the ubiquitous waste that litters the Arctic landscape is the fallout of a colonial past, then the prospect of far more waste generated through northern resource development may characterize what Derek Gregory refers to as Canada's "colonial present" and its forecasted future.[91] Municipal, solid, mining, and myriad other forms of waste constitute an anthropogenic legacy and capitalism's profound fallout underwritten by "ideologies and discourses that facilitate resource development and environmental transformations."[92] In significant ways, modern waste management is a manifestation of the West's colonial tradition, and its implementation requires an assimilation to predetermined neoliberal market-based definitions of what waste is and how it should be managed. For most Euro-Canadian communities, waste is "out-of-sight and out-of-mind"—"an ironic testimony to a desire to forget."[93] In this way, waste, both conceptually and materially, marks the success of the neocolonial project—its proliferation and technomanagement are predicated on an Enlightenment-rooted settler cosmology that emphasizes dominance over nature. In the northern Canadian waste landscape, this equates to teaching the colonial subject, in the first instance, to waste in new magnitude and kind and then to adopt neoliberal ways of dealing with waste's proliferation, that is, waste as profit.

Yet within an Anthropocene logos, as Chakrabarty points out, the neocolonial subject may now be subsumed within a universalized *Homo sapiens*—a species for whom, in functioning as a geophysical force, sovereignty is no longer possible. He explains:

It has to be one of the profoundest ironies of our modern history that increasing use of such energy [fossil fuels] should have now transformed our collective image, in our own eyes, from that of an autonomous if not sovereign and purposeful agency—from the level of individuals to the level of groups—to that of a force, which is defined as "the sheer capacity to produce pull or push on an object by interacting on it merely as another object." In other words when we say we are acting like a force, we say we don't have any sovereignty. We are like another object. A geophysical force has no sense of purpose or sovereignty.[94]

On one hand, then, the Anthropocene, as discourse, is a universal decolonizing project that challenges humanity's separation from, and superiority over, nature. A humanity based on a universalized (post) sovereignty, however, erases indigenous ways of knowing and being in favor of globalized technologies—geoengineering and "big science." Chakrabarty's characterization of sovereignty is based on a knowable, stable, and predictable geologic—one that Inuit scholars argue has never, and could never, exist.[95] Inuit did not sustain an "anthropogenic" sovereignty prior to colonization;[96] yet Inuit struggling for self-determination are required to adopt these frames in negotiations with Canada's federal government.[97] Technomanagerial approaches to the Anthropocene's ubiquitous, toxic, and indestructible wastes hinge on a sovereign approach to human–nature relations. The dangerous irony of the Anthropocene, then, is less that the possibility of sovereignty has collapsed and more that the various technologies predicted to "solve" our global environmental problems are framed through an understanding of sovereignty that always separates waste from resource, dirt from clean, and uncivilized from civilized—a configuration that, as the Anthropocene has already begun to show us, is inevitably doomed to failure.

NOTES

The authors gratefully acknowledge the financial support of the Social Sciences and Humanities Research Council of Canada (Insight grant 435-201300560) in conducting this research. The title of this chapter derives from the term used by white explorers to describe land in Canada's North. See, e.g., John Amagoalik, "Wasteland of Nobodies," in *Inuit Regain Control of Their Lands and Lives,* ed. Jens Dahl, Jack Hicks, and Peter Jull (Copenhagen: International Work Group for

Indigenous Affairs, 2000). The term is sometimes still used today, nearly always in discussions of Arctic sovereignty. See, e.g., Francis Harris, "Canada Flexes Its Muscles in Dispute over Arctic Wastes," *The Telegraph,* August 22, 2004, http:// www.telegraph.co.uk/news/worldnews/northamerica/canada/1496727/Canada -flexes-its-muscles-in-dispute-over-Arctic-wastes.html.

1. Iqaluit is the only city in, and the territorial capital of, Nunavut, Canada's largest and newest territory. In 2011, the population of Nunavut was just under thirty-two thousand people. Statistics Canada, *Focus on Geography Series, 2011 Census,* Catalog No. 98-310-XWE2011004 (Ottawa: Statistics Canada, 2011). Inuit make up approximately 85 percent of the territory's population, though this is significantly lower in Iqaluit. City of Iqaluit, *About Iqaluit: Demographics,* http:// www.city.iqaluit.nu.ca/. The median age of Inuit living in Nunavut is twenty-one. Statistics Canada, *Age Distribution and Median Age of Inuit by Area of Residence— Inuit Nunangat,* 2011, http://www12.statcan.gc.ca/. None of the communities in Nunavut are connected by roads, and the land area of territory is nearly 1.9 million square kilometers. Statistics Canada, *Focus on Geography Series, 2011 Census.*

2. The dump is reported to have self-ignited on May 20, 2014. Peter Varga, "City Can't Douse Iqaluit's Latest Massive Dump Fire," *Nunatsiaq News,* May 21, 2014, http://www.nunatsiaqonline.ca/stories/article/65674city_cant_douse _iqaluits_latest_massive_dump_fire/. This spontaneous ignition is caused by bacterial metabolism of the dump's abundant organic and inorganic material. The Iqaluit dump ignited spontaneously several times prior to the May 2014 fire. Fires in January 2013, December 2013, January 2014, and March 2014 lasted for less than a day each but are thought to have contributed to the current landfill fire. A fire starting September 26, 2010, lasted for thirty-six days. Tony Sperling, "Iqaluit Landfill Fire Control," PowerPoint presentation given to Iqaluit City Council, June 12, 2014, slides 6–9.

3. Nunavut Department of Health, "Bulletin: Questions and Answers Iqaluit Dump Fire—Air Quality," released July 18, 2014. The press release was distributed July 18; however, the "women of childbearing age" clause was amended on July 31 to only warn "pregnant women, as well as those who may become pregnant" against breathing in the dump smoke. Nunavut Department of Health, "Bulletin: Questions and Answers Iqaluit Dump Fire—Air Quality," released July 31, 2014. By this time, information from the original press release had already been reported widely. Dr. Maureen Baikie, the territory's chief medical officer, reported that an eight-week air quality monitoring study in Iqaluit showed that, for a given twenty-four-hour period, pollutants in the smoke are "at values that are well below environmental guidelines and standards." Peter Varga, "Iqaluit Dump Fire Smoke Not a Public Health Emergency, GN Says," *Nunatsiaq News,* August 4, 2014, http://www.nunatsiaqonline.ca/stories/article/65674iqaluit_dump_fire_smoke _not_a_public_health_emergency_gn_says/. For a more in-depth discussion, see Alexander Zahara, "The Governance of Waste in Iqaluit, Nunavut" (master's thesis, Queen's University, 2015).

4. Sperling, "Iqaluit Landfill Fire Control," slide 57.

5. The dump fire was eventually extinguished on September 16, 2014.

6. Robert V. Eno, "Crystal Two: The Origin of Iqaluit," *Arctic* 56, no. 1 (2003): 63–75.

7. Environmental Sciences Group of Royal Roads Military College, *Environmental Study of a Military Installation and Six Waste Disposal Sites at Iqaluit, NWT,* vol. 1, *Site Analysis* (Ottawa: Indian and Northern Affairs Canada/Environment Canada, March 1995).

8. Terry Dobbin (Iqaluit City Councilor), letter to the editor, "Iqaluit Needs Help with Contaminated Site Cleanups," *Nunatsiaq News Online,* January 14, 2013, http://www.nunatsiaqonline.ca/stories/article/65674iqaluit_needs_help_with _contaminated_site_clean-ups/.

9. Warwick Anderson, "Crap on the Map, or Postcolonial Waste," *Postcolonial Studies* 13, no. 2 (2010): 169–78.

10. Myra J. Hird, "Waste, Environmental Politics, and Dis/Engaged Publics," *Theory, Culture, and Society* (forthcoming).

11. Sarah A. Moore, "Garbage Matters: Concepts in New Geographies of Waste," *Progress in Human Geography* 36, no. 6 (2012): 787.

12. See Mary Douglas, *Purity and Danger: An Analysis of the Concepts of Pollution and Taboo* (London: Routledge, 1966), and Julia Kristeva, *Powers of Horror: An Essay on Abjection,* trans. Leon S. Roudiez (New York: Columbia University Press, 1982).

13. Dipesh Chakrabarty, "Postcolonial Studies and the Challenge of Climate Change," *New Literary History* 43, no. 1 (2012): 1–18.

14. *Iqalummiut* is the term used locally to describe those living in Iqaluit and includes both Inuit and Qallunaat (non-Inuit) community members.

15. Qikiqtani Inuit Association, *Qikiqtani Truth Commission Final Report: Achieving Saimaqtigiiniq,* 2010, http://www.qtcommission.com/.

16. As *Windspeaker* columnist Zebedee Nungak remarks, "traditionally, Inuit society was garbage-less. All our stuff was either edible by dogs, or naturally degradable." Nungak, "Introducing the Science of Qallunology," *Windspeaker* 24, no. 18 (2006), http://www.ammsa.com/publications/windspeaker/introducing -science-qallunology.

17. *Iqaluit* is Inuktitut for "place of many fish." The Hudson Bay Company established an outpost in the area in 1914.

18. Qikiqtani Inuit Association, *Qikiqtani Truth Commission Final Report.*

19. Eno, "Crystal Two: The Origin of Iqaluit," and Mélanie Gagnon and Iqaluit Elders, *Inuit Recollections on the Military Presence in Iqaluit* (Nunavut, Canada: Nunavut Arctic College, 2002).

20. See Qikiqtani Inuit Association, *Qikiqtani Truth Commission: Community Histories 1950–1975,* 2013, http://www.qia.ca/en/node/17, for detailed community histories, including explanations of why colonization in Canada's North did not occur until the twentieth century. Frank James Tester, "Can the Sled Dog Sleep? Postcolonialism, Cultural Transformation and the Consumption of Inuit

Culture," *New Proposals: Journal of Marxism and Interdisciplinary Inquiry* 3, no. 3 (2010): 7–19, provides further discussion of socioeconomic changes during this time.

21. Frobisher Bay was the name given to the community by European settlers until the city council voted to change it to Iqaluit in 1987. During this time it was common to use the terms *native, metis,* or *Eskimo* when referring to Inuit people. These terms are now considered pejorative or simply incorrect. *Eskimo,* for example, is a Cree term meaning "eater of raw meat." Quotations from J. Fried, "White-Dominant Settlements in the Canadian Northwest Territories," *Anthropologica* 5, no. 1 (1963): 57–67.

22. Fried, "White-Dominant Settlements in the Canadian Northwest Territories," 58.

23. John J. Honigmann and Irma Honigmann, "How Baffin Island Eskimo Have Learned to Use Alcohol," *Social Forces* 44, no. 1 (1965): 73–83.

24. Gagnon and Iqaluit Elders, *Inuit Recollections on the Military Presence in Iqaluit,* 28.

25. Marie Lathers, "Towards an Excremental Posthumanism: Primatology, Women, and Waste," *Society and Animals* 14, no. 4 (2006): 419. See also Alexander R. D. Zahara and Myra J. Hird, "Raven, Dog, Human: Inhuman Colonialism and Unsettling Cosmologies," *Environmental Humanities* 7, no. 1 (2015): 169–90.

26. P. Whitney Lackenbauer and Ryan Shackleton, *When the Skies Rained Boxes: The Air Force and the Qikiqtani Inuit, 1941–64* (Toronto: Munk School of Global Affairs, 2012), 8.

27. Anderson, "Crap on the Map," 170–71.

28. Gagnon and Iqaluit Elders, *Inuit Recollections on the Military Presence in Iqaluit.*

29. Lackenbauer and Shackleton, *When the Skies Rained Boxes,* 10.

30. Gagnon and Iqaluit Elders, *Inuit Recollections on the Military Presence in Iqaluit.*

31. E.g., see Phyllis Harrison, ed., *Q-Book: Qaujivaallirutissat* (Ottawa: Department of Northern Affairs and National Resources, 1964), and Charles Thompson, *Patterns of Housekeeping in Two Eskimo Settlements* (Ottawa: Northern Science Research Group, Department of Indian Affairs and Northern Development, 1969).

32. Gagnon and Iqaluit Elders, *Inuit Recollections on the Military Presence in Iqaluit*; Harrison, *Q-Book*; and Lackenbauer and Shackleton, *When the Skies Rained Boxes.*

33. Matthew Farish and P. Whitney Lackenbaur, "High Modernism in the Arctic: Planning Frobisher Bay and Inuvik," Journal of *Historical Geography* 35, no. 3 (2009): 520.

34. Ibid., 518. The quotation is from Alvin Hamilton, minister of the Department of Northern Affairs and National Resources under Prime Minister John Diefenbaker.

35. Ibid., 523, emphasis original.

36. Qikiqtani Inuit Association, *Qikiqtani Truth Commission Final Report*; Gagnon and Iqaluit Elders, *Inuit Recollections on the Military Presence in Iqaluit*; Thompson, *Patterns of Housekeeping in Two Eskimo Settlements*.

37. Warwick Anderson, "Excremental Colonialism: Public Health and the Poetics of Pollution" *Critical Inquiry* 21, no. 3 (1995): 640–69.

38. Thompson, *Patterns of Housekeeping in Two Eskimo Settlements*, 13, 23, 17, 27, 14–15, 23.

39. The Department of Northern Affairs and National Resources later became the Department of Indian Affairs and Northern Development in 1985 and Aboriginal Affairs and Northern Development Canada in 2011. Note the reiterated association between the aboriginal peoples and development.

40. Harrison, *Q-Book*, 8, 10, 64.

41. John S. Milloy, *A National Crime: The Canadian Government and the Residential School System, 1879–1986* (Winnipeg: University of Manitoba Press, 1999), provides a detailed history and description of Canada's residential school systems from 1879 to 1986. The closing events for Canada's Truth and Reconciliation Commission on residential schools were held in Ottawa in 2015.

42. Qikiqtani Inuit Association, *Qikiqtani Truth Commission Final Report*.

43. Thompson, *Patterns of Housekeeping in Two Eskimo Settlements*, 20, 29.

44. *Nunavut* means "our land" in Inuktitut. Prior to April 1, 1999, Nunavut was part of the Northwest Territories (NWT).

45. Prior to colonization, Inuit did not have surnames and, because Inuktitut was an oral language, first names did not have consistent spelling. In 1941, all Inuit were given E-numbers (Eskimo-numbers), which allowed the government to accurately collect "census information, trade accounts, medical records and police records." The E-number system ended after 1968, when the NWT's Project Surname requested that all Inuit select a surname to be used by government officials. See Sarah Bonesteel, *Canada's Relationship with Inuit: A History of Policy and Program Development* (Ottawa: Indian and Northern Affairs Canada, 2006), 38.

46. The term *Inuit* means "real human beings." *Inuk* is singular.

47. Gary W. Heinke and Jeffrey Wong, *Solid Waste Composition Study for Iqaluit, Pangnirtung, and Broughton Island of the Northwest Territories* (Northwest Territories: Department of Municipal and Community Affairs, 1990).

48. Exp Services Inc., *City of Iqaluit Solid Waste Management Plan* (Brampton, Ont.: Exp Services, 2013), prepared for City of Iqaluit.

49. Zebedee Nungak, "Ratcheting Garbage to a Federal Affair?," *Windspeaker* 22, no. 8 (2004), http://www.ammsa.com/publications/windspeaker/ratcheting-garbage-federal-affair.

50. John Sandlos and Arn Keeling, "Claiming the New North: Development and Colonialism at the Pine Point Mine, Northwest Territories, Canada," *Environment and History* 18, no. 1 (2012): 5–34.

51. Leo Heaps, *Operation Morning Light: Terror in Our Skies—The True Story of Cosmos 954* (New York: Paddington Press, 1978).

52. Joanna Kafarowski, "Gender, Culture, and Contaminants in the North," *Signs* 34, no. 3 (2009): 494–99.

53. "Pedal to the Pipeline," *Up Here: Life in Canada's Far North,* July/August 2014, http://uphere.ca/.

54. Government of Canada, Arctic Shipping Pollution Prevention Regulations (C.R.C., c. 353), Section 28: Sewage Deposit, http://laws-lois.justice.gc.ca /eng/regulations/C.R.C.,_c._353/.

55. Larissa Pizzolato, Stephen E. L. Howell, Chris Derksen, Jackie Dawson, and Luke Copland, "Changing Sea Ice Conditions and Marine Transportation Activity in Canadian Arctic Waters between 1990 and 2012," *Climate Change* 123 (2014): 161–73.

56. Rachel W. Obbard, Saeed Sadri, Ying Qi Wong, Alexandra A. Khitun, Ian Baker, and Richard C. Thompson, "Global Warming Releases Microplastic Legacy Frozen in Arctic Sea Ice," *Earth's Future* 2, no. 6 (2014): 315–20.

57. David Ljunggren, "Every G20 Nation Wants to Be Canada, PM Insists," Reuters, September 25, 2009, http://www.reuters.com/.

58. Michael Asch, "Governmentality, State Culture and Indigenous Rights," *Anthropologica* 49, no. 2 (2007): 281. The quotation is that of Asch paraphrasing Foucault.

59. In *R. v. Sparrow,* S.C.R. 1075 (1990), the Supreme Court of Canada declared, "There was from the outset never any doubt that sovereignty and legislative power, and indeed the underlying title, to such lands vested in the Crown." Ibid., 283.

60. The Canadian national anthem goes, "O Canada! Our home and native land! / True patriot love in all our sons command. / With glowing hearts we see thee rise, / The True North strong and free!"

61. Canada vies for its share of this pie with Russia, Norway, Sweden, the United States, Greenland, Iceland, and Finland.

62. Jessica Shadian, "Remaking Arctic Governance: The Construction of an Arctic Inuit Policy," *Polar Record* 42, no. 3 (2006): 249.

63. Chris Southcott, "Can Resource Development Make Arctic Communities Sustainable?," *Northern Public Affairs,* Spring 2012, 48–49.

64. Government of Canada, "High Investment Potential in Canadian Northern Oil and Gas," *Northern Oil and Gas Bulletins* 1, no. 1 (June 1994), https://www .aadnc-aandc.gc.ca/.

65. Shadian, "Remaking Arctic Governance," 250.

66. Government of Canada, *Canada's Northern Strategy,* http://www.north ernstrategy.gc.ca/, emphasis added.

67. Jack Kloppenburg Jr., "No Hunting! Biodiversity, Indigenous Rights, and Scientific Poaching," *Cultural Survival Quarterly* 15, no. 3 (1991), https:// www.culturalsurvival.org/publications/cultural-survival-quarterly/panama/no -hunting-biodiversity-indigenous-rights-and-scient.

68. Michael Bravo, "Science for the People: Northern Field Stations and Governmentality," *British Journal of Canadian Studies* 19, no. 2 (2006): 221–45.

69. E.g., see Warren Bernauer, "The Uranium Controversy in Baker Lake," *Canadian Dimension* 46, no. 1 (2012), https://canadiandimension.com/articles /view/the-uranium-controversy-in-baker-lake, and CBC News North, "Clyde River's Fight against Seismic Testing in Federal Court," April 20, 2015, http:// www.cbc.ca/news/canada/north/clyde-river-s-fight-against-seismic-testing-in -federal-court-1.3039744.

70. See, e.g., Kafarowski, "Gender, Culture, and Contaminants in the North," and Sandlos and Keeling, "Claiming the New North."

71. Shadian, "Remaking Arctic Governance," 253.

72. For an example, see Southcott, "Can Resource Development Make Arctic Communities Sustainable?"

73. The quotation is from Mary Simon's presentation to the International Conference on Arctic Cooperation: Militarization and the Aboriginal Peoples, Toronto, October 26–28, 1988, as cited in Shadian, "Remaking Arctic Governance," 256.

74. For a discussion of how Inuit knowledge has been considered in social science climate change research, see Emilie Cameron, "Securing Indigenous Politics: A Critique of the Vulnerability and Adaptation Approach to the Human Dimension of Climate Change in the Canadian Arctic," *Global Environmental Change* 22, no. 1 (2012): 103–14.

75. Frank James Tester and Peter Irniq, "*Inuit Qaujimajatuqangit*: Social History, Politics and the Practice of Resistance," *Arctic* 61, suppl. 1 (2008): 48– 61; Cameron, "Securing Indigenous Politics"; and Qikiqtani Inuit Association, *Qikiqtani Truth Commission: Community Histories 1950–1975*.

76. Sharon Ehaloak, paraphrased in Michele LeTourneau, "Planning Commission Slams Ottawa," *Northern News Service*, June 23, 2014, http://www.nnsl.com/.

77. Statistics Canada, *Median Total Income, by Family Type, by Province and Territory* (Ottawa: Statistics Canada, 2012), Table 111- 0009-CANSIM.

78. Information obtained from Aboriginal and Northern Affairs Canada via Access to Information Request: A-2013-01167.

79. Statistics Canada, *Smoking 2013* (Ottawa: Statistics Canada, 2013), http:// www.statcan.gc.ca/.

80. Department of Health and Social Services, *Nutrition in Nunavut: A Framework for Action* (Nunavut: Government of Nunavut, 2007).

81. Dr. Eduardo Chachamovich and Monica Tomlinson, with Embrace Life Council, Nunavut Tunngavik Inc., and the Government of Nunavut, *Learning from Lives That Have Been Lived: Nunavut Suicide Follow-Back Study 2005–2010* (Montreal: Douglas Mental Health University Institute, n.d.).

82. Sarah Rogers, "Boy, 11, Becomes Nunavut's Latest Suicide Statistic," *Nunatsiaq News Online*, July 1, 2014, http://www.nunatsiaqonline.ca/stories /article/65674_11-year-old_boy_is_nunavuts_latest_suicide_statistic/.

83. Sperling, "Iqaluit Landfill Fire Control," slide 2. Other engineers would emphatically define Iqaluit's municipal solid waste site as a dump, not a landfill.

84. Dru Oja Jay, "What If Natives Stop Subsidizing Canada," *The Media Co-op* (blog), January 7, 2013, http://www.mediacoop.ca/blog/dru/15493. See also the many responses given to the *National Post* when they asked readers how to go about "solving Canada's native issue." Paul Russell, "Todays Letters: Ideas for Solving the 'Native Issue,'" *National Post,* January 14, 2013, http://news.national post.com/full-comment/letters/todays-letters-ideas-for-solving-the-native-issue.

85. See Zahara, "Governance of Waste in Iqaluit, Nunavut."

86. CBC News North, "Iqaluit to Seek Military's Help in Tackling Dumpcano," August 14, 2014, http://www.cbc.ca/news/canada/north/iqaluit-to-seek-military -s-help-in-tackling-dumpcano-1.2736154.

87. For Rachel Qitsualik's discussions of Inuit self-sovereignty through Inuit cosmology and history, which she then compares with "anthropogenic" under-standings of sovereignty, see Rachel Qitsualik, "Inummarik: Self-Sovereignty in Classic Inuit Thought," in *Nilliajut: Inuit Perspectives on Security, Patriotism, and Sovereignty,* ed. Scot Nickols, Karen Kelley, Carrie Grable, Martin Lougheed, and James Kuptana, 23–34 (Ottawa: Inuit Tapiriit Kanatami, 2013).

88. Interview with Inuit Iqaluit resident (respondent 1), conducted on June 25, 2014.

89. Interview with Inuit Iqaluit resident (respondent 2), conducted on June 22, 2014.

90. These assertions of the absence of waste prior to colonization may be in-terpreted as reiterating the common colonial "noble savage" trope of the mythical Inuit living in harmony with nature—what postcolonial scholars have noted is invariably a construction of the colonial gaze. For a detailed discussion of how the "noble savage" and "dismal savage" tropes have been used in academic waste literature to silence indigenous voices and ontology, see Deborah Bird Rose, "Decolonizing the Discourse of Environmental Knowledge in Settler Societies," in *Culture and Waste: The Creation and Destruction of Value,* ed. Gay Hawkins and Stephen Muecke, 53–72 (Lanham, Md.: Rowman and Littlefield, 2003). We thank an anonymous reviewer for pointing out that tropes may also be used as a political strategy by indigenous people.

91. Derek Gregory, *The Colonial Present: Afghanistan, Palestine, Iraq* (Malden, Mass.: Wiley-Blackwell, 2004).

92. Arn Keeling and John Sandlos, "Environmental Justice Goes Under-ground? Historical Notes from Canada's Mining Frontier," *Environmental Justice* 2, no. 3 (2009): 123.

93. Myra J. Hird, "Waste, Landfills, and an Environmental Ethics of Vulner-ability," *Ethics and the Environment* 18, no. 1 (2013): 106.

94. Dipesh Chakrabarty, "History on an Expanded Canvas: The Anthro-pocene's Invitation," a keynote presentation delivered at the Anthropocene Proj-ect: An Opening, Berlin, Germany, January 10–13, 2013, http://hkw.de/en/app /mediathek/video/22392.

95. Emilie Cameron, Rebecca Mearns, and Janet Tamalik McGrath, "Translating Climate Change: Adaptation, Resilience, and Climate Politics in Nunavut, Canada," *Annals of the Association of American Geographers* 105, no. 2 (2015): 274–83, and Rachel A. Qitsualik, "Inummarik: Self-Sovereignty in Classic Inuit Thought," in Nickols et al., *Nilliajut: Inuit Perspectives on Security, Patriotism, and Sovereignty,* 23–34.

96. Qitsualik, "Inummarik: Self-Sovereignty in Classic Inuit Thought," 27.

97. For a more detailed discussion of Inuit and Western governance systems, see Jackie Price, "Tukisivallialiqtakka: The Things I Have Now Begun to Understand—Inuit Governance, Nunavut, and the Kitchen Consultation Model" (master's thesis, University of Victoria, 2007).

7

Gender Abolition and Ecotone War

JOSHUA CLOVER AND JULIANA SPAHR

We begin with a poem. We are both sometimes poets, so this seems apt. Moreover, poetry has not only a thick precapitalist history (in distinction, famously, to the novel, much less the newer media) but a historically privileged relation to representing the Anthropocene: it is at its beginnings often an anthropogenic mode for formalizing and cataloging ecological data such as the sorts of fish and of winds. It is such a poem we have chosen: the Hawaiian creation chant of the *Kumulipo*.

We want the poem to stand as an allegory for the historical development this essay traces. The allegory is not, however, in the poem's content, nor in its form—even if we linger on these for a moment, even if these are necessary elements in what will happen. The allegory blooms in the poem's material entanglement, its historical fate: how it was taken up and transformed by capital toward certain ends that it could not have foreseen.

The particular transformation in which we are interested concerns the remaking of an aggregate arrangement, various and elaborated and tending toward a whole, into a systematic differential purpose-built for the accumulation of capital. The distinction between difference and differential from which our argument develops identifies the historic internalization of the social into the political–economic, in a manner that preserves and produces difference at the level of lived experience only to homogenize it at the level of value production, where all difference becomes a potential lever for accumulation. We shall return to this analysis; for the moment, we might say that this transformation of difference into differential is one way to describe the character of the Anthropocene.

No such historical transformation happens in an instant, even in a given locale. Correspondingly, the dating of the Anthropocene remains open to general debate and to specific inquiries in cases like ours of Hawai'i. We hope the tracing of this allegory and this history will lead us toward a useful sense of how we date the era, toward a politics adequate to the present and an idea of where to intervene.

The *Kumulipo* is a good example of what poetry can look like before the Anthropocene. It is written in a social order both precapitalist and pre-Western contact. It enacts poetry's long history of engaging ecocomplexes. It is said to have been composed around 1700 by Keaulumoku, who, like Homer, may or may not be an avatar for a collective poet. Like many creation chants, it narrates the genesis of the world by listing a series of births. Unlike many creation chants, it tracks an evolutionary course, moving more or less up a phylogenetic chain. So the list begins with slime, then coral, then the burrowing worm, then the starfish, the sea cucumber, the coral-dwelling sea urchin, the kumimi crab, the whale. Humans do not show up until the eighth section of sixteen. The poem thus pivots on the following line: "from embryo the infant child has formed until now."[1] The chant is enumerative, but not merely enumerative. About sixty lines in, it begins a transition from the ocean to the area where the ocean and the shore meet, a new contrast or tension: the 'aki'aki seaweed next to the manienie shore grass, "the fragrant red seaweed living in the sea / Kept by the succulent mint living on land."[2]

Once set forth, the conjoined difference of land and sea becomes an organizing principle for the poem, alongside occasional clusters: a list of fish, a list of birds, a list of seaweeds, a list of taros. The concerns of the *Kumulipo* are larger than the charismatic megafauna that dominate the concerns of mainstream environmentalism. Still, these lists, as many lists in literature of this sort, tend to be anthropocentric; they are the plants and the animals that humans might need to survive. Despite its interest in the food plants and animals, however, the *Kumulipo* does not make a distinction between human and nature. It puts humans, one more list among the lists, in their place on land, while pointedly embedding them in the conjoined unity of land and sea that the poem works so hard to convey.

The meeting of land and sea is a paradigmatic *ecotone,* the meeting of two biomes: a transition zone, a contact zone, a space of flows. And those more knowledgeable about things Hawaiian, such as Rubellite Kawena Kinney Johnson, point to how the poem notices not only the dependencies between land and sea but also more complicated ecotones: open ocean, reef zone, coastal wetlands, dry and wet forest areas. It is also, and we think this is important, a beautiful poem that is expansive and inclusive.

And yet, ironically or inevitably, it becomes not just a poem elaborating the ecotone but itself part of that ecotone and its transformation. The poem is in circulation at the very moment of Western contact. It is said that the *Kumulipo* was chanted to James Cook on his landfall at Hawai'i: a consequential meeting of land and sea, to say the least. Cook, some say, was thought to be Lono-i-ka-makahiki (the Hawaiian deity of fertility, agriculture, and rainfall) come to life. This is 1788.

Let us make a claim, then, one that we will have to make good on. The "Anthropocene" is not simply a period but a set of forces. It is, among other things, the name for the set of forces that drive toward the meeting of *Kumulipo* and Cook. England's maritime and global power, of which Cook is an early emissary, will extend itself around the globe. Carl Schmitt's brief book *Land and Sea* offers a different sort of creation myth from the *Kumulipo,* but a related reminder.[3] Inevitably, with Schmitt, capital and empire trace the spatial dispensation of the globe, what he will later call *The* Nomos *of the Earth*—in this case the ambiguous undulations of the land–sea relation across centuries.[4] In the era after the Westphalian interstate system is settled, it becomes increasingly the case that land is the place of politics, sea the space of economy. This division corresponds to the rise of imperial capitalism; per Walter Raleigh, "whoever controls the seas controls the world trade; whoever controls world trade holds all the treasures of the world in his possession, and in fact, the whole world."[5] This is "the world" seen from Europe, the world as it will be organized by the first capitalist world empire. The *ur*-ecotone of land and sea, which initially appears as more or less primordial and natural, has become historical and social.

When exactly the Anthropocene began is much debated. Paul Crutzen and Eugene Stoermer, who proposed the term in 2000, begin by locating it "since the industrial revolution in 1750."[6] There has been some suggestion that Crutzen now wants to place the beginning of the Anthropocene with the first nuclear tests.[7] These are two of the three most persuasive datings on offer, basing themselves firmly in stratigraphic data. Simon L. Lewis and Mark A. Maslin, in a recent and critical revisiting, similarly offer two alternatives: 1610 and 1964.[8] The latter date aligns with Crutzen's second proposition concerning changes wrought by nuclear fallout. This underscores an initial problem with the periodizing hypothesis: if purely stratigraphic, it suggests, at a practical level, that our largely postnuclear age has solved its problem, and moreover that the ongoing climate collapse is extrinsic to the Anthropocene proper. In trying to locate the social existence of the Anthropocene, we are compelled to take more seriously the remaining two dates bequeathed us herein, designating colonialism at a global scale and the rise of industrial production. An influential essay by Dipesh Chakrabarty uses 1750 as well for its working assumption.[9]

We might add here that the 1610 dating shares some logical puzzles with the 1945/1964 holding. In Lewis and Maslin, their technical rationale comes from the dip in atmospheric CO_2: "the impacts of the meeting of Old and New World human populations—including the geologically unprecedented homogenization of Earth's biota—may serve to mark the beginning of the Anthropocene."[10] The tension between 1610 and the latter eighteenth century is between the colonization's privative destruction of common life and the coming of capitalist modernity with its compulsions toward ever-increasing productivity. Here the case of Hawai'i proves not unique but perhaps uniquely suggestive in the relative unity of these two events; the moments of its contact with empire and of the launch of the Industrial Revolution that will swiftly bestride the planet are one.

As the Anthropocene develops, the *Kumulipo* is carried along into the contemporary by its role in the complicated history that is the Pacific. A poem of beginnings, it is present no less at the ends of things. It was translated into English in 1897 by Queen Liliuokalani while she was under house arrest in Iolani Palace, having suffered a coup d'état by the emissaries of Anglophone capital.[11] Three moments then: *composition, contact, coup*. This alliteration feels easy. If it offered a complete story, it would be another wherein a poem exists both within colonial capture and as struggle through resistive translation, a struggle that has had uneven success.

But this is only part of the story. Squarely amid these events falls the

Great Māhele, the moment in the 1830s when Hawai'i produces its first constitution and bill of rights, taking on the formal characteristics of a modern sovereign state, albeit one that would shortly be subjected to the iron law and discipline of colonization and international markets.

The variegated array of oppositions or confrontations or pairings figured by this history that begins with the land and sea and then swiftly proliferates can scarcely be enumerated, much less resolved, herein. It would take a poem as sustained as the *Kumulipo* just to name them. But to quickly enumerate some of the issues: the Great Māhele generated more than a constitution and bill of rights. As Lilikalā Kame'eleihiwa notes, it "transformed the traditional Land systems from one of communal tenure to private ownership on the capitalist model."[12] Kamehameha III, in an attempt to avoid losing the lands to the takeover by Americans (but not in the name of America at this point), divides the islands among 245 chiefs. The islands are apportioned into wedges, pointedly, including both the shore and the interior, a literalization of the attention to the intersections between these zones that defines the *Kumulipo*. Land and sea—every wedge a contact zone now, every wedge a site for differential flows.

One can often hear it said that Kamehameha III was wily in this move to privatize the islands because these wedges are ecologically attentive in how they acknowledge the relationship between land and sea. But we can't help noticing how the poem's ecopoetics are so easily applied to the onset of Western capitalist modernity and, in fine dialectical fashion, mediate this onset as well. Most of this land, of course, ends up sold or leased to those who are not Hawaiian. As Kame'eleihiwa writes, "in the sweep of history, it is but a short step from the 1848 adoption of private ownership of 'Āina to the 1893 overthrow of the Hawaiian government."[13]

This is what is sadly compelling about the trajectory of the *Kumulipo*: its own transformation—we almost want to say transubstantiation—over the period we are considering and the way this is entangled with the problem of capital as such. If the poem of *ecotone* produces an *ecopoetics* at its inception, this is transformed into a full-blown *ecopolitics* by the time of Hawai'i's extended confrontations with Western powers and concomitant collapse of sovereignty at the end of the nineteenth century. State of nature to nature of state.

But this genitive inversion risks concealing what will turn out to be its content: how the chant becomes saturated with capital, with the logic of private property rights, with enclosure and primitive accumulation in the style that is specific to a variety of Pacific archipelagos, and, within that, the historical onset of wage and commodity relations, the possibility for exploitation through a new mode of production that will restructure circulation in turn and in full, drawing Hawai'i into a global space of flows.

This is not the poem's original content but becomes its unstated and unsayable substance. We see here in the story of the *Kumulipo* an ecological account of capital's internalization, and leveraging, of differentials toward the maximized rates of value accumulation—the way in which islands, nations, people, are brought into the "world-system" of capital.

And now another story with a similar structure, a structure that becomes evident when set next to the previous tale. This one about gender. The gender distinction does not arise with capitalism, obviously. And yet just as capitalism was spectacularly successful in using the ecotones that are represented in the *Kumulipo,* capitalism has been spectacularly successful in using the gender distinction toward its own ends. When Sylvia Federici narrates capitalism's onset, she points first to a feudal system in failure, to a crisis that went on for more than a century, endured from 1350 to 1500. And then she points to how the European ruling class response was what we now call primitive accumulation, or the conquest, enslavement, robbery, and murder that would be among, as she notices, the "bloodiest and most discontinuous in world history."[14]

Departing from Marx's focus on how capitalism produced and generalized the waged industrial proletariat, Federici enumerates how capitalism takes up and preserves the gender distinction to make possible its profound transformations. Women who refuse are called witches and hunted down. And primitive accumulation, she notes, depends on raced, gendered, and aged difference. And it is through these, she writes, "imposed divisions—especially those between women and men—that capitalist accumulation continues to devastate life in every corner of the planet."[15] We note her term "division" as a suggestive mediation of our terms "difference" and "differential," to which we will return shortly.

Much of the mainly Italian Marxist feminism of the 1970s explores the impact of this subjugation hundreds of years later. When Mariarosa Dalla Costa and Selma James turn their attention to this in *The Power of Women and the Subversion of the Community,* they speak of the role of the working class housewife as "indispensable to capitalist production."[16] The subjugation of women to the role of housewife who cares and feeds and otherwise maintains labor power, and provides this service to capital without any direct wage—here Leopoldina Fortunati has provided the most rigorous account—is a necessary condition for capital's capacity to extract surplus value toward accumulation on a world scale, capital's sine qua non.[17]

These materialist-feminist arguments are of their time. In many ways, these responses are entangled with the global crisis of capitalism arising in the period 1968–73, a crisis that raised specific questions around value production and productive labor and the related struggle over who ought be calculated as the properly revolutionary subject. It was distinctive in how it invited reconsiderations of capitalist value production that did not limit themselves to the assumption that value arises only in the scene of industrial and manufacturing production. The question of *where* value is produced arrives with a concomitant question: *and by whom?*

This is only one of a wide variety of contradictory responses to this moment offered by the various and divergent ideologies that get grouped under the term *feminism*. Feminism is all too frequently another tool that capitalism is able to use for its own ends; much of first world feminism takes the form of calls for more and better paid work for women, and not always all women at that. This makes a feminist-based theorization of, and resistance to, the environmental destruction of the Anthropocene complicated and perhaps contradictory, though it seems fair to note that ecological and feminist thought are historically conjoined, not least in the ways in which they can and have been used to affirm and manage capitalist accumulation, particularly in moments of crisis.

That said, the feminist inquiry that oriented itself from the question of value production indicates the moment in which a gendered critique *internal* to Marxist political economy becomes possible. The moment that is "Wages for Housework" provides an interesting example of what an anticapitalist feminism might look like. Kathi Weeks usefully summarizes many of the reasons to be suspicious of this thirty-year-old feminist project: methodological fundamentalism, universalizing claims, and the reductionism haunting the claim that the role of the working class housewife is the determinant position of all other women, and so on. Still, the series of short manifestos demanding wages for housework can be understood to mobilize the rhetoric of better-paid work for women so as to critique how capitalism uses the gender differential to preserve the necessary space of unpaid labor toward the reproduction of labor power, the laboring body, and its support apparatus in the domestic sphere. Per Weeks, this "disturbs the model of separate spheres, demanding that we map across the borders of the public and the private, between the realms of work and family."[18] In Dalla Costa and James's terms, the gendered family and its domestic sphere function to preserve the proletariat in its capacity to valorize capital. Without this unpaid "women's work," capital could not generate accumulation; such preservation of both capital and proletariat nexus is therefore necessarily at the expense of women. They write,

> On this family depends the support of the class, the survival of the class—but *at the woman's expense against the class itself.* The woman is the slave of a wage-slave, and her slavery ensures the slavery of her man. Like the trade union, the family protects the worker, but also ensures that he *and she* will never be anything but workers. And that is why the struggle of the woman of the working class against the family is crucial.[19]

It is worth lingering, at this pass, on the distinction we have drawn between difference and differential. One might bracket the question of whether gender difference exists in any essential way and still recognize two things. One, it had salience as a lived experience before the advent of colonialism, or capitalism, or the Anthropocene. Two, capitalism seizes upon it, transforms its social character, and becomes itself the producer of the gender difference. It is often overlooked that Judith Butler's celebrated argument regarding gender as performance, *Gender Trouble: Feminism and the Subversion of Identity,* takes its subtitle directly from "The Power of Women and the Subversion of the Community." The space between the accounts is clear enough. For Dalla Costa and James, the production of gender, of the subject "woman" (epitomized for them in that ceaseless supplier of domestic labor, the housewife), is unpaid labor for capital: "*The role of women,* in other words, has always been seen as that of a psychologically subordinated person who, except where she is marginally employed outside the home, is outside production; essentially a supplier of a series of use values in the home."[20]

Gender functions *for capital* not as difference but as differential, as a socially arbitrated and ideologically naturalized gap in wage levels (whether women are waged or not) across which surplus value flows. It is a sort of development of underdevelopment at the level of the household. The underlying argument is importantly elaborated in the essay "The Logic of Gender: On the Separation of Spheres and the Process of Abjection," written by the Endnotes collective, who name the sphere of labor not directly mediated by the market as "abject." Abject labor is wageless; wageless work makes women; the abject and unwaged work of women makes valorization possible at the levels necessary for capital's self-expansion. As they remind us, this sphere of labor "is obviously not abject *per se*—it exists as abject because of capital, and it is shaped by it. There is always this remainder that has to remain outside of market-relations, and the question of who has to perform it in the family will always be, to say the least, a conflictual matter."[21] "Wages for Housework," clarified thusly, identifies the making-inoperable of capital with the annihilation of an unpaid and gendered domestic sphere and thus cannot but take an abolitionist position. Indeed, we might suggest that the idea of gender abolition *is* the idea of annihilating the value-productive differential as applied to the specific category of gender and, furthermore, that this identity is itself an artifact of capital rather than of any given analysis.

This line of reasoning brings us again to the matter of the Anthropocene. We find ourselves now in what is not a *similar* but the *same* crisis of accumulation that arises in the 1960s and is often assigned to the global collapse of profitability in 1973, its underlying volatility never having been resolved. But we discover now an added valence. In our moment, the crisis cannot be located in the limits of value production but is located in the limits posed by ecological destruction. We say "limits" here knowingly, with some ironic despair, aware that we might expect so much more devastation that we will look back at this moment and wonder at how blithely we kept onward. And it has been interesting in these last few years to see Marxism begin its turn toward ecology, for example, in the work of John Bellamy Foster, Matteo Gagliardi, Minqi Li, and Jason W. Moore.

The turn is late. It is easy to blame Marxism for its perverse failures to grapple with changes in this most material of conditions, and we sometimes do, but the belatedness should not disqualify it. For Marxism provides us not simply with the necessary ruthlessness of its critique but with the analytic capacity to name the dynamic of destruction adequately. As each intensification of crisis presents a new set of underthought problems and limits for accumulation, we should expect, indeed *demand,* of our moment a flowering of Marxist-ecological thought equivalent to the moment of Marxist feminism. Similarly, we should demand of our Marxist feminism an attention to the ecological.

But we cannot simply leap from problematic to problematic—not even additively, when, as Hegel reminds us, "the truth is the whole." The task before us is to think the two moments of crisis together: episodes that seem to belong temporally to the 1970s and the present, while being marked with the problematics of feminism and ecology. Inasmuch as we have already insisted that from the perspective of capitalist accumulation, this is a single crisis developing over time and appearing differently in different moments, we can in turn insist that an adequate and absolute opposition to crisis capitalism (which is to say, capitalism *tout court*) must turn to synthesize the problematics of ecology and feminism at the level of the whole.

We might understand the conceptualization of the Anthropocene as a registration of the need for such a new totalization of "nature and culture" or, more capaciously, nature and history. Such efforts have arrived too often at the problem of "modernity" and within various progress narratives, indexing the particulars of ecological anthropogenesis to concrete developments. The era has been aligned with the development of the modern world system, where the two hemispheres become connected and trade becomes global, with Watt's steam engine, just four years before Cook arrives in Waimea Bay, with the technologies of ecocide, with fossil fuels taking pride of place. These form themselves into a cruel litany, a verso to the *Kumulipo*'s recto.[22] But there is a risk in identifying the Anthropocene, via its coincidence with industrial technologies or through an accounting of specific damages, with technical developments, as if these were a constitutive part of what capitalism is. Such imaginings have led to the idea that we can develop our way out of ecological crisis. For all the weight on *industrial,* on the dark satanic mills and chlorofluorocarbons, capitalism is not technology. *Capitalism is a real relationship among people*—one that internalizes relationships that precede it and is compelled to preserve these relationships through technological development and systemic expansion. It makes these relations historical.

Capitalism depends on multiple differential relationships. Gender has already provided us one clear example via the Marxist feminist analysis, wherein the seemingly natural gender difference is remade in a new social mode—*capitalist patriarchy,* let's say—necessary for accumulation. Race is an equivalently clear example of this historical seizure of exploitative relations for a particular differential mode.[23] No less the ecological.

Rather than saying, as people sometimes like to say in response to libertarian market utopians, that *state makes markets*—rather than saying this, we will insist that *capital makes differentials.* And, as the dialectic turns, *differentials make capital.* The drive to bring together the most cost-effective means of production with the lowest wages is intrinsic to capital's expansion and intensification, which is to say, it constitutes the Anthropocene; this can be done only through the production of social relations in which multiple differentials are presupposed. And this presupposition in turn can articulate why the many redistributive solutions on offer have little purchase on the problem; maldistribution is a form of appearance for necessary differentials, not an incidental outcome. Maldistribution is itself a constitutive part of value production rather than an unfortunate effect. There is no such thing as capitalism without ongoing and intensifying maldistribution.

In contemporary popular discourse, the reality of long-term intensifying maldistribution has had no greater proponent than Thomas Piketty.[24] In many regards, however, Piketty considers this maldistribution a political outcome rather than the condition of possibility for capital; inevitably, his only imagined remedies prescribe conventional political struggles toward mild wealth redistribution. The destructive inadequacy of such a "solution" is only multiplied when the argument is then applied to ecological catastrophe.

This is precisely the course plotted by law professor Jedediah Purdy. In his essay "Time Bomb," Purdy calls for "real conflict, not its facsimile."[25] This call depends from the revelations provided by Piketty in tandem with the latest United Nations climate reports. The lesson he takes from this combination, following Piketty, is that "climate change also presents distributive questions." This is inarguable. Immediately confusing these effects with causes, however, Purdy enters into a desultory fantasia wherein mild redistributive measures would some-how affect the direction or even rate of climate change:

> Other big questions for climate policy are even more explicitly distributive. Suppose there were a successful effort to charge for greenhouse-gas emissions—a carbon tax. Where would the pay-ments go? Would emissions rights be doled out free to industry according to historical levels of pollution—basically a subsidy for past polluters? Would they be sources of public revenue? Or might they create something like Alaska's oil-financed Permanent Fund, a stream of payouts to individual citizens? The latter alternatives would announce, in effect, that the global atmosphere belongs to the people of the world, that it is a global commons and that the right to use it comes from these owners and must benefit them. (James Hansen, the eminent climate scientist, calls this idea "cap and dividend.")[26]

As must always be the case, redistributive fantasies imagine a capitalism that somehow works for the mass of people, ostensibly in some way that also benefits ecology—by the simple measure of closing the differentials between rich and poor, climate secure and climate vulnerable, and so on. This misrecognizes what capitalism is at the most basic level; capital cannot expand (and expand it must) absent these differentials. This misrecognition finally flowers into the purest of absurdities: "Inequal-ity is driven by global capital flows."[27] In truth, global capital flows are driven by inequality: by wage differentials between places, genders, races; by the difference in resource extraction costs; by the kinds of exploitation that become possible only when some are dispossessed and others are not. These are aspects of the social relation from which value and profit arise.

The clarity of Purdy's error provides occasion to offer, as already sug-gested, a different alignment: between gender and the Anthropocene, as two social relations that have been both transformed and totalized into a kind of unity by the expansive and intensive drive of capital. Part of us wants to assert that the gender differential is being in part abolished by capitalism as more women enter both more and less developed econo-mies. As many have noted, there has been an uneven but continuing feminization of labor, both literally and figuratively, in the high-wage nations, a fact of deindustrialization and of declining real wages, which require higher amounts of wage labor from families. The expanding care industry, a result of women of caregiving age entering the workforce and having to hire care workers to do the reproductive labor that was once done by the housewife, has provided us with capital's version of "Wages for Housework."

But it is striking that this has not led to some imagined homogenization of the workforce, some dire equality of all against all, reduced to the lowest common denominator of simple labor. Instead, the feminization of labor seems like a series of moves within the preservation of differentials, driven by tendential wobbles in the trajectory of accumulation. As Jasper Bernes and Maya Gonzalez put it in a recent talk, "paradoxically, women enter the workforce as permanents and bring with them, as a structuring condition, the subordinate status that previously attended their intermittent participation."[28] Gender differentials are still necessary both to provide unpaid reproductive labor and to drive down wages. The gender differentials proceed entangled with a host of other productive differentials (and here we mean productive for capital), many of which are immediately apparent as ecological differentials. Here we might consider the economic differences between Global North and Global South, between high- and low-wage nations that allow for global wage arbitrage; we might draw forth the necessary differentials among resource extraction, production, assembly, and consumption-led nations. The preservation of these differentials, just as with the gender difference, allows for surplus value to flow.

Perhaps we are saying something as simple as that *differentials are capital's ecology*: not *difference*—we are not picking a fight with post-structuralists here—but rather the differentials that allow value to flow, to valorize and realize itself. This is true whether the differentials are familiarly ecological (as in the case of resource extraction or forcing other regions to bear one's toxic burden) or whether they do not appear particularly ecological at all (as in the case of childcare). Feminism, when it applies its attention to how differentials are used by capitalism and to further capitalism, might provide a useful tool in this complicated moment, but it is certainly not the only or sufficient analytic framework. These differentials exist at every stratum, from the household to the geopolitical, from the brute materiality of the shipping container to the ethereal whirring of financial circuits, from the sex work down the street to the start-up known as the Dating Ring currently flying New York women *of dateable age* to San Francisco to service the Bay Area's "soldiers of code."[29] The carbon footprint is just a beginning.

Ecological differential, and accompanying concepts such as "metabolic rift," leads us inexorably back to the term *Anthropocene*. A certain amount of acidic ink has already been spilled on this word. And much of this ink, such as Jason Moore's and others' insistence on the term *Capitalocene,* is legitimate—in part because it helps us spot the pitfalls in the path that is Chakrabarty's "Climate of History." In this essay, he claims that "the whole crisis cannot be reduced to a story of capitalism." And then he adds, "Unlike in the crisis of capitalism, there are no lifeboats here for the rich and privileged."[30] One gets the sense that he has little idea what the rich and privileged have been up to: lifeboat sales are up! But more significantly, the logic wherein a causal analysis can be disallowed because at some level of unfolding the causal dynamic will take down those who have most benefitted from it is an odd one.

Chakrabarty's essay is exemplary of certain conceptions of the Anthropocene as effacing previous differentials while disclosing a new, primary differential at the species level. This sentiment is vexed in several regards; we note merely that it is precisely the incapacity to think the Anthropocene *as itself constituted by compelled differentials and unfreedoms at every stratum* that makes analyses such as Chakrabarty's curiously inert and, moreover, lacking a logic whereby ecological struggles might both attune themselves to and solicit the engagement of other political antagonisms.

This is not to deny that there are clear gains in the language of the Anthropocene. To greatly foreshorten the arguments, one might point to Marxism's notable failure to think nature adequately in ways beyond its metabolic role in value-formation. The term *Anthropocene* might best be thought of as a struggle for a cognitive grasp on a unification of human and natural history that is at once more expansive and increasingly more pressing than modes of production construed narrowly as internal to but autonomous from the eco-epochal. These cognitive gains are useful to us to the extent that they do not forfeit the specificity of the Anthropocene as a fact of industrial capitalism, that strange fact that many partisans of the term seem intent on affirming and denying simultaneously. This contradiction may concern a certain difficulty in defining "industrial capitalism" in the first place. Otherwise, we are fine with the term *Anthropocene,* as long as it does not do what many fear it might: lead us away from the *Capitalocene.*

We have by now set forth more threads perhaps than can plausibly be tied up herein. It is late to be confessing this, but this essay is part of a larger project, one still very much in progress. In this essay, we were invited to think what happens when one puts the word *feminism* next to the word *Anthropocene* and how it might change this in-progress work. It has let us think about differentials and the flows across them, and the fate of these things in the era that some call the Anthropocene, and how we might attempt to puzzle our way out of them. The larger project is for now called "Ecotone War." An ecotone, as we have been suggesting, it not simply a meeting or an overlap, the intersection on a Venn diagram of ecologies. The regimes are in tension, *tonos.* The relationship is uneasy.

Nonetheless, the ecotone in its initial formulation, as a contact zone between differing ecologies, does not mean to be antagonistic. A space of flows is not itself a problem. Certainly we are not arguing that difference as such is a problem. The ecotone presented *within* the *Kumulipo* is not itself the sort of differential designed for value production. The ecotone toward which capital turns the *Kumulipo,* the ecotone of Cook's landfall, of the Great Māhele—that is a different matter. What Marx allows us to describe is the way that, in a certain historical passage, such spaces of flow must become spaces of value flow. Marx is clear that accumulation, labor exploitation, and ecological change mutually reinforce capitalism. Moore in his work builds from Marx's observations that changes in these dynamics are in this regard constitutive: "Every phase of capitalism emerges through a revolution in nature-society relations—new metabolic rifts, and much beyond—that creates new possibilities for the expanded accumulation of capital."[31] Britain's nineteenth-century industrialization, he points out, could not have happened without the agricultural revolution of the American Midwest. As he argues, left ecology has been limited by viewing "biospheric challenges as *consequences* of capitalism—rather than *constitutive* of the capitalist mode of production."[32]

It may be requisite to grasp both as true. As noted earlier, we see no real basis for the distributionist imaginary within which capital might develop its way out of crisis. Even John Bellamy Foster seems to fall prey to this as (writing with Brett Clark and Richard York) he ends *The Ecological Rift* with a call for "sustainable development" or an "ecology of consumption" in dialogue with an "ecology of production," a rationale that will prove consonant with a defense of, for example, Hugo Chávez's oil empire as a sort of positive entry in the ecological ledger because it funds a sort of socialism.[33] There is no exit from the Anthropocene via technological change. If there is an exit, it will be via an exit from the social relation that defines capital.

This will explain our insistence, apposite to Moore, on using the term *crisis* regularly herein. Crisis reduced to economistic terms is often understood as a more dramatic version of a business cycle; a properly Marxist account would insist that, as the world-system of capital expands, its crises expand as well toward some horizon beyond which they cannot continually recycle themselves. Just as economic crisis constitutes capital with its creative destruction, while signaling its self-undermining character, ecological crisis signals the limits of the capitalist world-system's ability to reproduce itself on an expanded scale. Like capital, ecological crisis is not simply cyclical but self-reinforcing, self-expanding—not like a wheel of fortune but like a Fibonacci sequence, and not amenable to the kind of reset function that "creative destruction" imagines.

In this larger project, we are trying to think with provocation, to insist on it really, to attempt to begin to be able to provide a reply to that Facebook moment when friends link to the latest scientific data on the melting of Artic sea ice, the melting of the tundra, the acidification of the ocean, and/or species extinction and then say, I can't get out of bed after reading this.

We want to get ourselves out of bed.

There is a risk in what we have provided to this point of falling into what might sometimes feel like a resolution, one routed through certain philosophical rhetorics of difference: largely ethical theorizations imbricated with ideas of allowing for the otherness of the Other. That might allow us a conclusion at once ethically clear and convivial: we call for difference not differential, heterogeneity not totalization, and so on.

We don't think it is that easy. We do not understand the transformation of difference to differential as a choice that was made and can be unmade. It is immanent to capital. When we come upon the *Kumulipo* within the context of 2015, we cannot read it as a representation of a lost world; to have such an understanding is always to misrecognize the mythic aspect of creation myths. Rather, the poem's blank enumeration enables its mobility and lability, enables it to testify about this present moment into which it is drawn. The story of the *Kumulipo* is indicative because it leads us to the coincidence of the colonial and capitalist turns that constitute the Anthropocene—but also because, in so doing, it leads us to the ur-ecotone of land and sea, which becomes within the period since the eighteenth century both literally and metaphorically the ur-ecotone of production and circulation. This is central to the history offered by Greg Dening, for example, in his study *Islands and Beaches*.[34] Anticolonial struggles might be thought of as a conflict that returns always to contact, located in the ur-ecotone where land and sea meet; this increasingly coincides with the struggle of capital itself.

And now we have arrived at the key terms of *struggle* and *intervention*. We are advantaged in approaching this by the manner in which capital struggles with itself. With the decline in profits from global manufacturing, a decline that manifested in the 1960s and entered into crisis in the 1970s, capital increasingly seeks its profits in circulation. As always, we glimpse this in the ascent of finance, the vast build-out in global shipping with which finance is entangled, the extension of supply chains, and the concomitant rise of logistics and resilience strategies. The disunity of production and circulation—trouble in the ur-ecotone of capital—takes the form of bubbles and blowouts, the spiraling crisis of the last forty-odd years. These ecotones are one, *Kumulipo* and capital. Where the poem was, now we find the port.

We hope by now the correspondences of our argument are at least available, if not in any regard complete. There are ecotones, which become productive within capital. They become productive because value can flow across them and continue in its expanded circuit; in return, capital weaponizes these ecotones into necessary, if veiled, antagonisms so that they can be preserved in all their value-capturing capacity. *The Anthropocene is not itself an ecotone but is the name for the making-productive of all these ecotones, and the mode of management which endeavors to preserve them as productive differentials.*

But we do not wish to discover in the immanence of this structure the despair of recognition that the enemy, being everywhere in general, is nowhere in particular. We have been trying to set forth a logic wherein practical choices can be made—choices that nonetheless elude the seemingly practical logic of redistribution, of pushing some value that has been drawn from one side of an ecotone to the other, back across the differential, and then watching it, nightmare-like, flow back again: the inevitable consequence of a politics of redistribution rather than abolition at every level.

Thus the siting of the port as an ecotonality where material intervention is possible. It is a transitional space—*transit,* after all—wherein the unity of conjoined spheres is mediated, where the conditions of one become the necessities of the other, and vice versa. A place where the mechanism requires and remakes differentials also discloses its own vulnerabilities in our present circumstance. The port is precisely the management of the differential, an apparatus through which value flows and is captured; it is like a condensation of the logic of the Anthropocene itself. Ports are the places where the underlying social relations of capital now present themselves. South African dock workers have realized this for some years now. In 2008, they refused to unload a Chinese ship loaded with armaments for Zimbabwe and, in 2009, to unload ships carrying goods from Israel, in solidarity with the Palestinians.

The year 2011 saw two port actions in the United States in that brief, heady moment that gets called by the name "Occupy": the November 2, 2011, shutdown of the Oakland port and then, a few weeks later, the less photographically spectacular but potentially more interesting West Coast follow-up, which suffered from an obeisance to pro-capital labor unions but presented as a horizon of the coordination of militant action among multiple locations, cities, states.

The problems with these actions are obvious: the uneasy relationship between anticapitalists and the strong unions of the port, the militarized port space, the flexible logistics networks between various ports along the West Coast. The failed Longview action (which, if it had happened, might have been the third port shutdown) was about all of these, but that is another sad and complicated story.[35] And there are many ways to think about these provisional and partial interventions: about their relation to port workers, especially the mainly unionized longshoremen and mainly nonunionized truck drivers; about their relation to property and dispossession in Oakland; about the conditions wherein it is possible to rally more than twenty thousand participants, perhaps far more; and about their limits: how even with such participation, it was able to interfere finally with but a fraction of the shipping industry for a brief period of time.

We do not intend to be nostalgic about those few weeks, that brief month or so. But we might echo here the recent arguments that have defined the left over the last twenty years: that workplace-based struggles—from factory occupations to worker-organized calls for better pay—are every day a less useful horizon for struggle in the Anthropocene. Most of the critiques of workerist activism eventually present some chart showing declining union membership or increasing provisionality of labor or any of the various ways that deindustrialization can be visualized. All well and fine, but we might add to this that the more pressing reason for skepticism regarding worker-based struggles is that, as labor has increasingly been compelled to take a preservationist stance in the face of global surplus population production, labor struggles that do exist no longer preserve an anticapitalist horizon and cannot but affirm the very differentials on which capital depends. Moreover, the shrinking space of industrial and manufacturing production in capitalism's historical core asks us to turn our analysis from production to circulation as a space of struggle—not struggles to circulate, to distribute *better*, but to make the operation of capital impossible.

We recognize that this analysis and our own lives have not yet earned the stridency of the term *war*, yet we want to insist on it here as aspirational.

If the port ecotone has a contemporary Other, it is the far less locatable space of banking itself, and specifically debt, where the compulsions of production are transformed into great bouts of circulatory liquidity. We take it as entirely unsurprising that the port shutdown should reappear on our shores (and reappear changed, having superseded the closed purview of union organizing) at the precise moment that struggle over debt achieves a qualitative intensification. Debt itself is the measure of a differential and, to revisit an earlier theme, a gendered one; the vast run-up of household debt since the 1970s is the same fact as the decline in manufacturing profitability, as the decline in real wages; it is itself an expression of the gender differential, of the necessary and necessarily unpaid labor required by capital, amplified by crisis.

So we recognize that these struggles take as their horizon abolition of both the ecological and the gender differential, of the relations wherein capital can continue to valorize and realize itself, wherein it must proceed with the ecological annihilation named the Anthropocene. We argue that these are conjoined struggles: that the struggles against capital and against gender cannot involve a rebalancing of them, as these equilibria, even when "working," are an ecocide machine, and thus that these struggles must be toward abolition of each, must become an *ecotone war* that will define the near future if we are to escape the Anthropocene alive.

NOTES

1. Rubellite Kawena Kinney Johnson, "The Kumulipo Mind—A Global Heritage—Kumulipo Version 2000," *Scribd,* April 19, 2013, http://www.scribd.com/, line 649.

2. Ibid., 66–67.

3. Carl Schmitt, *Land and Sea,* trans. Simona Draghici (Washington, D.C.: Plutarch Press, 1997).

4. Carl Schmitt, *The* Nomos *of the Earth in the International Law of the* Jus Publicum Europaeum, trans. G. L. Ulmen (New York: Telos Press, 2003).

5. As quoted in Schmitt, *Land and Sea,* 47.

6. Paul Crutzen and Eugene Stroermer, "Have We Entered the 'Anthropocene'?," Opinion section, *International Geosphere-Biosphere Programme (IGBP),* October 31, 2010, http://www.igbp.net/.

7. Paul Voosen, "Geologists Drive Golden Spike toward Anthropocene's Base," September 17, 2012, http://www.eenews.net/.

8. Simon L. Lewis and Mark A. Maslin, "Defining the Anthropocene," *Nature* 519, no. 7542 (2015): 171–80.

9. Dipesh Chakrabarty, "The Climate of History: Four Theses," *Critical Inquiry* 35, no. 2 (2009): 197–222.

10. Lewis and Maslin, "Defining the Anthropocene," 175.

11. Liliuokalani (Queen of Hawaiʻi), *The Kumulipo: An Hawaiian Creation Myth* (Boston: Lee and Shepard, 1897; repr., Kentfield, Calif.: Pueo Press, 1978).

12. Lilikalā Kameʻeleihiwa, *Native Land and Foreign Desires: Pehea Lā E Pono Ai? How Shall We Live in Harmony?* (Honolulu, Hawaiʻi: Bishop Museum Press, 1992), 8.

13. Ibid., 16.

14. Silvia Federici, *Caliban and the Witch: Women, the Body and Primitive Accumulation* (Brooklyn, N.Y.: Autonomedia, 2004), 62.

15. Ibid., 64.

16. Mariarosa Dalla Costa and Selma James, "The Power of Women and the Subversion of the Community," *Pétroleuse Press* (Winter 2010), http://petroleusepress.com/download.

17. Leopoldina Fortunati, *The Arcane of Reproduction: Housework, Prostitution, Labor, and Capital* (Brooklyn, N.Y.: Autonomedia, 1995).

18. Kathi Weeks, *The Problem with Work: Feminism, Marxism, Antiwork Politics, and Postwork Imaginaries* (Durham, N.C.: Duke University Press, 2011), 310.

19. Dalla Costa and James, "Power of Women," 25.

20. Ibid., 16, emphasis added.

21. Endnotes, "The Logic of Gender: On the Separation of Spheres and the Process of Abjection," *Endnotes* 3 (September 2013), http://endnotes.org.uk/issues/3.

22. Paul J. Crutzen, "Geology of Mankind," *Nature* 415, no. 6867 (2002): 23; Crutzen and Stroermer, "Have We Entered the 'Anthropocene'?"

23. Chris Chen, "The Limit Point of Capitalist Equality," *Endnotes* 3 (September 2013), http://endnotes.org.uk/issues/3.

24. Thomas Piketty, *Capital in the Twenty-First Century* (Cambridge, Mass.: Harvard University Press, 2014).

25. Jedediah Purdy, "Time Bomb," *POLITICO,* July 13, 2014, http://www.politico.com/magazine.

26. Ibid.

27. Ibid.

28. Jasper Bernes and Maya Gonzalez, "Home Is Where the Work Is: Looking Back at Feminization," lecture, Cruel Work: A Symposium on Feminism and Work, Mills College, Oakland, Calif., February 8, 2014.

29. Nitasha Tiku, "Startup Flying Dateable Women to San Francisco Like It's Imperial Japan," *Valleywag* (blog), March 4, 2014, http://valleywag.gawker.com.

30. Chakrabarty, "Climate of History," 221.

31. Jason W. Moore, "The End of the Road? Agricultural Revolutions in the Capitalist World-Ecology, 1450–2010," *Journal of Agrarian Change* 10, no. 3 (2010): 392.

32. "Transcending the Metabolic Rift: A Theory of Crises in the Capitalist World-Ecology," *Journal of Peasant Studies* 38, no. 1 (2011): 12.

33. John Bellamy Foster, Brett Clark, and Richard York, *The Ecological Rift: Capitalism's War on the Earth* (New York: Monthly Review Press, 2010), 418.

34. Greg Dening, *Islands and Beaches: Discourse on a Silent Land—Marquesas, 1774–1880* (Chicago: Dorsey Press, 1980).

35. Explaining many of these complications is Jack Heyman, "The ILWU Longshore Struggle in Longview and Beyond," *CounterPunch,* August 12, 2012.

8

The Anthropocene Controversy

JILL S. SCHNEIDERMAN

WHAT'S IN A NAME?

In *Life on the Mississippi,* a memoir of his days piloting a steamboat on the Mississippi River, American writer and humorist Mark Twain wrote,

> The military engineers of the Commission have taken upon their shoulders the job of making the Mississippi over again—a job transcended in size by only the original job of creating it. They are building wing-dams here and there, to deflect the current; and dikes to confine it in narrower bounds.... They are felling the timber-front... and ballasting it with stones.... One who knows the Mississippi will promptly aver—not aloud, but to himself—that ten thousand River Commissions... cannot curb it or confine it, cannot say to it, Go here, or Go there, and make it obey... cannot bar its path with an obstruction which it will not tear down, dance over, and laugh at.... But a discreet man will not put these things into spoken words; for the West Point engineers have not their superiors anywhere; they know *all* that can be known of their abstruse science; and so, since they conceive that they can fetter and handcuff that river... it is but wisdom for the unscientific man to keep still, lie low.... Otherwise one would pipe out and say the Commission might as well bully the comets in their courses and undertake to make them behave, as try to bully the Mississippi into right and reasonable conduct.[1]

As an earth scientist with a profound engagement with questions of social justice, I love this passage in which Twain foregrounds the issue of the earth's agency in relation to human attempts to control it. Now, almost two centuries after Twain wrote these words, we are, to use his language, "piping out" on the issue of human attempts to "bully" the earth. Recognizing that we live in a geological moment that allows us to observe the earth "tearing down, dancing over, laughing at" our efforts to restrain it, we geologists are trying to put this recognition into words. But we are embedded in controversy swirling around the proposal to acknowledge a new geological epoch. Scholars in the humanities are struggling with the concept and term too, and their perspective matters, especially if geologists crown a new epoch.

Nobel laureate Paul Crutzen and ecologist Eugene Stoermer proposed the term *Anthropocene* in 2000 in an obscure newsletter of the International Geosphere-Biosphere Programme. They intended the term to denote the contemporary global environment dominated by human activity. Suggesting that modern technology began to transform earth-system behavior and to substantially affect environmental processes, they presented the term *Anthropocene* to identify the time interval beginning, in their view, with the Industrial Revolution and the start of the human ability to shape earth's environment.[2]

The notion of the Anthropocene, however, has been expressed in the scientific literature for decades in several forms. In fact, since the early 1980s, Stoermer had been using the word *Anthropocene*; in the 1990s, the Chinese scientific literature under the influence of Chen Zhirong of the Institute of Geology and Geophysics at the Chinese Academy of Sciences referred to the Anthroposphere; and in his 1992 book *Global Warming, New York Times* journalist Andrew Revkin utilized the terms *Homogenocene* and *Anthrocene*.[3] Since Crutzen and Stoermer's introduction of the term at the beginning of the new millennium, the concept has enthralled thinkers from diverse arenas. Before 2003, the term produced 416 Web hits, while in 2011, that number had increased to more than 450,000.[4] The logarithmic increase in use of the word is obvious when one types into Google Ngram viewer the search term "Anthropocene" (Figure 8.1). Three scientific journals focusing on the topic have been established, *The Anthropocene, The Anthropocene Review,* and *Elementa,* and the term has been covered by an innumerable number of mainstream media outlets.[5] Recently, an exhaustive review of the current state of the debate in *Nature* by geographers from the

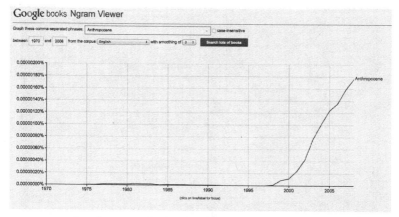

FIGURE 8.1. Google Ngram for "Anthropocene," showing rapid increase in use of the term.

University of Leeds reveals the rapid escalation of engagement with the idea by the scientific community.[6]

The word *Anthropocene* has become synonymous with the idea of human beings as a new driver of earth systems owing to the impact of anthropogenic changes to the earth's lithosphere, biosphere, atmosphere, and hydrosphere. In the geoscientific community, however, the idea of the Anthropocene as a formalized epoch on the geologic time scale (Figure 8.2) defined by rigorous stratigraphic standards is debatable.[7] Critics of a formalized Anthropocene epoch in the geologic time scale argue that it cannot be defined stratigraphically across the globe; that human activity is already a consideration in other geologic time periods; that it is better to view the Anthropocene culturally than geologically; and finally, that the word *Anthropocene* is semantically troubling for science. To counter these criticisms, proponents in the geoscience community produce global stratigraphic evidence to delineate the Anthropocene from the current geologic time period; argue for the distinction of the Anthropocene from other neighboring time periods; emphasize the need for a multidisciplinary approach to the question of an Anthropocene epoch; and defend the usage of the word, particularly in the practice of stratigraphy.

Scholars from academic realms beyond the geosciences are also debating the suggestion to designate as the Anthropocene the geological epoch in which we currently live. Numerous theorists have begun to highlight the limitations of the proposed nomenclature and have

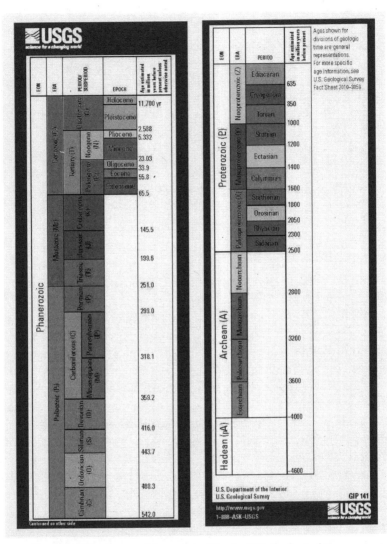

FIGURE 8.2. Geologic time scale approved by the U.S. Geological Survey, 2010. Courtesy of the U.S. Geological Survey.

contemplated the possibility of other monikers, such as Capitalocene, Chthulucene, Androcene, Corporatcene, Plasticene, or, one of my favorites, Petrolcene.[8] These proposals, whether taken at face value or not, imply that naming the Anthropocene is more than a geological endeavor. Rather, social concerns are legitimate matters in the debate, namely, unequal power relationships between varied groups of people, colonialism and European expansion into the Americas, impacts of globalized trade, economic growth, and reliance on fossil fuels. In this chapter, I explain why scientists and humanists are right to question the proposed time designation, reserve judgment on the geological facts of the scientific issue, and promote debate about which name to use should geologists recognize a new epoch of geologic time.

The Great Devonian Controversy

Today's controversy about using the term *Anthropocene* to designate the current geologic epoch parallels what historian of science Martin Rudwick dubbed the "Great Devonian Controversy."[9] Rudwick's scholarship on the disagreement about the dating of fossiliferous coals in England should remind us that arguing about the names of geologic time periods has an honorable place in the history of the science. The naming of what we now refer to as the Devonian period—a significant time between 416 and 358 million years ago in the Paleozoic era, when life abounded in the seas, plants and vertebrate animals proliferated and diversified on land, and which was named for Devon, England, where the rocks from this period were first studied—created controversy in the 1830s. An important debate in the geology then was the relative importance of fossils over rocks as the main criterion for determining the relative ages of rock strata.

Those involved in the scientific program of stratigraphic research at that time found consistent stratigraphic ordering of Britain's young rocks to be relatively simple because they are arranged almost like a layer cake, younger strata above older ones. But the more ancient rocks, from the Paleozoic era of our modern time scale (approximately 600 million to 225 million years ago) were more difficult to order. "Coal Measures" that formed from extensive fossil forests (the Carboniferous period of today's time scale, dating from about 360 to 280 million years ago) appeared near the top of the old (Paleozoic) rock pile and held economic as well as stratigraphic significance. But if geologists of the time could not determine what came before and after the coal layer, in the search for this source of energy, funds would be wasted in drilling through strata misinterpreted as young but actually older than coal. Arguments about whether rocks that contained plant fossils were old (Silurian) or young (Coal Measures) were resolved with an innovative suggestion that they were neither: the rocks containing the plants were representatives of a previously unrecognized time (the Devonian Period) in between the Silurian-aged rocks and the coal-bearing layers.[10]

Obviously, as we know, scientific knowledge is a social construct; scientific knowledge is not nature communicating directly with us about facts separate from the human context.[11] This is evident when one considers not only the name "Devonian" for a specific interval of geologic time but the names for the other periods of geologic time as well: the Cambrian, the classical name for Wales, and the Ordovician and Silurian, named after ancient Welsh tribes, were periods defined using stratigraphic sequences from Wales. As the Devonian was named for the English county where it was first studied, other periods of geologic time were named by different investigators for the locations at which they were first examined: Permian for a sequence of rocks in the region of Perm, Russia; Triassic for the triad of three distinct stratigraphic layers found throughout Germany and northwestern Europe; Jurassic for the extensive exposures of marine limestone in the Jura Mountains of Switzerland; Cretaceous for the extensive beds of chalk in the Paris basin (*creta*, Latin for "chalk").[12] Furthermore, since the first formation of the earth, multitudes of life-forms have developed and an increased array of diverse fossil organisms are available for distinguishing between episodes of geologic time. Thus, periods of the Cenozoic era are subdivided into epochs on the basis of the proportions of species of marine invertebrates in the fossil fauna still alive today. In sum, the justification for naming geologic periods has varied depending on the namer: geologic epochs have been named for locations, for physical divisions of rock layers, for the composition of such layers, and in case of the current Cenozoic era, for the types of fossils they contain.

Nevertheless, the consideration of the social setting in which science gets done does not imply that physical facts do not exist or, if they do, are irrelevant—a point that feminist philosopher of science Sandra Harding makes in defining feminist empiricism.[13] For example, the geologic record has recorded in thick layers of sediments the events of a period of time between 416 and 358 million years ago, but the rocks themselves might have been named something other than Devonian. The names given to all episodes of geologic time are based on social decisions. And as a geologist, I assert that we are right to debate the question of *what* we shall call the epoch in which we find ourselves to be living as both a scientific and a social decision.

Learning from Linnaeus

To choose smartly the name of a geologic epoch requires us to ask an additional question, that is, *why should* we, or, in the case of an already chosen name described above, *why did* we choose a particular name? My favorite example that illustrates the importance of asking this subsequent question comes from the scholarship of feminist historian of science Londa Schiebinger in her prize-winning book *Nature's Body: Gender in the Making of Modern Science,* in which she asks the question, why are mammals called mammals?[14] Throughout the book, Schiebinger shows that seventeenth- and eighteenth-century European social and political struggles influenced taxonomy and physical anthropology. Thus, natural historians of that time created a peculiar and enduring vision of nature that embodied the sexual and racial tensions of the time period. Schiebinger's chapter on the choice by renowned taxonomist Carl Linnaeus to name warm-blooded, hairy animals "Mammalia," even though *mammae* are not a pronounced unifying characteristic of this group, relates to my argument.[15] As Schiebinger points out, milk-producing mammae function only in half of these animals (the females), and only then for part of the time when they are lactating. Schiebinger reasons that Linnaeus could have chosen hair, three ear bones, or a four-chambered heart—ungulates, sloths, bats, sea cows, humans, and apes share these characteristics—as the defining feature of this group, but instead he made the female mammae the icon of the group. In doing so, he paved the way for thinking about females solely in terms of sexuality and underscored eighteenth-century women's position as nurturing caretakers.

Schiebinger asks, why did Linnaeus choose the name "Mammalia" when he might have chosen "Pilosa" (the hairy ones) or "Aurecaviga" (the hollow-eared ones)? She answers that cultural forces and pressing political trends molded his view of nature. As a physician and father of seven children, Linnaeus revered the maternal breast during this time when doctors and politicians were praising the virtues of mother's milk. Linnaeus was involved in the struggle against wet nursing that emerged alongside political realignments that undermined women's public power and attached new value to women's domestic roles.[16] Learning from Linnaeus and Schiebinger, we are right to ask, in my opinion, why choose *Anthropos* (Greek for human) as the namesake of a new epoch of geologic time? What do we obscure and what do we privilege with such a choice?

What Names Obscure / What Names Reveal

In considering the scientific community's questioning of the presence or absence of a new epochal boundary in the latest part of the Cenozoic era, I recall debates of twenty-five years ago about possible causes of the extinction that marked the end of the Mesozoic–Cretaceous/ Paleogene (Tertiary) boundary. These discussions had some geoscientists postulating a singular theory of mass extinctions all caused by asteroid impacts supposedly occurring every 26 million years. The purported cause of the asteroid impacts was the passing through the Oort Cloud of a hypothesized companion star to this solar system's sun that theoretically would produce periodic showers of comets raining down destruction on earth.[17] Scientists named the theoretical companion star "Nemesis," after the goddess of revenge. Though several studies claimed to have found periodic variations in such impacts, those simple periodic patterns seem to be statistical artifacts.[18] Recent results indicate that there is no evidence for periodicity in asteroidal impacts—so much for naming a supposed companion star of our sun after the goddess of destruction. Similarly, before attempting to name or critique a proposed name for a new epoch of geologic time, it is critical to understand the development of the geologic time scale as well as the structure of the scale itself.

DEEP TIME

Until eighteenth-century Scottish physician and gentleman farmer James Hutton made the discovery that paved the way for a science of geology, those who wondered about the age and history of earth could imagine only immense expanses of time. Anthropologist Loren Eiseley put it well when he wrote in *The Firmament of Time,*

> Time and Raindrops! It took enormous effort to discover the potentialities of both those forces. It took centuries before the faint, trickling from cottage eaves and gutters caught the ear of some inquiring scholar. . . . They could not hear it because they lived in a time span so short that the only way geologic change could be effected was by the convulsions of earthquakes, or the forty torrential days and nights that brought the Biblical Deluge.[19]

Still, as early as the fourth century BCE, Greek philosopher Aristotle speculated that the earth must have a long history. In attempting to answer the question of why fossil seashells were found entombed in mountaintop rocks, Aristotle supposed that oceans must have formerly covered terrestrial regions and therefore assumed slowness in geographical change and unlimited time to accomplish it. In the *Metamorphoses,* the Roman poet Ovid referred to these transpositions from land to sea, and Renaissance polymath Leonardo da Vinci, too, presumed that mountains must once have been coastline years in the past in order to contain seashells. In the eleventh century, the Persian polymath Ibn Sina speculated that long periods of time would be needed for the formation and destruction of mountains, and in China, Shen Kuo surmised enormous periods of time necessary to explain fossil shells embedded in rocks of high mountain ranges. These earliest inquiries about the earth's age and history fed the search for such understanding and led to the establishment of geology as a modern science.

Relative Time

In the late eighteenth century, Hutton developed a principle of an endlessly cycling *world machine*. Using that principle along with his subjective belief in the existence of a benevolent God, as well as field evidence from outcrops of rock, Hutton convinced his contemporaries that the earth was ancient—perhaps millions of years old. The "paradox of the soil," he said, was that in order to sustain life, soil depleted by farming must have a mechanism to refresh itself, replenish diminished nutrients, and survive to grow crops once again. This cycle would take time, because in his worldview, a benevolent God would never craft an earth that did not have a mechanism by which to recycle itself.[20] A closed loop of soil recycling would take enormous amounts of time—hence an ancient earth—and would be an ever-cycling world machine that would always sustain all living beings. In Hutton's most famous words, the earth showed "no vestige of a beginning—no prospect of an end."[21]

At an outcrop at Siccar Point, Scotland, Hutton found field evidence of vast time in the form of an angular unconformity—juxtaposed geological strata representing two different sets of environmental conditions—and hence a protracted gap in time (Figure 8.3). John Playfair, Hutton's confidant in science, wrote of their excursion to Siccar Point that, upon gazing at the unconformity, "the mind grew giddy" looking into the "abyss of time."[22] After Hutton, geologists attempted to determine the relative age of a rock outcrop, its history of deposition and deformation, and its spatial and chronological relationship to strata elsewhere on earth. Thus in the earliest stages of its development, the science of geology depended solely on relative dating of events based on the relative ages of rocks as determined by their contained fossils and stratigraphic positions. Units of geologic time were named as they were recognized and studied. As the section of this chapter dedicated to the Devonian controversy illustrates, the standard geologic time scale grew unsystematically.

Absolute Time

The earliest efforts to assign actual ages in millions of years to rock formations and to determine the age of the earth were done by estimating the amount of salt in the ocean, the average rate of deposition of sediment, and the rate of cooling of the earth. These attempts suggested only that the traditional concept of a six-thousand-year-old earth seemed impossible given geological observations. They led thinkers of the eighteenth and nineteenth centuries to suppose that the earth was at least tens of millions of years old. A means to measure geologic time, however, appeared only at the turn of the twentieth century with the discovery of radioactivity. Indeed, radiometric dating techniques

FIGURE 8.3. Angular unconformity at Siccar Point, Scotland, showing a gap in time between the deposition of two different sets of strata reflecting different environments of deposition. (Child standing on the unconformity surface.) Photograph courtesy of Jill S. Schneiderman.

have changed the way humans view our place in the vast expanse of time.

The titanic stretch of time that encompasses the first formation of the earth to the present moment is almost incomprehensibly enormous. The oldest materials known on earth (4.4 billion years old) are tiny grains of the mineral zircon found in sandstone from western Australia. The oldest rocks on earth (4.02 billion years old) come from northwestern Canada. Rocks of 3.4–3.6 billion years, metamorphosed lava flows and sediments, have been found in southern Africa and the Great Lakes region of North America as well as in western Australia. The debris from which the sedimentary rocks formed must have come from even older rocks of earth's earliest crust. Based on these facts, as well as the fact that the majority of the seventy well-dated meteorites (fragments of asteroids representing some of the most primitive material in the solar system) have ages of 4.4–4.6 billion years, scientists consider the earth to be 4.6 billion years old.[23]

Divisions of Geologic Time and the Significance of Mass Extinctions

Geologic time cannot be grasped using units of measurement for human history: months, years, decades, centuries, millennia, are too short for geologic time. Instead, geologic time is measured in eons, eras, periods, epochs, and ages—divisions of billions of years into millions, hundreds of thousands, and thousands. It is necessary to understand the way in which geologists divide up time in order to comprehend the geological debate about entry into a new epoch.

Eon is the largest division of the geologic time scale; the whole of geologic time comprises four eons: Hadean, Archean, Proterozoic, and Phanerozoic. Since the three oldest eons have few if any fossilized remains of ancient living creatures, each of these eons is minimally subdivided. In contrast, though it represents only 13 percent of earth history, the Phanerozoic is fossil rich, and geologists section it finely. Paleozoic, Mesozoic, and Cenozoic eras of the Phanerozoic eon are split into periods, and periods are partitioned into epochs, each recognized by its distinctive fossil flora and fauna (Figure 8.2).

The major boundaries between eras and periods are marked by mass extinctions—times when the earth loses more than 75 percent of its species in a geologically short interval. This has happened only five times ("the Big Five") in the past 540 million years or so (Figure 8.4). The first mass extinction event marks the end of the Ordovician period (443 million years ago), when roughly 86 percent of species were wiped out in no more than 2 million years. Since most life in the Ordovician existed in the sea, the numbers of marine organisms (e.g., trilobites, brachiopods, and graptolites) were reduced drastically. One current hypothesis for this extinction event is the onset of a severe global cooling with alternating glacial and interglacial episodes and associated cycles of falling and rising sea levels.

The most devastating mass extinction marks the end of the Paleozoic era (approximately 250 million years ago). Geologists often refer to this extinction event as the "Great Dying," because 96 percent of marine species died out in less than two hundred thousand years. It took millions of years to recover from this extinction event, and all life on earth today is descended from the 4 percent of species that survived it. Proposed causes of the event include global warming and ocean acidification triggered by a huge volcanic event.

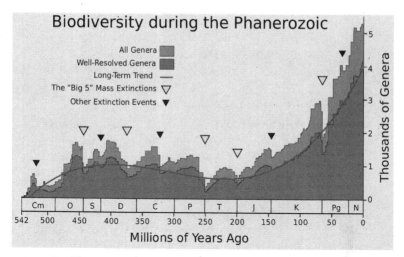

FIGURE 8.4. Phanerozoic diversity versus time and the five main mass extinctions. Albert Mestre, Wikimedia Commons, CC BY-SA 3.0. Originally in Robert A. Rohde and Richard A. Muller, "Cycles in Fossil Diversity," *Nature* 434 (March 10, 2005): 208–10.

Presumed to be the result of an asteroid impact, the extinction most prominent in the popular imagination ended the Mesozoic era.[24] Though infamous for the death of dinosaurs, scores of organisms— ammonites, flowering plants, and flying reptiles—perished. The impact in what is today's Yucatán peninsula caused a global transformation that included rapid cooling in a geological instant. It is in the context of identifying boundaries of geological time on the basis of extinctions of organisms that controversy about the Anthropocene takes place.

AMENDING THE GEOLOGIC TIME SCALE

Human Beings, the Sixth Mass Extinction, and a New Epoch

Most scientists would agree that humans are living through a sixth mass extinction because the world's species are vanishing at an unnaturally rapid rate. Some groups of human beings are altering the earth's landscape in sweeping ways: they have hunted to extinction animals such as the passenger pigeon and the West African black rhinoceros; chopped down broad swaths of forest; effected large-scale transfer of species from their natural habitats to new continents; created free-floating giant islands of plastic; and pumped billions of tons of carbon dioxide into the atmosphere and oceans, transforming the climate.[25] In fact, although percentages are still being debated, a 2007 report from the Intergovernmental Panel on Climate Change suggested that perhaps 30 percent of all species face an increased risk of extinction in the twenty-first century if the planet keeps warming rapidly.[26]

Although we have known about this vector of change, we have done little to shift its direction.[27] Toward the latter half of the nineteenth century, British naturalist Alfred Russel Wallace observed,

> We live in a zoologically impoverished world, from which all the hugest, and fiercest, and strangest forms have recently disappeared. . . . Yet it is surely a marvelous fact, and one that has hardly been sufficiently dwelt upon, this sudden dying out of so many large mammalia, not in one place only but over half the land surface of the globe. We cannot but believe that there must have been some physical cause for this great change; and it must have been a cause capable of acting almost simultaneously over large portions of the earth's surface, and one that, as far as the Tertiary period at least is concerned, was of an exceptional character.[28]

To explain the zoological impoverishment, Wallace hypothesized "a Glacial epoch":

> We have proof in both Europe and North America, that just about the time these large animals were disappearing, all the northern parts of these continents were wrapped in a mantle of ice; and . . . the presence of this large quantity of ice (known to have been thousands of feet if not some miles in thickness) must have acted in various ways to have produced alterations of level of the ocean as well as vast local floods, which would have combined with the excessive cold to destroy animal life.[29]

Though Wallace limited his supposition specifically to Europe and North America, some scientists assert that the extinction of the Cenozoic megafauna has been caused not by ice but by humans.[30] Though there is no agreement on this matter, when the chronology of extinction that began forty thousand years ago is compared with the pulses of

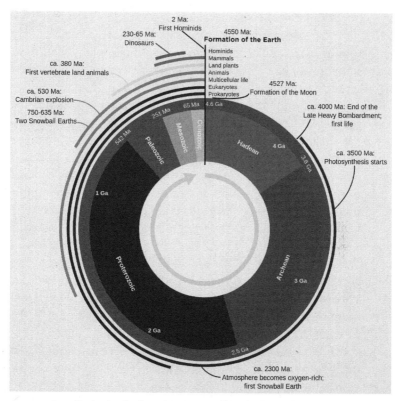

FIGURE 8.5. Geologic clock with events and periods. Ma = one million years ago; Ga = one billion years (gigayear) ago. Woudloper, Wikimedia Commons, public domain.

human migrations, the arrival of humans is a reasonable answer to the megafauna's disappearance. By this marker, we have moved into a new epoch. This is all the more remarkable given that, if we use a twenty-four-hour clock as an analogy for the whole of geologic time, humans appear very late in time—a fraction of an instant before midnight at the end of the twenty-four hours (Figure 8.5).

Some proponents of a new epoch cite distinct stratigraphic markers, such as human-induced erosion of landscapes through agriculture, construction, and dams, and the presence of mineraloid substances, such as plastic and glass in most recent sediments.[31] Furthermore, they assert that not only dramatic biotic change but also increased sensitivity to greenhouse gases make it likely that the earth has entered a stratigraphic interval unlike any previous interglacial during the Quaternary period. Since the markers of human actions will likely be visible in the geological record for millions of years to come, it is sensible to suggest that a new epoch has begun. To these scientists, the only question that remains is what to call this new epoch.[32]

The proposal to name an Anthropocene epoch originates in the awareness that human beings, acting in ways that are out of sync with the pace of geological time, are the chief cause of most contemporary global change. Nonetheless, one can argue that the choice of that particular name does not do justice to the true causes of the epochal change. The Anthropocene does not acknowledge that some groups of human beings have had greater effects on the planet than others. As Londa Schiebinger points out in her study of the use of the peacock flower as an abortifacient by West Indian women under colonialism, narratives mask or expose histories that depend on the perspective of the teller.[33] Scholars in the humanities and social sciences declare that the Anthropocene narrative represents humanity as an undifferentiated species assuming power over the rest of the earth system. But in the crucial field of climate change, for example, a large segment of humanity has not participated in the fossil fuel economy that has led to global warming.[34] So the choice of a name for the new epoch has the potential to obscure or reveal the agents of such change. That name will affect the stories people compose about the continuing development of human societies. Given the centrality of the concept of geologic time in the science of geology, as well as the implications beyond the natural sciences of a proposed new epoch, it behooves us to examine any proposals for a new division of time and the name selected to describe it.

The In/Significance of Stratigraphy

The formal administration of stratigraphic units within the geologic time scale is the work of the International Commission on Stratigraphy (ICS) and its parent organization, the International Union of Geological Sciences. The development, recognition, and amendment of the time scale through formal stratigraphic practice requires a systemized approach to define, delineate, and correlate sequences of rocks and to identify stratigraphically constrained units of time based on contained rocks, minerals, and fossils as well as chemical and physical parameters.[35]

The current chair of the ICS has argued that a specific time-stratigraphic unit cannot be found to define the Anthropocene because some areas of the world, such as the Americas, were cultivated later than other regions, including China and the Middle East.[36] This disparity in the onset of agriculture between locations based on levels of development across human history is also evident in Europe, where sediments from the advent of the Industrial Revolution are readily present in soils but found only there, not uniformly elsewhere. Another argument used to dismiss the Anthropocene designation is that stratigraphic boundaries can range up to many thousands of years, and because attempts to define a boundary for the beginning of the Anthropocene have focused on changes over the course of centuries, not millennia, any effort to identify stratigraphic boundaries in a traditional sense might be futile.[37] This concern is echoed by those who claim that introducing the Anthropocene into the geological time scale would create more problems than solutions, because it would force geologists to reexamine criteria for defining a geologic epoch.[38] Certain indicators of the Anthropocene also do not leave abrupt boundary layers in strata that would delineate the Anthropocene clearly. For example, although the rise of greenhouse gases in the atmosphere is well documented, this change did not occur rapidly enough to produce a discernible boundary layer based on the chemical signature of the greenhouse gases.

In response to the claims that the Anthropocene cannot be defined stratigraphically at a sufficient level to merit formal recognition as a geological epoch, other geoscientists offer several examples of distinct stratigraphic indicators as evidence of the Anthropocene—for example, human-induced erosion and denudation of landscapes through agriculture, construction, and, indirectly, the damming of rivers equates to a distinct lithostratigraphic signal.[39] Mineralogical, biological, and chemical evidence also offers distinct signals of a new geological epoch.[40] For example, the production of *mineraloids,* such as plastic and glass, amounts to the creation of new minerals that signal a new phase in the mineralogical evolution of the earth.[41] Human modification of the landscape is responsible for significant increases in terrestrial erosion and sedimentation and *has* produced mappable rock units of artificial deposits.[42] Increased extinction rates since the Holocene began *have* diminished certain kinds of creatures in the fossil record. Burning of fossil fuels *has* changed carbon and nitrogen ratios globally and caused particles from combustion to appear in sediments worldwide.

Proposals for the inception of a formal Anthropocene epoch that geologists are examining for their potential use as a globally synchronous marker include the following: impacts of early humans, including use of fire more than 2 million years ago; megafauna extinction fifty thousand to ten thousand years before present (BP); origin of farming eleven thousand years BP; extensive farming beginning eight thousand years BP; rice production starting sixty-five hundred years BP; production of anthropogenic soils five thousand to three thousand years BP; cross-continental mixing of humans and other biota beginning in 1492; decrease of atmospheric carbon dioxide in 1610; industrialization since 1760; detonation of nuclear weapon detonations in 1945; persistent application of industrial chemicals since 1950; and a global carbon-14 peak in 1964.[43]

Though most of the controversy within the discipline rests on stratigraphic principles, the proliferating use of the concept of the Anthropocene beyond geoscience also rankles some geoscientists. It has led them to ask if the drive to recognize the Anthropocene is political rather than scientific.[44] Given the use of the term by scholars from the humanities and social sciences, geoscientists argue that the Anthropocene should be considered only an epoch of *human* history marked by calendars and cultures rather than stratigraphic units.

Irrespective of what geoscientists think and how it affects the decision whether to define a new epoch called the Anthropocene, it's clear that the term has captivated popular and scholarly imaginations and developed a life beyond the geosciences.[45] This widespread appeal might be attributed to the fact that, as Ellis and Trachtenberg claim, the designation of a new epoch, regardless of what it is named, has moral content at its core.[46] Or perhaps that the study of the Anthropocene requires investigations not only in earth, life, and climate sciences but also in ethics, policy, cognition, and economic systems, to name just a few other relevant arenas, has caused numbers of civically minded people to awaken to reality. The multiple intersections make the recognition of a new epoch relevant beyond scientific enterprises. The Call of the Anthropocene pulls us to change our ways, to recognize the hundreds, if not thousands of years of human dominance of earth as well as social struggles between oppressors and oppressed.

Feminist scholars of science studies, such as Sandra Harding and Donna Haraway, have also theorized and demonstrated that knowledges are site specific. They are situated in space and time; they privilege varied but not subjective perspectives. To the extent that acknowledgment of a new epoch can enable perception of systems of oppression that have led humanity down this path, the stratigraphic debate is much less interesting than dialogues about the Anthropocene in which scholars across disciplines are engaged. Conversations such as these should challenge geoscientists to acknowledge that the concept of the Anthropocene requires cultural as well as geological engagement.[47]

Naming the Current Epoch

If one accepts the idea that there is convincing geological evidence for a new epoch (as I do), then there is clearly a need to name that epoch.[48] As I pointed out earlier in this chapter, the history of science shows that it is healthy for science to endure questioning about nomenclature from within and outside of the scientific community. So it is a good sign that scholars from varied disciplines have taken interest in and continue to challenge and propose alternative names for this new epoch. I believe that Crutzen and Stoermer, as well as subsequent geoscientists, intended well when they proposed the Anthropocene epoch. Without being an apologist for the geoscientific community, I think it is fair to say that Crutzen and Stoermer urged recognition of a new geological epoch to focus attention on the supersized and damaging effect of our temporally and spatially limited species, Anthropos, on the planet, all living beings and human cultures. Nonetheless, critiques from outside the geosciences enable the critical partial perspective from which most geoscientists do not see. Powerful critiques, especially from feminist and postcolonial theorists, rest on the self-centeredness of the name and studied ignorance of intersecting systems of oppression. The proposal to name an Anthropocene epoch contrasts with earlier discoveries in science, such as the Copernican revolution and Darwin's evolution by natural selection, that have shifted views away from the notion that humanity occupies the center of the universe and the highest rung on a ladder of evolution. If one concludes that the time has come to recognize a new epoch in history, whether human and/or geological, informed critiques of the move to name the new epoch lead to the need to reconsider divisions of geologic time and remain open to alternative nomenclature.

What matters to geologists when dividing deep time are global-scale changes driven by mechanisms such as plate tectonics, ongoing volcanic eruptions, or asteroidal impacts. Nonetheless, human beings, though geological latecomers, have induced intense global-scale changes. Altering the composition of the atmosphere, effecting changes in sea level, and reconfiguring the land surface logically lead to the proposition that the present should be identified as a new epoch rather than what is currently known as the Holocene epoch. Economic, political, social, and ethical implications will follow from wider understanding that human exploits are forcing thorough changes to a currently inhabitable earth. Much is at stake in this controversy, for unlike other geological units of time, the name and definition of this one will have consequences outside the geological sciences. If the epoch were to be viewed as starting with the use of fire, culpability for global environmental change would rest with all of humanity. In contrast, if the epoch were to be seen as beginning with industrialization, then responsibility for the global environmental crisis would reside historically with Europeans and North Americans, who would end up with proportionate obligations to the global community. Nonetheless, geologists from the ICS will use scientific evidence alone to decide whether to designate a new unit of geological time that acknowledges global environmental change induced by human beings.

CONCLUSION

In *Vibrant Matter: A Political Ecology of Things,* political theorist Jane Bennett theorizes a "vital materiality" that runs through and across bodies both human and nonhuman.[49] Her theory is congruent with that of sociologist of science Bruno Latour, who embraces the notion of the Anthropocene because, in his words, it holds promise for bypassing the so-called Great Divide of nature–culture.[50] The ideas of both these scholars also resonate with those of James Lovelock, the independent scientist, environmentalist, and futurist who evinced the idea of Gaia as neither person nor organism but the property of all the feedback systems that have operated, on the whole in a balanced way, so that over the last billion years of planetary history, life has been able to survive on earth. Perhaps Mark Twain said it best in concluding his essay "Was the World Made for Man?":

> Man has been here 32,000 years. That it took a hundred million years to prepare the world for him is proof that that is what it was done for. I suppose it is. I dunno. If the Eifel Tower were now representing the world's age, the skin of paint on the pinnacle knob at its summit would represent man's share of that age; and anybody would perceive that the skin was what the tower was built for. I reckon they would, I dunno.[51]

Metaphors such as this one help cultivate humility in the face of one particular fact: human beings occupy only a microsecond of geologic time. Poised as we are at this moment between the geological past and an uncertain future, an understanding of geological time and the scales by which we measure it, along with the societal implications of the choices made to identify and name its units, will help us choose language that fosters justice for the planet and all beings that inhabit it.

AFTERWORD

At the time of this writing, the Anthropocene Working Group (AWG) of the Subcommission on Quaternary Stratigraphy (a constituent body of the ICS, which is the largest scientific organization within the International Union of Geological Sciences) was set to provide its summary of evidence and provisional recommendations on a potential new geological time interval at the thirty-fifth International Geological Congress in South Africa. Reports have suggested that majority AWG opinion may comment as follows:[52]

- The Anthropocene concept articulated by Crutzen and Stoermer in 2000 is geologically real and is of ample scale to be considered as part of the geological time scale.
- The appropriate designation for the Anthropocene is "epoch" (rather than "age," "period," or "era").
- If the Anthropocene is adopted as an epoch, it would mean that

the Holocene epoch has ended but that we continue to exist within the Quaternary period and Cenozoic era.

- Impacts of human activity on earth are discernible in the stratigraphic record going back thousands of years beyond the Holocene. However, extensive and roughly synchronous worldwide changes to the earth system in terms of greenhouse gas levels, ocean acidification, deforestation, and biodiversity deterioration occurred during the "Great Acceleration" in human activity from the start of the Industrial Revolution in 1750 to the present. But the strongest and most distinctive collection of signals imprinted on recently deposited sedimentary layers coincides with the mid-twentieth century. Therefore the mid-twentieth century represents the best beginning of a potential Anthropocene epoch.

- Changes to the earth system that typify the potential Anthropocene epoch include noticeably accelerated rates of erosion and sedimentation; far-reaching chemical changes to the carbon, nitrogen, and phosphorus cycles; the onset of significant changes to the global climate and sea level; and biospheric changes such as unparalleled levels of species invasions across the earth. These are geologically long term and effectively irreversible changes to the earth system.

- Plastic, aluminum, concrete, and fly ash particles; fossils; artificial radionuclides; and changed carbon and nitrogen isotope patterns are signals in recent strata of changes made to the earth system by human activity. Many of these signals will remain in the earth's strata as a permanent record of past processes.

- A physical reference point in strata at one carefully selected place on earth where the best combinations of stratigraphic signals can be found would be used to mark the beginning of the Anthropocene. Once such a location is identified and confirmed, it would form the basis for the preparation of a proposal to the ICS to define a formal Anthropocene unit.

- The majority of members of the AWG have voted that the Anthropocene is stratigraphically real and that it should be formalized as an epoch of geological time. Most members of the AWG would take the time period around 1950, shortly after scientists exploded the first atomic bomb, as the beginning of the epoch and would expect plutonium fallout to be a primary signal of the onset of the Anthropocene.

NOTES

This chapter appeared in slightly different form as Jill S. Schneiderman, "Naming the Anthropocene," *philoSOPHIA* 5, no. 2 (2015): 179–201.

1. Mark Twain, *Life on the Mississippi* (Boston: J. R. Osgood, 1883), 206–7.

2. Paul J. Crutzen and Eugene F. Stoermer, "The Anthropocene," *Global Change Newsletter* 41 (2000): 17–18.

3. As noted in James Syvitski, "The Anthropocene: An Epoch of Our Making," *Global Change* 78 (March 2012): 14.

4. Ibid.

5. M. Ellis and Z. Trachtenberg, "Which Anthropocene Is It to Be? Beyond Geology to a Moral and Public Discourse," *Earth's Future* 2 (2014): 122–25.

6. Simon L. Lewis and Mark A. Maslin, "Defining the Anthropocene," *Nature* 519 (March 12, 2015): 171–80.

7. J. Zalasiewicz et al., "Are We Now Living in the Anthropocene?," *GSA Today* 4, no. 2 (2008): 4–8; Whitney J. Autin and John M. Holbrook, "Is the Anthropocene an Issue of Stratigraphy or Pop Culture?," *GSA Today* 22, no. 7 (2012): 60–61.

8. Donna Haraway, "Anthropocene, Capitalocene, Chthulucene: Staying with the Trouble," *AURA* (Aarhus University Research on the Anthropocene) (blog), May 9, 2014, http://anthropocene.au.dk; a video of the talk is available at http://vimeo.com/97663518; Peter Rugh, "Learning to Live in the Anthropocene," November 22, 2013, http://www.commondreams.org/; Christina Reed, "Plastic Age: How It's Reshaping Rocks, Oceans and Life," January 28, 2015, http://www.newscientist.com/.

9. Martin J. S. Rudwick, *The Great Devonian Controversy: The Shaping of Scientific Knowledge among Gentlemanly Specialists* (Chicago: University of Chicago Press, 1985).

10. Ibid., 57–60, 314–15.

11. Donna Haraway, "Situated Knowledges: The Science Question in Feminism and the Privilege of Partial Perspective," *Feminist Studies* 14, no. 3 (1998): 575–99.

12. John McPhee, *Basin and Range* (New York: Farrar, Straus, and Giroux, 1981), 95–100.

13. Sandra Harding, "Introduction: Beyond Postcolonial Theory: Two Undertheorized Perspectives on Science and Technology," in *The Postcolonial Science and Technology Studies Reader,* ed. Sandra Harding, 1–32 (Durham, N.C.: Duke University Press, 2011).

14. Londa Schiebinger, *Nature's Body: Gender in the Making of Modern Science* (Boston: Beacon Press, 1993).

15. Londa Schiebinger, "Why Mammals Are Called Mammals," ibid., 40–74.

16. Londa Schiebinger, "Why Mammals Are Called Mammals: Gender Politics in Eighteenth-Century Natural History," *American Historical Review* 98, no. 2 (1993): 383.

17. An asteroid is the remnant of a shattered planet or another asteroid that originally formed at about the same time as the earth. The Oort Cloud is a spherical cloud of icy planetesimals believed to surround the sun.

18. C. A. L. Bailer-Jones, "Bayesian Time Series Analysis of Terrestrial Impact Cratering," *Monthly Notices of the Royal Astronomical Society* 416, no. 2 (2011): 1163–80.

19. Loren Eiseley, *The Firmament of Time* (Lincoln: University of Nebraska Press, 1960), 10–11.

20. As quoted in Stephen Jay Gould, *Time's Arrow, Time's Cycle: Myth and Metaphor in the Discovery of Geological Time* (Cambridge, Mass.: Harvard University Press, 1987).

21. James Hutton, "Theory of the Earth; or an Investigation of the Laws Observable in the Composition, Dissolution, and Restoration of Land upon the Globe," *Transactions of the Royal Society of Edinburgh* 1, no. 2 (1788): 304.

22. As cited in Sir Archibald Alison et al., ed., *Great Men of Great Britain: Original Memoirs* (London: Charles Griffin, 1866), s.v. "Hutton, Dr. James."

23. USGS Geology in the Parks, "The Age of the Earth," October 31, 2014, http://geomaps.wr.usgs.gov/parks.

24. Anthony D. Barnosky et al., "Has the Earth's Sixth Mass Extinction Already Arrived?," *Nature* 471 (March 3, 2011): 51–57.

25. Elizabeth Kolbert, *The Sixth Extinction: An Unnatural History* (New York: Henry Holt, 2014); Jenna R. Jambeck et al., "Plastic Waste Inputs from Land into the Ocean," *Science* 347, no. 2663 (2015): 768–71.

26. Intergovernmental Panel on Climate Change Core Writing Team, "Summary for Policymakers," in *Climate Change 2007: Synthesis Report. Contribution of Working Groups I, II and III to the Fourth Assessment Report of the Intergovernmental Panel on Climate Change,* ed. R. K. Pachauri and A. Reisinger (Geneva: IPCC, 2007), https://www.ipcc.ch/.

27. See Naomi Klein, *This Changes Everything: Capitalism vs. the Climate* (New York: Simon and Schuster, 2014).

28. Alfred Russel Wallace, *The Geographic Distribution of Animals: With a Study of the Relations of Living and Extinct Faunas as Elucidating the Past Changes of the Earth's Surface* (Cambridge: Cambridge University Press, 1876), 150–51.

29. Ibid., 151.

30. See Gary Haynes, ed., *American Megafaunal Extinctions at the End of the Pleistocene* (Dordrecht, Netherlands: Springer, 2009).

31. Patricia Corcoran, Charles Moore, and Kelly Jazvac, "An Anthropogenic Marker Horizon in the Future Rock Record," *GSA Today,* 24, no. 6 (2014): 4–8.

32. Zalasiewicz et al., "Are We Now Living in the Anthropocene?," 4.

33. Londa Schiebinger, *Plants and Empire: Colonial Bioprospecting in the Atlantic World* (Cambridge, Mass.: Harvard University Press, 2007).

34. Andreas Malm and Alf Hornborg, "The Geology of Mankind? A Critique

of the Anthropocene Narrative," *Anthropocene Review* 1, no. 1 (2014): 62–69.

35. Autin and Holbrook, "Is the Anthropocene an Issue of Stratigraphy or Pop Culture?," 60.

36. C. Schwägerl and A. Bojanowski, "The Anthropocene Debate: Do Humans Deserve their Own Geological Era?" *Spiegel Online* (website), July 8, 2011: http://www.spiegel.de.

37. Autin and Holbrook, "Is the Anthropocene an Issue of Stratigraphy or Pop Culture?" 60–61.

38. Schwägerl and Bojanowski, "Anthropocene Debate."

39. Zalasiewicz et al., "Are We Now Living in the Anthropocene?"; J. Zalasiewicz, C. Waters, and M. Williams, "Potential Formalization of the Anthropocene: A Progress Report," in *Part XVII, Theme C: Applied Stratigraphy/The Quaternary System and Its Formal Subdivision, STRATI 2013: First International Congress on Stratigraphy: At the Cutting Edge of Stratigraphy,* ed. Rogério Rocha, João Pais, José Carlos Kullberg, and Stanley Finney, 999–1002 (Dordrecht, Netherlands: Springer Geology, 2014); J. Zalasiewicz, M. Williams, W. Steffen, and P. J. Crutzen, "The New World of the Anthropocene," *Environmental Science and Technology* 44, no. 7 (2010): 2228–31.

40. Zalasiewicz et al., "Potential Formalization of the Anthropocene."

41. The idea that human invention has produced new minerals is also in keeping with the recent propositions by mineralogists that, when one looks at the entirety of earth history, it appears that minerals, like organisms, also evolve.

42. J. Zalasiewicz et al., "The Technofossil Record of Humans," *Anthropocene Review* 1, no. 1 (2014): 34–43.

43. Colin N. Waters et al., "Evidence for a Stratigraphic Basis for the Anthropocene," in *STRATI 2013: First International Conference on Stratigraphy,* ed. R. Rocha et al., 989–93 (Cham, Switzerland: Springer, 2014); Lewis and Maslin, "Defining the Anthropocene," 171–80. Also see the afterword of Stanley F. Finney and Lucy C. Edwards, "The 'Anthropocene' Epoch: Scientific Decision or Political Statement?," *GSA Today* 26, no. 3 (2016): 4–10.

44. Finney and Edwards, "'Anthropocene' Epoch."

45. E.g., the Deutsches Museum in Munich, Germany, had a *Welcome to the Anthropocene* exhibition, running December 5, 2014, through January 31, 2016, that presented geology and environmental issues in relation to the proposed Anthropocene epoch.

46. Ellis and Trachtenberg, "Which Anthropocene Is It to Be?"

47. Ibid.

48. As I referred to earlier in this chapter, perhaps we should propose a name that is consistent with previous schemes of naming segments of the geologic time scale. Understanding the consistent semantics (as opposed to the inconsistent rationale for names of periods of the Paleozoic and Mesozoic, as discussed earlier in this chapter) is an important tool for settling on a name that achieves

the purpose of acknowledging a new epoch while at the same time avoiding the pitfall of the homogenization all of humanity.

As many people know, the suffix -zoic means "life"; thus Paleozoic is "ancient life," Mesozoic equates to "middle life," and Cenozoic refers to "new life." Mentioned earlier in this chapter, the epochs of the periods of the Cenozoic era are named to indicate the proportion of present-day (Holocene) organisms in the fossil record since the beginning of the Cenozoic era roughly 65 million years ago. Paleocene is derived from the Greek word palaios, meaning "ancient" or "old," and kainos, meaning "new"; Eocene is from eos, meaning "dawn" of the new; Oligocene is from oligos, meaning "few" or "scanty" new; Miocene is from meion, meaning "less" new; Pliocene is from pleion, meaning "more" new; Pleistocene is from pleistos, meaning "most" new; and Holocene is from holos, meaning "whole" or "entirely" new. Therefore, why not label the new epoch with a name that acknowledges the much less contested sixth extinction and increased diminishment of species on earth in this epoch? What could we name such an epoch?

When I asked a classics scholar what would be the Greek for diminished amount of new life, she explained that the antonym of pleistos (as in Pleistocene) would be elachistos and would be the prefix that might help me come up with a name that would acknowledge the diminished amount of species compared to the Holocene epoch. Though it isn't the most elegant English, Elachistocene would mean "least amount of new," and I propose that name instead of "Anthropocene," for it adheres to the geological schema yet avoids the homogenization of humanity so problematic in the term Anthropocene.

Though I would make a friendly amendment to Haraway's suggestion to name the new epoch the "Chthulucene" ("subterranean born") and propose "Chthulucene" as the name for the period to which the Elachistocene belongs, might we take the opportunity of naming our new geological epoch to consider the designation of the era as well? Theologian and scholar Thomas Berry wrote prolifically, pushing what he called "The Great Work"—the effort to carry out the transition from a period of devastation of the earth to a period when living beings and the planet would coexist in a mutually beneficial manner; the result would be the erosion of the radical discontinuity between the human and the nonhuman. This vision of the Ecozoic stands in stark contrast to the notion of the Eremozoic era imagined by renowned entomologist E. O. Wilson—the Age of Loneliness, when other creatures are brushed aside or driven off the planet.

49. Jane Bennett, Vibrant Matter: A Political Ecology of Things (Durham, N.C.: Duke University Press, 2010).

50. Bruno Latour, "Agency at the Time of the Anthropocene," New Literary History 45, no. 1 (2014): 1–18; Latour, "Facing Gaia: A New Enquiry into Natural Religion," lecture series, University of Edinburgh, February 2013, http://www.ed.ac.uk/schools-departments/humanities-soc-sci/news-events/lectures/gifford-lectures.

51. Mark Twain, "Was the World Made for Man?," in *Letters from the Earth,* ed. Bernard DeVoto, with a preface by Henry Nash Smith, 211–16 (New York: Harper and Row, 1962).

52. Press release, University of Leicester, August 29, 2016, http://www2.le.ac .uk/offices/press/press-releases/2016/august/media-note-anthropocene-working -group-awg.

FIGURE 9.1. Natalie Jeremijenko, *Tree Logic*, 1999. Massachusetts Museum of Contemporary Art (Mass MoCA). Photograph by Flickr user sharon_k. CC BY-SA 2.0.

9

Natalie Jeremijenko's New Experimentalism

DEHLIA HANNAH IN CONVERSATION WITH NATALIE JEREMIJENKO

In the courtyard outside the Massachusetts Museum of Contemporary Art (Mass MoCA), six live maple trees are suspended upside down from a high truss (Figure 9.1). Installed as a permanent exhibit in 1999, Natalie Jeremijenko's *Tree Logic* has undergone continuous transformation since the first set of trees adapted to their habitat and outgrew their steel containers and ultimately had to be replaced. If one visits the museum shortly after a new generation of trees has been planted, one observes straight-trunked, young saplings with their leaves and branches pointing directly toward the ground. Over time, the trees turn to grow upward toward the sun, forming strange and contorted-looking shapes in the process. Inside the planters, their roots also reverse course in response to the pull of gravity, an expression of gravitropism.

Tree Logic was also part of Mass MoCA's 2000 group exhibition *Unnatural Science,* in which context the contortions of the trees—both logical and physical—provoked audiences to voice enduring concerns about what science does to nature in the pursuit of knowledge. Indeed, the denatured trees illustrate well Francis Bacon's infamous maxim that "nature exhibits herself more clearly under the trials and vexations of art than when left to herself."[1] Although the trees appear as though they had been sculpted by human hands, the artwork actually exhibits the eminently natural phototropic response of the plants to their contrived environment. Meanwhile, in the woods out behind the mu-seum, retired generations of twisted trees have been replanted upright, only to reverse their direction of growth once more—a dubious return to nature that effectively constitutes a second phase in this ongoing artistic experiment.

Tree Logic was the provocation that eventually brought the authors of this chapter together for a conversation about the philosophical significance of art and experimental practices for this book. Natalie Jeremijenko is an artist and associate professor of visual art at New York University's Steinhardt School of Culture, Education, and Human Development, where she directs the xDesign Environmental Health Clinic. Holding degrees in fine arts, neuroscience, biochemistry, and history and philosophy of science, as well as a PhD in computer science and engineering from the University of Queensland, she has taught at the intersections of visual arts and engineering at Yale; the University of California, San Diego; the San Francisco Art Institute; and the Royal Melbourne Institute of Technology and has exhibited her work widely, ranging from museums (such as New York's Museum of Modern Art) to Web platforms, rock music festivals, urban parks, highways, and polluted riverbeds.

Dehlia Hannah is a philosopher of science, technology, and aesthetic theory who wrote about the use of methods and media of scientific experimentation in contemporary art in her dissertation, "Performative Experiments." At Arizona State University, she is research cura-tor of the Synthesis Center and an assistant research professor in the School of Arts, Media, and Engineering. Her work as a postdoctoral fellow at the Center for 21st Century Studies, and as co-organizer of the Anthropocene Feminism conference, led to the exhibition *Placing the Golden Spike: Landscapes of the Anthropocene* at the University of Wisconsin–Milwaukee's Institute of Visual Arts (INOVA, March 26–June 12, 2015), which she a co-curated with INOVA's director Sara Kra-jewski. The exhibition, which included work by Jeremijenko, addressed the question currently being debated by geologists of where we ought to place a "golden spike" to mark the beginning of the Anthropocene. Our conversation excavates our ongoing projects of thinking through material practices of scientific and technological experimentation as sites of imaginative and political world-making—a matter that the concept of the Anthropocene makes vivid.

A CONVERSATION

DEHLIA HANNAH (DH): I would like to highlight one respect in which your work, Natalie, initially struck me as exemplary for thinking through anthropocene feminism, namely, your seemingly unsentimental attitude toward nature as it has been conceived in environmentalism and also in some feminist ecocriticism. Long before we were talking about the Anthropocene, works such as your *Tree Logic* and *OneTrees* (1999), which explored notions of genetic and environmental determinism, provoked a lot cultural anxiety about violating natural norms.[2] By forcing trees to grow upside down and propagating genetically identical organisms at the height of debates about genetic engineering, Frankenfoods, and the Human Genome Project, you disturbed a lot of assumptions about what counts as a natural process or entity, even though you're actually using pretty conventional botanical practices in both cases. The concept of the Anthropocene suggests that the era of nature is over—if it was ever a coherent concept to begin with. Is there any room for being mournful now that there is no place left untouched by human hands? What do you make of the Anthropocene?

NATALIE JEREMIJENKO (NJ): What the Anthropocene asserts is that we are these major biogeochemical forces in the world. It's very much a demand to recognize that we are interacting in and with these natural systems for better or for worse, in sickness and in health, that we are enmeshed in them. And so the question is, what is our response? What is our responsibility? I think it's this idea that we have this enormous effect—therefore *we can have* an enormous effect. We can design it—as opposed to the paradigm we've inherited from traditional environmentalism, which is "conserve, preserve, leave no trace, do not touch, do as little damage as possible." It's a gestalt shift toward understanding that there's no doing that, there's no being outside of the system: we are here. It's a test of our agency.

As far as nature goes—when would we go back to? Prior to World War II? Prior to World War I? Prior to getting thrown out of the Garden of Eden? What are we pointing to preserving?

DH: Well, that solves the problem of where we should place the golden spike—right outside the gates of the Garden of Eden! But getting back to the matter of getting back to nature (or not), let's talk about your approach to entangling and imbricating ourselves even further in our environments and also with their politics and economics. You've done things like wrestle with a rhinoceros beetle, kiss frogs with antifungal lip balm, feed nutritious and detoxifying food to fish, make cotton candy out of bee pollen (Figure 9.2), build bridges through urban spaces for bees and butterflies, cultivate wetlands with the explicit purpose of using them to remediate oil spills, eat and drink the milk of critters that are ecologically important, burn junk mail to create fertilizer for public parks, and use child labor to make art. In short, where old-school environmentalism would teach us to let nature go its own way, your approach is to experiment, manipulate, and intervene *more*.

That puts you in some interesting company from a philosophical perspective. There's a long tradition from romanticism to critical theory to feminism that construes the scientific and technological manipulation of nature in a very negative light. Francis Bacon, the so-called father of modern experimentalism, is a lightning rod for criticism. Johann Wolfgang von Goethe criticizes him for silencing nature through torture; Theodor Adorno and Max Horkheimer indict him for the instrumentalization of reason in the attempt to gain technocratic control over the world; Carolyn Merchant and Sandra Harding hold him responsible for advocating an exploitative and misogynistic attitude toward nature, women, and nonhuman Others. But by the early 1980s, with the rise of history and sociology of science, there was a call from the philosopher Ian Hacking to go "back to Bacon" and pay closer attention to experimental practices, a move that initiates what's known as the New Experimentalism in recent philosophy of science. Insofar as it is attentive to the materialities, contingencies, and context of scientific practice, it's an approach that's quite resonant with feminist epistemologies, especially with Donna Haraway and Karen Barad's excavations of the inextricable entanglement of social, discursive, and material phenomena. I've come to think of you, Natalie, as the Francis Bacon of anthropocene feminism, an experimentalist informed by the concerns of feminism and environmentalism but very willing to subject nature—or whatever passes for nature these days—to the vexations of art.

FIGURE 9.2. Natalie Jeremijenko, *FLOWERxFLOSS,* 2013. The project uses bee pollen and isomalt to create a cotton candy–type confection that promotes bio-diversity in the lower gut. Photograph courtesy of Natalie Jeremijenko.

NJ: That's exactly where I'd like to be situated, because it's fundamentally about who produces knowledge and how it's produced, whether
or not the peer-reviewed academic journal article is the icon of
knowledge or if there's a much more convivial, socially situated,
embodied, contextual knowledge production process that I think
is embodied by experiments, or what I call lifestyle experiments.

DH: So how do you go about opening up the space of inquiry so that
knowledge production is something that happens with the collaboration of many different people, critters, and nonhuman agents
or agencies?

NJ: There are a couple of contrasts to make. Let me address your comments by talking about some specific examples. There's a series of
projects around shorelines—*MUSSELxCHOIR*, the *Amphibious
Architecture* array—that really are about a huge cultural question
at stake post–Super Storm Sandy as we reinvent the relationship
between terrestrial and aquatic spaces. These are part of a larger
project called *Unshoreline*. Conventional urban designs have these
hard-edged promenades, and the reclamation and rejuvenation of
the waterfront are taking away from industry to create bike lanes
and highways. And yet I would argue that this fails drastically to
speak to what really can work and how could we redesign our relationship to natural systems in this context, which is a big public
question, because we all bear the risk of how our public infrastructure is designed. This is an example of socialized risk, and yet who
gets to design those interventions has been privatized. How they get
designed is through large city contracts awarded to master planners,
and the most invisible are the huge contracts to large corporate engineering firms that have a stranglehold on the public purse. They
have no incentive whatsoever to experiment. In contrast, I think it's
important to talk about small-scale material practices that really
do enlist diverse opinions. One example I want to share is from the
2013 Creative Time Sand Castle Competition at Rockaway Beach.

DH: Let me offer a bit of context: as I remember it, the 2012 competition was a lighthearted hipster affair, with a balanced showing of
kitschy and minimalist, conceptual sand castles. But the following
year's competition must have felt far more momentous—even the
decision to hold the competition was controversial. In the interim,
the entire beach had been washed away by Super Storm Sandy,

FIGURE 9.3. Rockaway Beach boardwalk after Super Storm Sandy, 2012. Photograph by Flickr user Roman Iakoubtchik. CC BY-SA 2.0.

uprooting the foundation of the wooden boardwalk and sending it crashing into nearby homes and businesses like a giant surfboard on the floodwater (Figure 9.3). The Rockaways suffered enormous damage from the storm, raising ongoing political debate in New York City about whether and how the shoreline and local community should be rebuilt for greater resilience, especially in light of the fact that the frequency of such extreme storms can only be expected to increase as a consequence of climate change.

NJ: I was one of a number of artists who were invited to participate in the competition last summer, so I took my Cross[x]Species Construction Company to build sand castles (Figure 9.4). The firm is made up of organisms that actually are involved in constructing and reconstructing beaches. All of the organisms that I brought along were named after politicians and activists who have actually created public spaces. I learned a really interesting lesson from Enrique Peñalosa the fish, who was a diggity fish. [DH: A former mayor of Bogotá and recent Colombian Green Party candidate, Enrique Peñalosa is an influential scholar of sustainable urban design and an advocate for the democratization of transportation.] He was in this front aquarium—and he was the diggiest fish that I could find. These cichlid fish dig in the sand to create their nests and then protect this territory and manipulate the local environment, not

FIGURE 9.4. Natalie Jeremijenko, Cross[x]Species Construction Company at 2013 Creative Time Sand Castle Competition, Rockaway Beach, New York. The "company" is made up of organisms and plants that purify water and sand. Photograph courtesy of Natalie Jeremijenko.

dissimilarly to the "man's house is his castle" kind of thing. I got this fish from the Petco on Union Square, where I'd gone in to find a diggity fish, and they'd actually given him to me for free because he was so aggressive and diggity in that he'd killed a couple of other fish. And he had been given to the store by a Good Samaritan who had found him in a plastic bag on the streets of New York City. So this the backstory to Enrique Peñalosa the fish, who was incredibly diggity. But when I put him in the tank at the competition and put in some local sand, he sulked; he didn't actually perform at all for this crowd (Figure 9.5)! He in fact just did nothing. I took him home upset with him because we didn't win the sand castle competition.

I kept getting these algae blooms in the tank, and I had never had algae blooms in the tank before. It was interesting to me because I'd swap out the water and then I'd get another algae bloom and then I'd swap out the water again. For three weeks this went on, where I kept getting these algae blooms in the tank, in this

FIGURE 9.5. Natalie Jeremijenko, Cross[x]Species Construction Company at 2013 Creative Time Sand Castle Competition at Rockaway Beach, New York. The aquarium on the right, which houses a cichlid fish, shows the unexpected algae blooms resulting from nutrient-rich sand imported to Rockaway Beach after Super Storm Sandy. Photograph courtesy of Natalie Jeremijenko.

little pocket ecosystem. And it wasn't until I came home, having been away for two or three days and Enrique Peñalosa the fish had jumped out and suicided to get out of the tank. That's when I realized it was the sand, because for the sand castle competition, we had to put in local sand. This was the big beach that residents were standing around saying, "We haven't had a beach like this in thirty years, but don't worry, it'll be gone next year."

After Sandy, Rockaway Beach was eviscerated and the Army Corps of Engineers came and dumped all this sand back on the coastline to create a beach. But of course, the sand is not from another beach, it's mined from a riverbed somewhere and it's full of nutrients. So here's this shocked ecosystem after a storm surge, and they come along and put this nutrient rich-sand that's leaching out into the coastline and creating algae blooms that could kill anything else. So what was interesting was that this small-scale pocket experiment demonstrated that these actions taken by the Army Corps and the politicians, in the so-called public interest, were not.

The other thing is that the boardwalk, where we were celebrating, was back in place. This is the same boardwalk that had lifted up and rammed into buildings and cars (Figure 9.3). They'd just reloaded the gun, if you will, putting it right back where it was! This public experiment enabled me to understand a little bit about what was going on with this complex ecosystem and then to propose a second experiment. This is an experiment using a material out of Lord of the Rings: it's a building cladding material that is UV-stable, which is interesting in itself, but what's amazing is that it has 100 percent solar throughput. So it's a real game changer. If we put this on the boardwalk, instead of killing everything underneath the boardwalk, you actually display the dune grasses and skipper moths and the organisms that really do build and stabilize a beach and create a healthy dune ecosystem, because, of course, the sunlight would pass through. If we could do a small-scale demonstration, people would come along and they'd see that they can ride over it, they can walk over it; it's not so great for high heels, but its fine for strollers and pedestrians. It would display the organisms underneath so then people can figure out for themselves, without the risk analysis and the engineering reports, that when a storm surge comes along, there's no big rigid mass to pick up and kill people and do damage. The water will go right through it. That kind of material demonstration can change what is demanded of public infrastructure. It's a way to explore what is possible and how we might change access to these delicate ecosystems that we really want to understand.

DH: This is a really nice example of what it could mean to build *with* the human and nonhuman inhabitants of a community in a way that takes account of new technologies as well as the way that ecosystems stabilize themselves. But before we move on, can you say a little bit more about Enrique Peñalosa the fish and his refusal to dig in the sand? I can think of some scholars in animal studies who'd construe this as an act of animal resistance. You might have read it as a labor action—but wasn't he also doing some knowledge production in his own right? Was he refusing to dig because of the algae, giving you a sign before you were ready to recognize it?

NJ: Well right, exactly. The water was too murky. The sand was too full of nutrients. He wasn't going to have any part of it. Looking at the environment through these organisms whose lives depend on them—they have both a legibility and an honesty that is very different from getting a water quality test back, some sort of instrumental reading of pH, for example. How does it actually work biologically? What are we seeing or not seeing? I think it's the intelligent responses of other, nonhuman organisms that really can help us understand this with a veracity that would be otherwise impossible, because we don't always know where to look.

DH: It seems like there's a consistent theme in your work where you set up situations in which we can learn to read the behaviors or responses of organisms to their environments as signs of what's going on there—such as water quality, air quality, whether it's a hospitable environment for both us and them. You frame those responses so that the whole system is more legible to us—sometimes by amplifying or isolating them, and sometimes by translating data collected using sensors or monitors into audible words, text messages, songs, light, and other signals we're familiar with. In one way, this is exactly what most scientific experiments are designed to do, to frame natural or artificial phenomena in a way that allows us to inspect them more carefully. But in your work, there's also the element of making these processes and the way we collect knowledge about them visible and aesthetically engaging. It's also about making that knowledge production public and political.

NJ: I suppose that's a theme song of mine. The *MUSSELxCHOIR* is a good example—

DH: Is *MUSSELxCHOIR* part of the Cross[x]Species Construction Company?

NJ: No, but mussels certainly could be recruited into it because they are the heavy lifters of water quality improvement. They form these massive mega-metropolises and the algae and fish attraction enables them to create habitats. They form these pliant mega-metropolises that actually absorb energy differently from oyster reefs, which are much more celebrated in urban design. Mussels are critically important organisms that I would argue should be actively cohabitated with. In fact, there's a long human history of coevolution or cohabitation with mussels if you look at the midden piles that are huge on a geological scale, that arguably are the womb of civilization.

There's a long history of living with and through mussels, so incorporating them back into the urban infrastructure, into this *Unshoreline,* is the project of the *MUSSELxCHOIR*—to celebrate and reveal the mussels. The mussels of the *MUSSELxCHOIR* are instrumented with sensors so, as they open and close, we can collect data on their gape angle. How much they open and close, their behavior, reflects the water quality and tells us a lot about what's happening in the water. They'll quite literally "clam up" if the water quality is too bad. They're tremendously sensitive to zinc and copper. They are actually used for commercial off-the-shelf water quality monitoring, but in my case, we're using the data that we get about their behavior to convert it into song—and launch their career as a rock band (Figure 9.6).

DH: Do they sing different songs based on the water quality? Is there a correlation between the sounds they make and what they experience?

NJ: Well, yes, but it's not actually data sonification; that's an entirely different field. I'm using this project to iconify the idea of natural intelligence. In the Venice lagoon [at the 2012 Venice Architecture Biennale], for example, we set the pitch according to the depth of the mussels so they played a version of the song "A Bicycle Built for Two"—a cover, if you will—which I call "A Bicycle Built for Too Many." [DH: In 1961, a computer was programmed to sing "Daisy Bell (A Bicycle Built for Two)," becoming a "hit song" in the history of artificial intelligence research, later sung by HAL in *2001: A Space Odyssey.*] That's explicitly to show that this computational model–based approach of taking complex systems and building representations of them in computers and then tweaking parameters in Monte Carlo simulations to make predictions is one paradigm—in fact, this is often what's referred to as running experiments. However, there are issues about how a model represents and what it represents, because it can only represent what we already know. [DH: Because we can only include known parameters in our representations.] Whereas the idea of natural intelligence that I'm trying to iconify with the *MUSSELxCHOIR* is that the mussels themselves are integrating over many parameters that we know and don't know, that we can measure and can't measure. They are actually capturing a certain kind of knowledge through their behavior and making it legible.

What are they thinking? What are they doing here? Just that

FIGURE 9.6. Natalie Jeremijenko, *MUSSELxCHOIR,* Melbourne, 2013. Mussels, which can filter as much as six to nine liters of water per hour, are fitted with sensors that measure the opening and closing of their shells as they react with the environment. The data are then converted to sound as part of a public display. The project uses the behavior of the organisms themselves as a biologically meaningful measure of pollutant exposure. *MUSSELxCHOIR* has also been installed in New York and Venice (at the 2012 Venice Architecture Biennale). Photograph courtesy of Natalie Jeremijenko.

they are there—like the fish in Amphibious Architecture (Figure 9.7)—demonstrates and demands that we recognize that this is a place that's inside natural systems, not culture or a city where nature is somewhere "out there." But it also forces us to understand data in a biologically meaningful way, in terms of how they affect organisms in the environment. If an Environmental Protection Agency data set said the water quality was healthy and the mussels died, who would you believe? The mussels. They have a higher standard of evidence, a higher literacy, and they're integrating over many more parameters. The demand to make sense of their behavior is really important. It's part of the idea that natural intelligence, as opposed to artificial intelligence, is an alternative to the computational model–based approach to irreducibly complex systems.

It's also an invitation for many people in situ to make sense of these systems, because it's more legible, spectacular, and visual. I've

FIGURE 9.7. Natalie Jeremijenko, *Amphibious Architecture,* 2009. Two networks of floating interactive tubes, in New York's East River and Bronx River, house a range of sensors below water and an array of lights above water. The sensors monitor water quality and the presence of fish, while the lights respond to the sensors and create feedback loops between humans, fish, and their shared environment. An SMS interface allows viewers to exchange text messages with the fish and to receive real-time information about the river (Figure 9.11). Photograph courtesy of Natalie Jeremijenko.

been thinking about the visuality in public health terms, in terms of the infectiousness of an idea, almost as though the more visual it is, the more eyeballs are infected with the idea that there is social and environmental transformation happening—as opposed to an oyster reef, an earnest, nice, oyster reef that people aren't seeing and hearing and that doesn't have a Facebook page, that people aren't downloading tunes from, like any of the fifteen or so oyster reefs around New York City. I think the visuality of these kinds of demonstrations is important—it's crucial in making these small-scale experiments legible to diverse sets of people with different interests, perspectives.

DH: I'd like to clarify how this kind of practice differs from data soni-fication, something that, moving beyond just data visualization, is being done a lot in the sciences and the arts lately. It seems like the key difference has to do with how the data are selected to be processed into sound or image. My understanding is that here you, in a way, let the mussels decide what's relevant to measure about their environment rather than preselecting the parameters. Does that appeal to us as complex data-processing organisms ourselves? Are we able to engage with complex phenomena that we can actu-ally see in a more substantive way than we can with a data set that describes a phenomenon, even if that also takes a visual form?

NJ: It's about recognizing that data are not transparent. That there isn't an easy mapping between what the mussel is singing and what that means is because whether you're doing data sonification or a mussel choir, there just isn't an easy mapping! The project recognizes the intellectual uncertainty that is always and already the condition of irreducible complexity. [DH: Something that representations tend to obscure.] The irreducible complexity of urban ecosystems defies representation by any neat little scatterplot or graph. These are dynamic, complex, unpredictable ecosystems, yet we still need to understand them. So whereas data sonification uses a limited set of parameters, the *MUSSELxCHOIR* is an invitation for un-derstanding the complexity of what it means to integrate mussels into our urban infrastructure, what it means to recognize that they are valuable, that we can learn from them, that they are dynamic, responsive organisms that we can have a mutualistic relationship with. It's an invitation to listen and make sense of a whole system rather than a didactic project of saying "this is what you can hear."

DH: So there is a correlation—

NJ: Each song tells a different story. For example, in the Venice lagoon, if the bass came in a lot, then the organisms deeper were active, versus the ones at the top that were tweeting away. So you could make sense of what difference depth makes to dissolved oxygen or algae concentration, and there are other things we could have asked more questions about based on the songs. It's not just a statistical correlation; it's an experiment, a query: how does depth affect the mussels at this site? Each song is an investigation of some aspect of the environment that we can really learn about from the mussels.

The *MUSSELxCHOIR* on tour has been really interesting (Figure 9.8). The mussels are held up in a vacuum, on stage, so they're more visible—eye to eye, mouth to mouth. Here people can more clearly investigate what they're doing and how they're coping in this little pocket environment. You can see differences between the backup singers on the bottom and the stars on stage, and the lights also turn on when they're active. The idea was to familiarize people with their behavior, to help people get to know these organisms.

DH: So is this the laboratory version of the field experiment you're conducting in the actual riverbeds?

NJ: If the laboratory experiment is a performance, then this is the live performance—Mussels: Live in Concert! It's really about creating the cultural thrill, like going to see a band: the mussel choir's in town!

DH: But it's also about showing how the mussel choir works, right? This is what fascinates me about this kind of artistic practice, which I've been calling "performative experimentation." It is like what goes on in the lab, but it has the added element of performing and exhibiting the performativity of science itself. There's an emphasis on performing how knowledge production happens, calling attention to the fact that the parameters have to be selected, the data have to be cleaned, exhibiting that there's a lot of openness and ambiguity in how data can be collected and interpreted.

NJ: It doesn't actually displace the science. Again, I think of it as an invitation. There are off-the-shelf systems that use mussels for water treatment. But knowing about the *MUSSELxCHOIR* makes those water treatment facilities that use them much more legible.

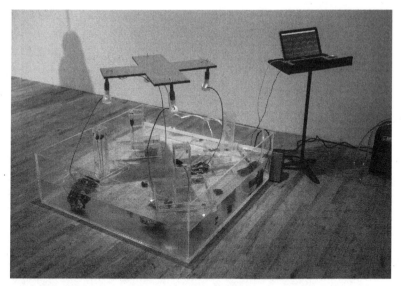

FIGURE 9.8. Natalie Jeremijenko, *MUSSELxCHOIR Performing Live!*, 2014, at Postmasters Gallery, New York. In this indoor, touring version of *MUSSELx-CHOIR*, the data collected from the sensors that capture the opening and closing of the mussels' shells are used to control both sound and lights to generate live performances. Photograph courtesy of Postmasters Gallery.

It's an invitation to learn how data are produced in a way that a white paper or a data stream isn't. When you tell the story that mussels or biomonitoring are involved, it's delightful, engaging in a different way...

DH: So it's an invitation to understand how knowledge is produced and also how infrastructure is or could be produced differently.

NJ: Right, and I'd argue it's also demonstrating an alternative to the ocean and coastal engineers who are doing our coastline design and might be concerned with wave energy absorption, and entering those alternatives into the public discourse about how we redesign our shorelines. Conventional engineering megaprojects—all of this stupid stuff about big gates and heavy equipment—are radically expensive. It's a great deal to demand from the public purse that any of these should happen, versus the idea that we can design *with* natural systems, which traditional engineering companies are the least qualified to do. Being unfamiliar with this approach, being risk averse, they have no incentive to innovate toward this kind of practice. But I would say that creating the framework where you can see how mussels work and understand how valuable they are to urban ecosystems means we can start to hold other alternatives accountable to shared environmental health. OK, so you want to put up a big sea gate: does it improve water quality as well as this much less expensive living system would do? No. Using the framework of shared human and environmental health is a radically different paradigm for how shoreline technology is usually evaluated, in terms of cost or risk. These demonstration experiments are aimed at changing the discourse, reconceptualizing the terms of the public debate. It's a critical methodology.

DH: One thing that stands out is that yours is a very constructive critical methodology. Criticism doesn't always come with a constructive alternative, but you very often mobilize the critique through the alternative—by showing that another way is possible, you call into question the way we're used to dealing with problems. Can you say more about how the political imperatives of environmental justice are given expression through these very practical investigations of what kinds of engineering alternatives might be available to us? Actually, there's a very old question about experiments, which is, why do we actually need to carry them out in the world, rather than just in thought? This seems crucial to the critical force of your work.

NJ: The idea of small-scale, participatory public experimentation is completely different from the expert model in which we get the expert in to tell us what we need to do, design it, and send the bill. In the conventional design processes that are informed by scientific consultants, there's no room for experiment, no room failure, no room for learning. I certainly don't know how we should reconstruct the shoreline, but I'm extremely skeptical of many of the plans that have been proposed. They haven't responded to the paradigm shift that recognizes that we can't design with force and mass; we have to design with buoyancy and tension, with living systems. So methodologically, how do you act in the context of this political, social, and environmental complexity, if you want to get something done? It's easy to be paralyzed by complexity, but these small-scale experiments point to a methodology for really investigating, does this work *here*? Does it work thirty feet away, where there's an oyster bed? It's a big contrast to the approach that the Department of Housing and Urban Development used in which they brought in ten teams of starchitechts who were all given big budgets to do what I call million-dollar Photoshops—master plans of shoreline development. Not a single experiment was done, not a cent spent on them. One percent of that budget would have paid for several of my experiments! And while you can do a nice rendering of oyster reefs here and a bike path there, you don't learn anything from a million-dollar Photoshop. It's a way to co-opt and enlist people, but there's no collective learning involved in that process. These approaches are not mutually exclusive, of course; they could have done both. Having these small-scale material experiments is the only way we can explore the cultural, technical, environmental, social, and political implications of changing our shared environmental commons.

DH: Let's talk about some more nature and technology, because there's a sense in which your approach is to work in harmony with natural systems, but you do so by embracing nature as a model for technology, engineering, and design—there doesn't seem to be any neo-Luddism lurking here. Again, to me, it's very Baconian. Bacon considered the ultimate aim of the new era of science to be the development of technologies useful for human ends. This was the ultimate purpose of learning how to study nature through observation and experiment, or that's how he pitched it to the King of England anyway, which is about the same position we're now in when we address city planning boards or university presidents. It seems to matter a lot how we construe nature, so how do you think about nature now that we find ourselves in this discourse of the Anthropocene?

NJ: As for nature, I don't find the concept useful, but at the same time, natural and living systems are really important to me. One of the paradigms I have recently discovered and tried to articulate is, amazingly, something that I learned about not in all of the evolutionary theory, biology, and molecular genetics, or any of the fields I've studied. I had never come across this one stunning idea that of the subset of symbionts that we know, mutualists dominate the world. Most of the world's biomass is made up of mutualists, where both parties benefit from the relationship and both do better in each other's presence. It's a startling fact about natural systems, and also that I could have gone through so much formal education in this area without hearing about it. I've heard about selective pressure, I've heard a lot about predator–prey relationships, and we know

FIGURE 9.9. Natalie Jeremijenko, *Signs of (Intelligent) Life,* 2014, at Postmasters Gallery, New York. Advertising is printed on Tyvek bags, which are also used to grow perennial flowers. The added greenery in the urban environment improves air quality and supports pollinators. As an example of mutualism—a symbiotic relationship in which both parties benefit—the signage cross-promotes both economic and ecological interests. Photograph courtesy of Natalie Jeremijenko.

that corals and pollinators are mutualists, but it's still just stunning to me that they're so prevalent is something I encountered in a little footnote in a paper. This idea of mutualism is what I find stunning about natural systems, and mutualistic systems design is what I take as the explicit exemplar—that we use our understanding of natural systems as templates for what works. What do mutualistic systems look like? This an essential part of what's been left out of our cultural stories about nature.

For instance, the *Signs of (Intelligent) Life* project is a very simple demonstration of that (Figures 9.9 and 9.10). These commercial signs could advertise whatever the business or .org you like on them, but they're also growing perennial flowers that increase leaf area index and have human health benefits; they support pollinators in a pollinator crisis, improve air quality, and also grow delicious

FIGURE 9.10. Natalie Jeremijenko, detail from *Signs of (Intelligent) Life*. Photograph courtesy of Natalie Jeremijenko.

new edibles, high-nutrition value flowers. It's about what works, and mutualism works. But it's a political paradigm, too: to be explicit about who's benefiting and make sure that there actually is shared benefit from the systems we design.

DH: It makes it very clear that it's a political question which systems or aspects of nature we adopt as models or select for amplification through culture and technology. In just the way Bacon thought art should learn to imitate nature, Dr. Frankenstein got the idea to enliven his monstrous being by watching lightning strike a tree. Your choice to be inspired by mutualism as an engineer and designer has different implications than electing to follow the "red in tooth and claw" notion of nature, of which we can of course also find examples to imitate.

NJ: Exactly. It's no accident that you hear a lot about this being a dog-eat-dog world and selective pressure and survival of the fittest.

DH: These stories serve a purpose, but where our purposes are different, we can also find exemplary narratives and material processes in natural systems . . .

FIGURE 9.11. Natalie Jeremijenko, detail from *Amphibious Architecture* (Figure 9.7). Screen capture of text message exchange between the passing fish and viewers. Image courtesy of Natalie Jeremijenko.

CAN THE SUBAQUATIC SPEAK?

Our conversation closed with a rapid-fire exchange about artistic production of situated knowledge and embodied practice as a response to
the epistemological demands of feminism. In addition to projects like
the *MUSSELxCHOIR* being an invitation for the public to participate
critically in scientific knowledge production and urban design, they
are also an invitation across species lines for fish and other critters to
participate in the creation and representation of our environmental
commons (Figure 9.11). To grasp the standpoint of nonhuman Others,
we have to set up situations in which we can watch, listen, and read
the signs of life.

NOTES

1. Bacon's use of the term *art* refers to craft or technology, not to fine art—but
the double meaning serves my purposes well here. Francis Bacon, "Of the Dignity
and Advancement of Learning, Books II–VI," in *The Works of Francis Bacon,*
ed. James Spedding, Robert Ellis Leslie, and Douglas Dennon Heath (London:
Longmans, 1870), 1:298.

2. In *OneTrees,* Natalie Jeremijenko cloned one thousand Paradox walnut trees
then displayed the seedlings at San Francisco's Yerba Buena Center for the Arts. In
2003, the trees were planted around the San Francisco Bay area. Because the trees
are genetically identical, as they matured, they manifested the social and environmental differences to which they had been exposed. *OneTrees: An Information
Environment* (project website), http://www.nyu.edu/projects/xdesign/onetrees/.

Acknowledgments

The idea for this volume emerged from a series of discussions among Rebekah Sheldon (2011–12 Provost Postdoctoral Fellow at University of Wisconsin–Milwaukee's Center for 21st Century Studies [C21]), 2013–14 C21 Provost Postdoctoral Fellow Dehlia Hannah, C21 deputy director Emily Clark, and me about C21's 2014 annual spring conference. In the context of the annual C21 theme, "Changing Climates," we were determined to do a conference that pushed some of the increasingly unproblematic uptakes of the concept of the Anthropocene by humanists and social scientists. Foremost among our concerns were two developments: the elision of earlier feminist critiques of nature and environmentalism that had in some ways anticipated the concept of the Anthropocene and the decidedly masculinist approach to "fixing" the Anthropocene through techniques of geoengineering. We thus invited plenary speakers and issued a call for papers to scholars who could expand and contextualize these concerns.

In addition to conceiving the concept of *anthropocene feminism*, Dehlia Hannah, Emily Clark, and I were part of the conference organizing committee. Along with Jennifer Johung (art history, University of Wisconsin–Milwaukee), we selected papers and formed panels for the conference's breakout sessions. The organizing committee succeeded in pulling off the conference with good spirit and aplomb. For that I want to thank C21 associate director John Blum, business manager Annette Hess, and the two C21 graduate project assistants, Matthew Boman and especially Audrey Jacobs, the latter of whom was responsible for the design of the conference website and program. An especially warm thank-you goes out to Marina Zurkow, who, although originally scheduled to participate as a plenary speaker but unable to make it, lent her images to our publicity materials. Thanks are also due Johannes Britz, provost and vice chancellor for academic affairs; Rodney Swain, dean of the College of Letters and Sciences; and Jennifer Watson, associate dean of the College of Letters and Science for their support of the event.

Finally, the editing and production of this book could not have happened without the extraordinary work of John Blum, who serves as C21's editor. John is a thoughtful, careful, and patient manuscript editor who brings a wealth of experience to the task of manuscript preparation. I would also like to thank Doug Armato, director of the University of Minnesota Press, for his role in bringing the center's book series to Minnesota, and Danielle Kasprzak, humanities editor at Minnesota. Finally, I thank Anne Carter and Mike Stoffel. Despite the incredible team of collaborators on this project, responsibility for any and all errors is mine.

Contributors

Stacy Alaimo is professor of English and director of environmental and sustainability studies at the University of Texas at Arlington. She is author of *Exposed: Environmental Politics and Pleasures in Posthuman Times* (Minnesota, 2016), *Undomesticated Ground: Recasting Nature as Feminist Space,* and *Bodily Natures: Science, Environment, and the Material Self* and coeditor, with Susan J. Hekman, of *Material Feminisms.*

Rosi Braidotti is a distinguished university professor and founding director of the Centre for the Humanities at Utrecht University. She is the author of *The Posthuman, Nomadic Subjects: Embodiment and Sexual Difference in Contemporary Feminist Theory,* and *Nomadic Theory: The Portable Rosi Braidotti.*

Joshua Clover is professor of English at the University of California, Davis. He is the author of *Red Epic* and of *1989: Bob Dylan Didn't Have This to Sing About.*

Claire Colebrook is Edwin Erle Sparks Professor of English at Pennsylvania State University. She is the author of *The Death of the PostHuman, Sex after Life,* and *William Blake and Digital Aesthetics.*

Richard Grusin is professor of English and former director of the Center for 21st Century Studies at the University of Wisconsin–Milwaukee. He is the author of *Premediation: Affect and Mediality after 9/11; Culture, Technology, and the Creation of America's National Parks;* and, with Jay David Bolter, *Remediation: Understanding New Media.*

Dehlia Hannah is research curator of the Synthesis Center and assistant research professor in the School of Arts, Media, and Engineering at Arizona State University. She is coeditor, with Sara Krajewski, of the exhibition catalog *Placing the Golden Spike: Landscapes of the Anthropocene.*

Myra J. Hird is professor in the School of Environmental Studies and director of the genera Research Group (gRG) at Queen's University, Canada. She is the author of *Sociology of Science: A Critical Canadian Introduction, The Origins of Sociable Life: Evolution after Science Studies,* and *Sex, Gender, and Science.*

Lynne Huffer is Samuel Candler Dobbs Professor of Women's, Gender, and Sexuality Studies at Emory University. She is the author of *Are the Lips a Grave? A Queer Feminist on the Ethics of Sex* and *Mad for Foucault: Rethinking the Foundations of Queer Theory.*

Natalie Jeremijenko is associate professor of art and art education and director of the xDesign Environmental Health Clinic at New York University. She has exhibited her art work at New York's Museum of Modern Art and the Venice Architecture Biennale.

Elizabeth A. Povinelli is Franz Boas Professor of Anthropology at Columbia University. She is author of *Economies of Abandonment: Social Belonging and Endurance in Late Liberalism; The Empire of Love: Toward a Theory of Intimacy, Genealogy, and Carnality;* and *The Cunning of Recognition: Indigenous Alterities and the Making of Australian Multiculturalism.*

Jill S. Schneiderman is professor of earth science at Vassar College. She is editor of *The Earth around Us: Maintaining a Livable Planet* and coeditor, with Warren D. Allmon, of *For the Rock Record: Geologists on Intelligent Design.*

Juliana Spahr is professor of English at Mills College. She is author of *Well Then There Now, The Transformation,* and *Everybody's Autonomy: Connective Reading and Collective Identity.*

Alexander Zahara is a PhD student in geography at the Memorial University of Newfoundland in St. John's, Canada. He is coauthor of "Developmental Exposure to Aroclor 1254 Alters Migratory Behavior in Juvenile European Starlings *(Sturnus vulgaris)*," in *Environmental Science and Technology.*

Index